The Italian Army in the Balkans 1940–41

The Invasion of Greece and Yugoslavia

Massimiliano Afiero

Helion & Company

Helion & Company Limited
Unit 8 Amherst Business Centre
Budbrooke Road
Warwick
CV34 5WE
England
Tel. 01926 499 619
Email: info@helion.co.uk
Website: www.helion.co.uk
Twitter (X): @helionbooks
Visit our blog https://helionbooks.wordpress.com/

Published by Helion & Company 2025
Designed and typeset by Mach 3 Solutions (www.mach3solutions.co.uk)
Cover designed by Paul Hewitt, Battlefield Design (www.battlefield-design.co.uk)

Text © Massimiliano Afiero 2024
Unless otherwise credited all images are from the author's collection. All images credited
www.movm.it and USSME (*Ufficio Storico dello Stato Maggiore dell'Esercito*) are reproduced
with kind permission.
Colour artwork by Renato Dalmaso © Helion & Company 2024
Colour vehicle artwork by David Bocquelet © Helion & Company 2024
Maps by George Anderson © Helion & Company 2024

ISBN 978-1-804515-30-3

British Library Cataloguing-in-Publication Data.
A catalogue record for this book is available from the British Library.

For details of other military history titles published by Helion & Company Limited contact the
above address or visit our website: http://www.helion.co.uk.

We always welcome receiving book proposals from prospective authors.

Contents

Glossary of Italian Ranks and Titles that Appear in the Text, and British Equivalents

Aiutante	Adjutant
Ammiraglio	Admiral
Artigliere	Gunner
Capitano	Captain
Capitano di Fregata	Frigate Captain
Capo Meccanico di Seconda Classe	Chief Mechanic, Second Class
Capo Meccanico di Terza Classe	Chief Mechanic, Third Class
Colonnello	Colonel
Generale	General
Generale di Brigata	Brigadier / Brigadier General
Guida del Gruppo	Team Leader (a rank in use in the Blackshirt units, equivalent to a Sergeant)
Maggiore	Major
Maresciallo	Marshal
Regia Aeronautica	Italian Royal Air Force
Regia Marina	Italian Royal Navy
Secondo Capo Meccanico	Second Chief Mechanic
Sergente	Sergeant
Sergente Artigliere	Artillery Sergeant
Sergente Maggiore	Sergeant Major
Sottocapo Artigliere	Sub-Chief Gunner
Sottotenente	Second Lieutenant
Tenente	Lieutenant
Tenente Colonnello	Lieutenant Colonel
Tenente Generale	Lieutenant General

Introduction

Having only entered the war in June 1940, Mussolini's Italy, after attacking France and launching an offensive in North Africa, decided to attack Greece in October 1940. According to most historians, the Greek campaign is explained by Mussolini's decision to respond in some way to the German expansion into the Balkans in 1940 by sending troops into Romania, but in reality the Balkans and consequently Greece itself had been part of Italy's strategic objectives since the First World War. Italian penetration had begun earlier with the conquest of Albania, which had, since 1923, rekindled old quarrels with Greece, when Italy had occupied Corfu.

With Italy's entry into the war in June 1940, the Greek Government and Crown began to take a pro-British attitude, even though a nationalist dictatorship on the fascist model had been established in the country, and things became increasingly complicated. The Italian General Staff then began to draw up plans for the invasion of Greece. The Italian military commanders and Mussolini himself, however, chose the wrong timing, attacking Greek territory during the autumn season from Albanian territory, in a mountainous region, and in the rain and mud. Without adequate logistical systems and without adequate equipment and weapons, it was inevitable that they would not achieve the hoped-for easy victory, suffering instead a bitter defeat. After a failing invasion of Greek territory, the Italian troops eventually had to fall back to Albania, threatened with being thrown back into the sea by Greek forces. There followed months of extremely hard defensive fighting that put a strain on the Italian logistical machine, which was never able to effectively support the frontline troops.

Reinforcements continued to arrive from Italy, and were sent to the front without adequate training and often without heavy weapons and artillery. Only in the spring of 1941, thanks to the intervention of the German armed forces in the Balkans, with the invasion of Yugoslavia and then of Greece itself, was the Italian offensive able to resume and the Greek Army finally defeated. The victory against Greece was dearly paid for and caused Italy heavy losses and above all, the decisive German intervention on the Balkan front put an end to the so-called 'parallel war' desired by Mussolini in his vain attempt to equal the German territorial conquests.

Only the Italian soldier emerged victorious from this tragedy, who, by his great sacrifice and self-denial, constantly demonstrated great courage and valour, making up for the shortcomings and deficits of the high command, as evidenced by the numerous *Medaglia d'Oro al Valor Militare*, awarded, many of which were *alla Memoria*, medals (posthumous). Among those decorated were not only soldiers from the Royal Army, but also men from the Navy and from the Air Force. And if the official historiography continues to describe the Italian intervention in Greece only as a shameful military defeat, it is necessary to remember that the rapid advance of the German armed forces into Greece was also due to the fact that the Greek Army had previously bled against the Italian forces. The end of hostilities, and after the conquest of the island of Crete, in which Italian forces also took part, was followed by the military occupation of Greece by the Italian and German armed forces.

Massimiliano Afiero

1

Historical Contrasts Between Italy and Greece

The reasons for conflict between the Kingdom of Italy and the Kingdom of Greece had distant origins and primarily concerned two issues: the Aegean islands and Albania. In 1912, as a consequence of the Italian-Turkish War that had begun the previous year with the invasion of Libya, the Italian Navy had occupied Rhodes and the Dodecanese islands,[1] territories that were part of the Ottoman Empire at the time. The government in Athens immediately made some claims, but then with the outbreak of the First World War, the issue was shelved. At the end of the war, the issue was taken up again, but an international conference organised in Lausanne proved Rome right and recognised Italy's possession of Rhodes and the Dodecanese in 1923.

The question of Albania, an independent country since 1912, over which Italy exerted a strong influence, was also a major cause of friction between Rome and Athens. The reason concerned in particular the definition of the southern border of the new state in Northern Epirus, where populations of Greek and Albanian origin were mixed. At the beginning of the First World War, the Greek Army occupied the southern regions of Albania, in order to support the local Greek population that had proclaimed the independence of the area as the Autonomous Republic of Northern Epirus. But in 1916, following a vast military operation in Albania, Italian forces occupied the region of Northern Epirus without resistance and drove out the Greek garrisons in the area without bloodshed. At the end of the war, on 29 July 1919, an accord was signed between the Greek Prime Minister, Eleutherios Venizelos, and the Italian Foreign Minister, Tommaso Tittoni, to

---

1   The Italian-Turkish War was fought by the Kingdom of Italy against the Ottoman Empire between 29 September 1911 and 18 October 1912 to conquer the North African regions of Tripolitania and Cyrenaica. In 1912, in order to force the Turks to surrender, the Italian Government decided to take the war to Turkish metropolitan territory by opening a second front in the Aegean Sea. And so, on 28 April 1912, the island of Stampalia was occupied, with the aim of occupying all of the Southern Sporades. Then on 4 May, the first landing of troops took place on Rhodes, the most politically and strategically important island. On 9 May 1912, the cruiser *Duca Degli Abruzzi* occupied Calchi, taking the garrison prisoner. In the following days, ships of the 1st and 2nd divisions occupied Scarpanto and Caso, while other units of the same divisions seized the R.N. *Roma di Nisiro*, the R.N. *Napoli di Piscopi*, the R.N. *Pisa di Calino*, the R.N. *San Marco di Lero*, and the *Amalfi di Patmo*. On 16 May, during the fighting at Psithos, the destroyers *Nembo* and *Aquilone* occupied the island of Lipso, while on the 19th the R.N. *Pegaso* seized Simi. Finally, on the 20th, the R.N. *Napoli* landed at Coo, bringing the total number of islands occupied during the series of actions to 13.

resolve the outstanding issues between the two countries, the Dodecanese islands and the Albanian border, but no agreement was reached. With Benito Mussolini's rise to government, the situation was resumed in an attempt to improve relations between Italy and Greece.

The Occupation of Corfu

In order to settle the border issue between Greece and Albania, the Conference of Ambassadors in Paris entrusted the task to a four-man Italian delegation led by *Generale* Enrico Tellini. However, the mission, which was intended to establish the border between the two countries, fell into an ambush, attacked by unknown persons near the village of Zepi in Greek territory, along the road from Ioannina to Kakavia; *Generale* Tellini, his driver and two other officers lost their lives. It was a real provocation, but the perpetrators were not immediately identified and, above all, it was not clear whether they were Greeks or Albanians. The Tellini mission had international status, but Benito Mussolini considered it a direct affront against Italy and immediately accused the Greeks of being responsible for the massacre. He therefore sent a peremptory ultimatum to Athens in which he demanded not only an official apology, but also a solemn funeral for the victims in the presence of the entire Greek Government, military honours from the Greek fleet and 50 million *lira* in compensation. The Greeks rejected Rome's demands and turned to the League of Nations. *Il Duce* then responded by sending a naval squadron to bombard Corfu, and the island was then occupied by Italian troops. The Paris Ambassadors' Conference again intervened to resolve the new crisis: Greece would apologise not to Italy but to the international community that had organised the mission led by Tellini. Italy would then receive compensation, not the requested 50 million, but an equitable amount to be defined. The island of Corfu was then cleared by Italian troops. However, the real perpetrators of the Zepi massacre were never identified.

In the following years, attempts were made to improve relations between the two countries and in 1928 a friendship treaty was even signed between Italy and Greece, which was to last 10 years, but was only a formal agreement. In fact, in the international arena, the government in Athens continued to consistently take sides against Italy, as in 1935, when it voted sanctions against the country.

The situation seemed to improve in April 1936, when the Greek Prime Minister, Ioannis Metaxas, established a fascist-inspired dictatorial regime in Athens, showing an ideological affinity with Mussolini's Italy: the Roman salute was introduced and an organisation similar to the *Opera Nazionale Balilla* was set up. But while Metaxas had admiration for the Axis forces, and in particular for National Socialist Germany, the Greek royal house (George II of Greece had been restored to the throne in 1935 after a brief republican interlude) sided instead with England. In the following years, *Genikós* (General) Metaxas continued to maintain cordial relations with Italy.

The Invasion of Albania

Tensions between Italy and Greece became critical again when, in April 1939, Italian forces invaded Albania.[2] The small Balkan state had already been occupied by Italian troops in 1917, then the Giolitti government renounced the protectorate and recognised Albania's independence. Over the years,[3] diplomatic attempts had been made to try to regain Albania in a peaceful manner and effectively forcing it to relinquish its sovereignty, but without success. King Zog I, corrupt and not much loved by the Albanian people, had also indicated that he wanted to withdraw from Italian influence and seek new political alliances, either with the British or with the Germans. It was precisely this last possibility that, in 1939, prompted Mussolini, also as a response to the German occupation of Czechoslovakia, to order the invasion and occupation of Albania.

Initially, the invasion plan was to commit a maximum force of 50,000 men, supported by 51 naval units and 400 aircraft. Later, the planned invasion force was increased to 100,000 men, supported by 600 aircraft. In the end, however, only 22,000 men actually took part in the invasion.

On 7 April 1939, Italian troops, led by *Generale* Alfredo Guzzoni, invaded Albania, simultaneously attacking all Albanian ports. The Italian naval forces engaged in the invasion included the battleships *Giulio Cesare* and *Conte di Cavour*, three heavy cruisers, three light cruisers, nine destroyers, fourteen torpedo boats, one minesweeper, ten auxiliary ships and nine transport ships. The ships were divided into four groups, which made landings at Vlora, Durrës, St John of Medua and Saranda.

In contrast, the regular Albanian Army had 15,000 poorly equipped soldiers, who had previously been trained by Italian officers. King Zog I and his military commanders had decided to organise resistance in the mountains, leaving the ports and main cities undefended. But the Italian officers present in Albania as military instructors had sabotaged this plan and the Albanians discovered that artillery pieces had been disabled and there was no ammunition. Thus, the main resistance actually came from the Albanian Royal Gendarmerie and small groups of patriots.

---

2   Albania represented a territory of considerable strategic importance for Italy. The Navy above all aspired to control the port of Vlora and the island of Saseno, located at the entrance to the Bay of Vlora, as they would allow Italy control of the entrance to the Adriatic Sea and would form a suitable base for military operations in the Balkans.

3   With Mussolini as head of the Italian Government, interest in Albania returned. Italy began its penetration of the Albanian economy in 1925, when Albania agreed to allow Italy to exploit its mineral resources. This was followed by the signing of the first Treaty of Tirana in 1926 and then a second in 1927, under which Italy and Albania entered into a defensive alliance. Additionally, the Albanian government and economy were subsidised by Italian loans and the Royal Albanian Army was not only trained by Italian military instructors, but most of its officers were Italian; other Italians held high positions in the Albanian government. One-third of Albania's imports came from Italy. Despite this strong Italian influence, King Zog I refused to give in completely to Italian pressure and in 1931 openly opposed the Italians, refusing to renew the 1926 Treaty of Tirana. After Albania signed trade agreements with Yugoslavia and Greece in 1934, Mussolini made an unsuccessful attempt to intimidate the Albanians by sending a fleet of warships.

In Durrës, Albanian forces, including gendarmes and volunteers, attempted to counter the Italian advance, but were only able to hold out for a few hours before being overwhelmed after being subjected to a heavy artillery bombardment from Italian ships. As soon as it was possible to complete the landings of light tanks from the Italian ships, Albanian resistance began to diminish and a few hours later the city was captured. Meanwhile, every other Albanian port also fell into Italian hands. King Zog, with his wife and son, fled to Greece taking most of the gold reserves of the Albanian Central Bank with them. When news of the King's escape began to spread, the angry Albanian population attacked the prisons, freed the prisoners and looted the royal palace. In general, the majority of the Albanians welcomed the Italians as liberators. At 9.30 a.m. on 8 April, Italian troops under *Generale* Messe entered Tirana and quickly captured all government buildings. Other Italian troops marched towards Shkodra, Fier and Elbasan. The Scutari garrison only surrendered towards evening after 12 hours of hard fighting.

During the Albanian campaign, four bersaglieri battalions were engaged, which, once landed, immediately moved inland. At St John of Medua, the 3rd Complement Battalion of the 8th Regiment landed, which, on 8 April, moved forward to the bridge over the Drinassa (Scutari), tenaciously defended by the Albanian soldiers. *Tenento* Riccardo Bombig, with a group of bersaglieri, threw himself forward across the crumbling parapets of the bridge in an attempt to overcome enemy resistance.[4] Although under fire from enemy weapons and amidst explosions, he and his companions succeeded in putting the Albanians to flight. At the very end of the action, however, he was hit by enemy fire and mortally wounded. He was decorated with the *Medaglia d'Oro al Valor Militare alla Memoria* (Gold Medal of Military Valour for his memory), with the following citation:

> Commander of an advanced company, who had already distinguished himself in the previous landing operation, with exceptional calm and serene disregard for danger, he kept his bersaglieri firmly in place when they were being beaten by violent fire. In order to attempt to cross a bridge, which was mined and partly broken, he dared to do so at the head of a few brave men. In the heroic attempt, he was mortally wounded by a machine gun barrage: an admirable example of a high sense of duty and personal valour. [Bridge over Brinassa – Shkodra, 8 April 1939]

Italian losses from 7 to 9 April in completing the occupation of Albania totalled 93 men, dead and wounded; 60 percent of these losses from the Navy.

On 12 April 1939, the Albanian parliament voted to depose Zog and unite the nation with Italy 'in personal union', offering the Albanian crown to Victor Emmanuel III. The parliament elected Albania's largest landowner, Shefqet Vërlaci,

---

4   Riccardo Bombig was born in Pula in 1913. After graduating as an accountant, he entered the Royal Military Academy in Modena in 1933, from which he graduated as an infantry second lieutenant. He was assigned to the 8th Bersaglieri Regiment and promoted to lieutenant five years later on the eve of his departure for the occupation of Albania as part of the Expeditionary Corps under the command of *Generale* Alfredo Guzzoni.

as prime minister, who would serve as interim head of state for five days until Victor Emmanuel III formally accepted the Albanian crown in an official ceremony at the Quirinal Palace in Rome.

On 13 April 1939, during the meeting of the Grand Council of Fascism, Mussolini said:

> Albania is the Bohemia of the Balkans, whoever holds Albania holds the Balkan region. Albania is a geographical constant of Italy. It assures us control of the Adriatic …. no one enters the Adriatic anymore …. we have widened the bars of the Mediterranean prison.

Once the occupation was complete, under the direction of *Tenente Generale* Francesco Jacomoni di San Savino, a rapid policy of fasciation was initiated, with the establishment of an Albanian Fascist Party and an Albanian Fascist Militia, as well as the integration of the local armed forces into the Italian military structure.

Greece's Fears

Naturally, the Italian occupation of Albania caused great concern to the government in Athens: Metaxas, fearing an imminent invasion by Italy after rumours had circulated that Italian troops were moving towards the Hellenic borders, immediately alerted two divisions of the Greek Army in Epirus and Macedonia, with orders to prepare to contain a possible attack. At the same time, he immediately sought the protection of Great Britain and France, who immediately offered their guarantees. And so, on 13 April 1939, British Prime Minister, Neville Chamberlain, announced that if Greece was invaded, the United Kingdom would intervene on its side. A few days later, the government in Paris also made a similar declaration. Mussolini, for his part, tried in some way to calm tempers, informing Metaxas, through his chargé d'affaires, that between the two countries 'cordial relations of friendship' were not in question.

Invasion Plans

The tension between Greece and Italy became critical again in mid-August 1939, when four Italian divisions stationed in Albania were moved very close to the border with Greece and at the same time Italian planes engaging in reconnaissance flights, frequently straying into Greek airspace.

On 16 August, Mussolini ordered the General Staff of the Royal Army to prepare a plan for the invasion of Greece. Re-elaborating some previous studies, the commander of the troops in Albania, *Generale* Alfredo Guzzoni, suggested a large-scale action involving a contingent of 18 divisions grouped in 6 Army Corps commands: four corps with twelve divisions were to move from the Coriza area eastwards in the direction of Salonika, with a supporting attack southwards in the direction of Ioannina led by an army corps with three divisions and another three divisions deployed to protect the frontier between Albania and Yugoslavia.

The pincer manoeuvre was then to close in on Athens. At the same time, however, Guzzoni asked for at least a year for preparations, especially to strengthen the road network to Greece and the capacity of the Albanian ports. In addition, the Army's chief of staff, *Generale* Alberto Pariani, asked for at least 20 divisions to be committed to the operation.

Also in August 1939, due to the state of tension with Italy, the Greek Government ordered a partial mobilisation of its armed forces and strengthened its defences on the Albanian border. At the time, the Greek military command was more concerned about a possible war against Bulgaria, because of the traditional Bulgarian claims on Thessaloniki and Western Thrace. In fact, work had been underway since 1936 to fortify the border between the two nations, with the construction of the so-called 'Metaxas Line'. The Italian military manoeuvres in Albania forced the chief of staff of the Greek Army, *Genikós* Alexandros Papagos, to reinforce the defensive device in the Epirus region. A first mistake on the part of the Italian strategists.

On 1 September 1939, German forces invaded Poland. Mussolini then decided to cancel any plans to invade Greece in order to concentrate on possible action in Yugoslavia.[5] At the same time, Greece declared its neutrality and Metaxas established contacts with Germany in order to mediate away Italian aims on his country. A few days later, Mussolini, in order to further ease the tension between Italy and Greece, sent Metaxas a note saying that Italy had no intention of taking '…the initiative of operations against Greece.' Italian troops in Albania were to remain 20 kilometres away from the Greek-Albanian border. And so, starting on 22 September 1939, the Greek Command began a gradual demobilisation of its troops in the area.

Plans Against Yugoslavia

Il Duce, however, ordered his generals to prepare attack plans against both Yugoslavia and Greece in order to face any eventuality. The main target for Mussolini continued to be Yugoslavia, against which an intervention plan was prepared, first called 'Exigency E' and then 'P.R. 12 bis'. The plan called for the use of five armies that were to operate near the Slavic borders, particularly in Styria and Carinthia, on the Julian and Friulian borders and on Albanian territory. The armed action was to be accompanied by a political action that was to favour the dismemberment of the country by appealing to the different ethnic groups that made up Yugoslavia: Slovenes, Croats, Serbs, Macedonians and Montenegrins, who had never fully integrated into the new Yugoslav state. In particular, attempts were made to exploit the nationalistic aspirations of the Croats. In the end, the plan against Yugoslavia was shelved on the orders of Mussolini himself, both because of the failure of the various ethnic groups to rise up and because of pressure from Hitler, who wanted to avoid forceful action in the Balkan area.

---

5   Mussolini had repeatedly considered invading Yugoslavia to claim possession of Croatia and Dalmatia. He was convinced that the Balkan country was just a British invention that came about with the Treaty of Versailles at the end of the First World War and as such had no right to exist as a united and independent state.

Plans Against Greece

For Greece, as mentioned above, a war plan had been prepared in August 1939 by *Generale* Guzzoni and Generale Pariani. The plan called for 20 divisions, which were to be deployed in two directions: the main one, with 12 divisions, was to be engaged in Macedonia with the objective of Thessaloniki; the second, with 3 divisions, was to be engaged in Epirus towards Gianina. The pincer action was then to close on Athens. Of the remaining five divisions, three were to be engaged in a defensive role guarding the borders between Albania, Yugoslavia and Greece, two others were to occupy Corfu and garrison the Ionian islands. This plan too, again due to German pressure, remained on paper, at least until Italy's entry into the war in June 1940. But once again, Minister Ciano wanted to speed things up by planning an intervention in Greece. To this end, he sent the Alpine captain, and writer, Curzio Malaparte, to Athens as a journalist and special observer.

At the end of March 1940, Malaparte arrived in Greece and met Francesco Anfuso, the Italian press attaché in the country. The two immediately began frequenting Athenian cultural salons to assess the country's political and social situation. After receiving first impressions from Malaparte, Ciano wanted to travel to Albania in person in May 1940, in search of alliances against Greece: he managed to make contact with numerous Albanian notables, including the brothers Dino, Gemil and Nebil. These claimed the restitution from Greece of Ciamuria, a territory between the Ionian coast and the town of Gianina, which had belonged to Albania until 1913, when it was assigned by the London Conference to the Greek state. On 23 May 1940, during a demonstration and in the presence of Ciano himself, the Albanian population clamoured for the annexation of Kosovo and Ciamuria to Albania and then to Italy. The same evening, Ciano met *Generale* Carlo Geloso, who had replaced Guzzoni as commander of the Italian forces in Albania, and ordered him to have the five divisions under his orders ready for an attack on Greece, because: 'the Hellenic territory was about to become a naval base for the English and French'. Geloso immediately reiterated that he had not received any directive to this effect from higher commands.

Ciano thought that the Greek Government would not oppose Italian demands for the occupation of Ciamuria, so there would be no need for a full-fledged military offensive, as envisaged in Guzzoni's plan, but only a peaceful march to occupy the claimed territories. Geloso immediately rejected the idea of advancing into Greek territory with only five divisions. Ciano then asked what Geloso thought was the most convenient strategic operational direction to attack Greece. Although still sceptical about the feasibility of the action, Geloso replied that it was necessary to immediately aim at isolating Greece from Turkey, aiming at the conquest of Salonika. To achieve this goal, which would lead to the conquest of part of Greek territory, at least 10–11 divisions would be needed. In the end, he was deemed too cautious by Ciano and so on 5 June 1940, Geloso was removed from command of the Italian troops in Albania and replaced by *Generale* Sebastiano Visconti Prasca.

On 10 June 1940, Italy entered the war against France and England and the plans to invade Greece as well as Yugoslavia were temporarily shelved. Mussolini continued to reassure Metaxas of Italy's peaceful intentions towards Greece. And while the Italian leadership continued to maintain a hostile attitude, in Athens the Italian ambassador, Emanuele Grazzi, attempted to maintain cordial relations with the Greek Government and reassured Metaxas about Italy's respect for the country's neutrality. The news of Italy's entry into the war, however, had provoked a wave of anti-Italian sentiment throughout Greece and the Greek press itself did not hide its sympathies towards France and England. On the Italian side, therefore, numerous episodes of Greek collaboration with the British continued to be denounced: in particular, the Italian governor of the Dodecanese, *quadrumvir* Cesare Maria De Vecchi, made repeated accusations about the support given by the Greeks to British ships in the Aegean Sea. Attacks on Italian submarines by British ships or aircraft from the Greek mainland were also reported, but there were also attacks by Italian aircraft against Greek shipping in the Aegean.

And so, at the end of the operations against France in the western Alps, Guzzoni's plan against Greece was again analysed. Mussolini ordered *Generale* Carlo Geloso to revise it, taking into account that the objective was no longer the occupation of the whole of Greece but an offensive in Epirus alone, particularly in Ciamuria. The new plan was to include the occupation of Epirus, Acarnania in Ciamuria up to Missolonghi and the Ionian Islands, with the employment of 10 divisions. The plan was later revised by the General Staff of the Royal Army, which increased the number of divisions to be employed to 11.

In the meantime, starting on 11 August 1940, Ciano launched a massive anti-Greek propaganda campaign: articles appeared in the press about the situation in Ciamuria, a region in Epirus inhabited by an Albanian minority, who were victims of abuse, massacres and deportations by the occupying Greek authorities. To this end, news of the murder of Albanian patriot Daut Hoggia was reported in the Italian press. Wanted by the Greek authorities for brigandage and murder, he was murdered by two of his compatriots to pocket the bounty promised by the Greek police. Instead, the Italian press turned him into a Chamurian patriot who was killed on the orders of the Athens government.

On 15 August 1940, a new incident occurred: the sinking of the old cruiser *Elli*, which was engaged in firing a few salvoes during the feast of the Virgin Mary on the island of Tinos in the Aegean. At the time, the command of the *Regia Marina* had ordered Italian submarines based in the Dodecanese to attack merchant traffic engaged in conducting business with the United Kingdom. Thus, the governor of the Dodecanese, De Vecchi, ordered *Tenento* Giuseppe Aicardi, commander of the submarine *Delfino*, to attack all shipping traffic off the Greek islands of Tinos and Siros. On 15 August, the *Delfino* was off the island of Tinos, the site of a shrine sacred to the Orthodox Church and at that time the celebration of the Assumption of Mary was underway. Having penetrated the harbour, the Italian submarine torpedoed and sank the old cruiser *Elli* anchored in the roadstead: one of the crew was killed and 29 more were injured. Two more torpedoes were fired and hit the quay where the procession was in progress and only by a miracle was a massacre of civilians avoided. The Greek Government immediately accused Italy, which for its part denied any involvement in the incident. And even when the Greek authorities recovered fragments of the torpedoes, which bore Italian markings, the Italian Government promptly reiterated that the torpedo factory in Fiume had supplied material to many foreign nations, including England itself.

Emergency G

The sinking of the *Elli* further complicated relations with Greece and at the same time increased pro-British sentiments in that country. Moreover, Italy's aggressive attitude convinced the Greek military leadership to intensify the reorganisation of the armed forces and to prepare defence plans to face an invasion of Epirus. More seriously for the future Italian offensive, the number of troops deployed on the border with Albania was increased.

Mussolini ordered the Army General Staff to once again review the plan of action against Greece, which from then on was designated as 'Emergency G'. The number of divisions to be committed in the offensive was decreased to nine and relied on a possible attack by Bulgaria so as to commit the bulk of the Greek forces away from the areas affected by the Italian offensive or a peaceful occupation of the disputed territories with the approval of the Athens government.

In the meantime, Italy's aggressive policy towards Greece attracted the attention of Germany and Hitler himself: the *Führer*, while recognising Greece as part of Italy's sphere of influence, wanted to postpone any action in the Balkans until after the defeat of England, above all to avoid any possible involvement of the Soviet Union in the region. And so, after the personal intervention of the German Foreign Minister, Joachim von Ribbentrop, and especially because he was busy preparing for an imminent Italian offensive against Egypt, on 22 August 1940, Mussolini ordered preparations for the attack on Greece, which had been initially planned for 1 September 1940, to be halted. Two days later, in a letter sent to Hitler, *Il Duce* declared: '…that the measures taken in Albania had only defensive value.'

Having moved the military attack against Greece to 1 October (and later to 20 October), Ciano continued his political action, attempting to establish relations between the highest echelons of the Greek armed forces, in order to favour a possible coup d'état to bring elements closer to the Italian Fascist regime into the government. In this way, a peaceful Italian occupation of Epirus and the Ionian Islands could have proceeded. In view of this possible eventuality, during the month of September 1940, three more divisions, the *Parma*, *Siena* and *Piemonte*, were sent to Albania, bringing the total number of forces at *Generale* Visconti Prasca's disposal to eight divisions. To Italian attempts to bribe some of his senior officers, Metaxas responded by having them arrested, in particular *Genikós* Platis, accused of being a fascist sympathiser. The only option that remained to Italy was the use of force.

On 4 October 1940, Mussolini met with Hitler in Brenner to discuss the situation in Europe and in particular in the Balkans. On this occasion, the *Führer* once again urged Il Duce to avoid any armed intervention in the Balkan area, predicting an imminent landing of German troops in England and thus a period of peace for the whole of Europe. But Hitler was lying, since the landing in England had been postponed *sine die* and, moreover, his troops were preparing to enter Romania. The suggestions to Mussolini were therefore simply a way to keep the Italians out of the Balkans.

So it was the Germans who finally convinced Mussolini to attack Greece. On 11 October they sent troops into Romania, at the request of the Romanian government,[6] officially to protect the Ploiesti oilfield. *Il Duce* reacted harshly to the German intervention, addressing Ciano: '…Hitler always puts me in front of a *fait accompli*. This time I will pay him back with the same coin: he will know from the newspapers that I have occupied Greece. Thus the balance will be restored…'

Ciano then asked if Badoglio, Chief of the General Staff, agreed and Mussolini replied: 'Not yet, but I will resign as an Italian if anyone finds it difficult to fight the Greeks.' Badoglio was informed two days later, on 13 October, and showed his opposition. By this time Mussolini had made up his mind and listened to no one, without giving the command time to at least review the attack plans.

On 15 October 1940, a meeting was called by Mussolini at Palazzo Venezia: among those summoned were Ciano, Badoglio, the Ambassador to Albania, Francesco Jacomoni, *Generale* Ubaldo Soddu, Under-secretary for War, the commander of troops in Albania, *Generale* Sebastiano Visconti Prasca, and the Under-Chief of the Army Staff, *Generale* Mario Roatta. Mussolini opened the meeting:

> The purpose of this meeting is to define the outline of the action, in its general character, which I have decided to begin against Greece. This action, at first, must have objectives of a maritime character and of a territorial character. The objectives of a territorial character must lead us to the seizure of the whole of the Albanian south coast, that is, to the occupation of the Ionian islands Zakynthos, Kefalonia, Corfu and the conquest of Thessaloniki. When we have achieved these objectives, we shall have improved our positions in the Mediterranean, vis-à-vis England. At a later stage, or in conjunction with these actions, the complete occupation of Greece, to put it out of action and to ensure that under all circumstances it will remain in our political-economic space. Having thus clarified the matter, I also set the date, which in my opinion cannot be delayed even by an hour; that is, the 26th of this month. This is an action that I have been maturing for months and months; before our participation in the war and even before the beginning of the conflict. Having established these essential points, it is now a question of examining how this action is to be carried out, and I have therefore sent for the *Tenente Generale* and the Commander of the troops of Albania to give us a political and military framework, so that we can determine all the appropriate measures to achieve our objectives in the best possible way and in the most convenient time. I would add that I see no complications in the North. Yugoslavia has every interest in remaining quiet, as is also apparent from public statements by official bodies that exclude the possibility of complications, except when it comes to defending

---

6   After being forced to cede the regions of Bukovina and Bessarabia to the Soviet Union, Romania also had to cede other territories to Hungary. In order to avoid the total dismemberment of the country, the Romanian government, headed by Ion Antonescu, sought the protection of Germany. The latter was particularly interested in protecting the oil wells in Ploiesti, which were indispensable for the German war economy.

the country. Complications of a Turkish nature I exclude, especially since Germany has established itself in Romania, and since Bulgaria has become stronger. It can be a pawn in our game, and I shall take the necessary steps to ensure that it does not miss this unique opportunity to achieve its aspirations for Macedonia and the outlet to the sea. Having established the objectives and the date, it is now a question of seeing the other aspects of the situation, so that we can – on the basis of them – determine the measures and means to be taken.[7]

Immediately afterwards, Jacomoni took the floor:

In Albania, this action is anxiously awaited. The country is impatient and full of enthusiasm; in fact, it can be said that the enthusiasm is so lively that it has had some disillusionment recently because the action has not yet begun.

Ciano briefed those present on the internal situation in Greece:

There is a clear split between the population and a ruling, political, plutocratic class, which is the one that animates the resistance and keeps the Anglophile spirit alive in the country. This is a very small, very rich class, while the other part is indifferent to all events, including that of our invasion…

Then it was the turn of Visconti Prasca, who stated that the 'Emergency G' plan had been prepared down to the last detail and that the Italian armies would overcome the Greeks in a few days. When asked by *Il Duce* about the situation of the forces, he replied:

About 70,000 men, plus special battalions. Compared to the troops in front of us – about 30,000 men – we have a superiority of two to one.

At the meeting, it was also considered that after the occupation of Epirus, new forces would be needed to proceed with the occupation of the entire Greek territory, bringing the total number of divisions committed to 20.

On 17 October, Badoglio informed *Generali* Pricolo and Roatta and *Ammiraglio* Cavagnari about the decisions taken at Palazzo Venezia. The Navy for its part was to organise and carry out two troop landings, one at Corfu and another in the Gulf of Arta. Cavagnari immediately advanced reservations about the feasibility of the operations and also stated that the action against Greece would lead to a greater British presence in the Mediterranean, threatening the fleet based in Taranto.

Instead, the *Regia Aereonautica* was to support troop movements and counter any movements of the Greek forces. Pricolo also complained about the short time

---

7   From the minutes approved by *Il Duce*, at Palazzo Venezia, on 16 October 1940-XVIII.

available to organise airfields in Albanian territory. Pricolo and Cavagnari therefore asked Badoglio for a postponement of the operations. Badoglio in turn turned to Ciano, Mussolini being absent at the time. Badoglio himself went so far as to threaten to resign if Greece was attacked. In a subsequent meeting with Mussolini on 18 October, the *Maresciallo* obtained a postponement of only two days. The attack on Greece was moved to 3 a.m. on 28 October 1940.

In the following days, *Generale* Visconti Prasca began to request new troops and materials for the forthcoming offensive, requests that naturally the Army General Staff could not fulfil. At the same time, *Generale* Francesco Rossi was sent to Albania to assess the situation on the ground on the eve of the offensive, and proposed a postponement of the operations due to the poor weather conditions, which were prohibitive for any air, sea or land operations. Even this proposal fell on deaf ears: Mussolini had already made up his mind and would not change it even when a letter arrived from King Boris of Bulgaria, informing him that he would not commit his troops against Greece. *Il Duce*'s reply was lapidary: 'We will do without him!'[8]

Apart from Bulgaria's failure to intervene, the Italian attack also lacked the element of surprise: the Greek Ambassador in Rome, Politis, also imitated by his colleague in Berne, informed Athens on 25 October that the Italian invasion could begin between 25 and 28 October. The Germans, of course, also knew about the Italian preparations and when, on 25 October, Hitler received a letter from Mussolini (readied since 19 October) in which *Il Duce* very vaguely hinted at his intention to occupy Greece, without indicating a precise date for the start of the offensive, the *Führer* proposed a meeting in person to discuss the matter: the meeting was then fixed for 28 October in Florence, practically a few hours after the start of the attack on Greece!

The Ultimatum to Greece

Before delivering the ultimatum to Greece, in order to somehow justify the attack, a few days' earlier border incidents were organised by the Italian authorities themselves, during which alleged Greek armed gangs had attacked Albanian border guard posts. There were also border incidents between Cyamurians, the Albanian ethnic minority on Greek territory, and the Greek authorities.

On 28 October 1940, at 3:00 a.m., the Italian Ambassador in Athens, Emanuele Grazzi, delivered to Metaxas the ultimatum prepared by Ciano and Mussolini:

> The Italian Government has had to repeatedly observe how, during the current conflict, the Greek Government has assumed and maintained an attitude that is in conflict not only with the normal relations of peace and good neighbourliness between the two nations, but also with the precise

---

8   On 16 October 1940, Ciano's chief of staff Filippo Anfuso had gone to King Boris III of Bulgaria with a letter from Mussolini requesting the country's intervention in the upcoming campaign against Greece. The reply was a refusal: the Bulgarian Army was insufficiently equipped for modern warfare and the country feared an attack from neighbouring Turkey.

duties that the Greek Government is bound by its status as a neutral state. On several occasions the Italian Government has found itself obliged to call the Greek Government to observe these duties and to protest against the systematic violation; a violation which is particularly serious because the Greek Government has tolerated the use of its territorial waters, its coasts and its ports by the British fleet in the course of its war operations, favoured the supply of supplies to the British Royal Air Force and permitted the organisation of a military intelligence service in the Greek Archipelago to the detriment of Italy. The Greek Government – which should have realised the serious consequences of its attitude – did not respond with any measures to protect its neutrality, but on the contrary intensified its favouring of the British armed forces and its collaboration with Italy's enemies. The Italian Government has evidence that such collaboration was planned and regulated by the Greek Government through military, naval and aeronautical agreements. The Italian Government is referring not only to the British guarantee, accepted by Greece as part of a programme of action directed against Italy's security, but to the explicit and precise commitments made by the Greek Government to make available to the Powers at war with Italy important strategic positions on Greek territory, including among these the air bases in Thessaly and Macedonia, intended for an attack against Albanian territory. The Italian Government – in this connection – must remind the Greek Government of the provocative action it has taken against the Albanian nation with the terrorist policy it has adopted against the peoples of Chiamuria and with the persistent attempts to create disturbances beyond its borders. It was also because of these facts that the Italian Government was – but to no avail – obliged to remind the Greek Government of the inevitable consequences that such a policy would have for Italy. This cannot be tolerated by Italy any longer. Greece's neutrality has increasingly become a mere semblance. Responsibility for this lies primarily with Great Britain and its intention to always involve other countries in the war. But it is now clear that the policy of the Greek Government has been and is directed towards turning Greek territory, or at least allowing it to be turned into a base for war actions against Italy. This could only lead to an armed conflict between Italy and Greece, a conflict that the Italian Government has every intention of avoiding. The Italian Government has therefore come to the determination to ask the Greek Government – as a guarantee of Greece's neutrality and as a guarantee of Italy's security – for the duration of the present conflict with Great Britain to occupy with its armed forces certain strategic points on Greek territory. The Italian Government asks the Greek Government not to oppose this occupation and not to hinder the free passage of the troops destined to carry it out. These troops do not present themselves as enemies of the Greek people and in no way does the Italian Government intend that the temporary occupation of certain strategic points, dictated by contingent necessity and of a purely defensive character, should prejudice the sovereignty and independence of Greece. The Italian Government requests the Greek Government that it immediately give its military authorities the necessary orders so that such occupation may take place in a peaceful manner. Should the Italian troops encounter resistance, such resistance will be met by force of arms and the Greek Government will assume responsibility for the consequences arising therefrom.

The ultimatum expired at 6 a.m., so it was effectively a declaration of war, as Metaxas himself reported to Grazzi: 'You know I could not accept even if I wanted to. It's 3 o'clock, before 6 o'clock I would have to summon the military leaders, hear the king, send orders not to resist to the most distant units. Anyway, what would be the strategic points that Italy wants to occupy?'[9]

Grazzi could not answer because he did not know what they were. Metaxas then concluded: 'So you see that it is war?'

After the meeting with the Italian ambassador, the Greek Prime Minister issued orders to complete the mobilisation of troops on the borders with Albania, Yugoslavia and on the Aegean islands. He then convened the council of ministers and called the British ambassador, Palairet, to ask for the support of the British fleet to deal with possible amphibious invasions (which were actually not included in the Italian plan of attack).

As promised by Mussolini, on 28 October 1940, Hitler learned the news of the Italian attack on Greece from the newspapers while his train was passing through Bologna station on its way to Florence for his meeting with *Il Duce*. Hitler had hoped to the last that he could dissuade Mussolini from his intentions and arrive in time to convince him, but to no avail. As soon as he got off the train in Florence, Mussolini went to meet him: 'Führer, we are marching. At dawn this morning the victorious Italian troops crossed the Greek-Albanian border'. At the sight of a less than pleased Hitler, Mussolini added: 'Don't worry. Everything will be over in a fortnight!'

Hitler's fears lay above all in the inevitable British intervention in Greece, from whose airfields bombardments against the Romanian oil wells, so valuable to the Third Reich's economy, could be carried out. To this end, even before the Italian offensive ran aground, Hitler ordered his General Staff to prepare an intervention plan against Greece, before the country turned into a British stronghold.

---

9   AA.VV., *Ottobre 1940: la Campagna di Grecia* (Campobasso: Italia Editrice, 1995), p.49.

Il Duce, Benito Mussolini, portrayed on a 1920s postcard.

Generale Enrico Tellini.

Italian troops landed at Corfu to militarily occupy the island (from *Illustrazione Italiana*, issue 36 of 9 September 1923).

The cover of the *Domenica del Corriere* of 9 September 1923 with the news of the Italian mission massacre.

On the morning of 7 April 1939, four Italian columns landed in Albania: at St John Medua, Durrës, Vlora and Santi Quaranta.

Greek Prime Minister Ioannis Metaxas in a 1937 photo.

Tenente Riccardo Bombig, decorated with the *Medaglia d'Oro al Valor Militare alla Memoria* (www.movm.it).

Italian troops land in the port of Durrës, April 1939 (USSME).

Landing of Italian
armoured units in an
Albanian port, April 1939
(USSME).

Albanian troops in the Italian Army immediately after the military occupation of the country
(USSME).

Generale Alfredo Guzzoni, commander of the Italian troops in Albania, in Fushe-Kruja, at the end of military operations, April 1939.

Generale Alexandros Papagos.

Minister Galeazzo Ciano.

Carlo Suckert, known as Curzio Malaparte.

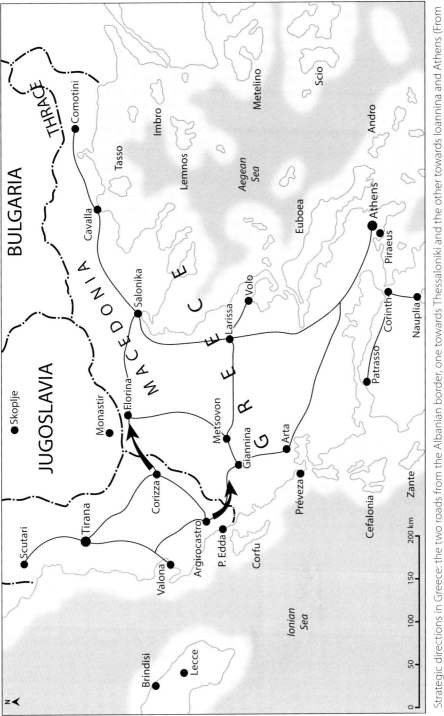

Strategic directions in Greece: the two roads from the Albanian border, one towards Thessaloniki and the other towards Ioannina and Athens (From the magazine *Chronicles of War*).

The Greek cruiser *Elli* under sail.

The Italian submarine *'Delfino'*.

Generale Carlo Geloso.

4 October 1940, Hitler and Mussolini during their meeting at the Brenner Pass in a railway carriage, during which they discussed England and the Balkans.

September 1940: Landing of Italian troops in the port of Durrës, Albania (USSME).

September 1940: Landing of Italian troops in the port of Durrës, Albania (USSME).

Gorizia, 9 October 1940: Mussolini reviews some units stationed in north-eastern Italy (USSME).

Generale Mario Roatta.

Generale Sebastiano Visconti Prasca in a
pre-war photo.

Hitler and Mussolini greet the crowd from the
balcony of Palazzo Vecchio in Florence, 28
October 1940. It was in Florence that Mussolini
informed Hitler that he had attacked Greece.

2

Opposing Forces

The plan for the invasion of Greece, prepared by the Italian General Staff, envisaged an offensive from Albanian territory to conquer Epirus, after which, having received the necessary reinforcements, the Italian troops would first push towards Athens and then proceed to occupy the whole territory. In planning the operations, the Italian generals did consider a landing of troops on the Greek coast in order to trap the enemy in a vice or at least divert valuable troops from the Greek-Albanian border. A landing operation in Corfu was hypothesised, but not realised due to logistical problems and bad weather conditions.

Italian Forces in the Field

By 28 October 1940, the total deployment of Italian forces in Albania was some 83,000 men: 5,000 in the Littoral sector, 25,000 in the Epirus sector, 43,000 in the Korcian sector and 10,000 in the Pindus sector. Visconti Prasca, had 8 divisions plus other smaller units along the Greek-Albanian border, deployed from west to east:

Coastal Sector

Littoral Regiment, deployed along the coast, under the orders of *Generale* Carlo Rivolta, comprising:

 3rd Grenadier Regiment of Sardinia
 7th Cavalry Regiment *Milan*
 6th *Aosta* Cavalry Regiment
 a Blackshirts battalion

A total of about 5,000 men

Epirus Sector

XXV Army Corps of the Ciamuria under the orders of *Generale* Carlo Rossi, charged with invading Epirus, comprising:

Siena Infantry Division under the orders of *Generale* Gualtiero Gabutti, with part of the *Guide* Cavalry Regiment for a total of 6 battalions (9,000 men and 44 artillery pieces).

Ferrara Infantry Division under the orders of *Generale* Licurgo Zannini, reinforced with Albanian bands and Blackshirts to a total of 8 battalions (12,000 men and 51 artillery pieces).

Centauro Armoured Division under the orders of *Generale* Giovanni Magli with four light tank battalions and a bersaglieri regiment (4,000 men, 163 tanks and 24 artillery pieces).

Pindo Sector

The Alpine Division *Julia*, under the orders of *Generale* Mario Girotti, was stationed close to the Pindus mountain range between the deployment of the XXV and XXVI Army Corps. It comprised 5 battalions, 2 artillery groups and a unit of Albanian volunteers, for a total of about 10,000 men and 20 artillery pieces.

Korciano Sector

XXVI Army Corps under the orders of *Generale* Gabriele Nasci, which was stationed in a defensive position along the western Macedonian border from Morova to Grammos. It comprised:

Piemonte Infantry Division, under the orders of *Generale* Adolfo Naldi (about 9,000 men and 32 artillery pieces).

Parma Infantry Division, under the orders of *Generale* Attilio Grattarola (about 12,000 men, 60 artillery pieces, motorcyclists, light tanks, army corps artillery and miners' units).

Venezia Infantry Division, under the orders of *Generale* Silvio Bonini (10,000 men 40 artillery pieces).

Arezzo Infantry Division, under the orders of *Generale* Ernesto Ferone, with two Albanian battalions (12,000 men and 32 artillery pieces).

To these forces stationed in Albania, were to be added those stationed in the Aegean, grouped in the Infantry Division *Regina*, under the orders of *Generale* Michele Scaroina: the division acted as a permanent garrison for the entire Italian Dodecanese. Apart from Rhodes, the main detachments were stationed in Leros, Coo, Scarpanto, Caso, Calino, Castelrosso, Stampalia, Patmo and Gaidaro.

Also in Brindisi, elements of the 47th Infantry Division *Bari* were preparing for an amphibious landing on Corfu, supported by a naval squadron comprising two old light cruisers, two destroyers, three torpedo boats and three transport ships. Another four divisions were being prepared for the second phase of the offensive, the march on Athens, with arrival at the front expected by mid-November.

Most of the Italian divisions were not at full strength in terms of men and materiel. The *Centauro* Armoured Division, for example, had an establishment of 5,000 men, 24 artillery pieces, 8 anti-tank guns and 170 light tanks. Additionally, it must be remembered that the Italian divisions were organised into only two regiments, while the Greek divisions had three. This was because after the Pariani reform of 1938, the Italian infantry divisions had abandoned the 'ternary' or 'triangular' system, with an establishment of three regiments with three battalions each, adopted by almost all armies in the world, to adopt the 'binary' system (two regiments with three battalions each). It was an expedient found by the Italian General Staff to increase the total number of divisions, but officially justified by wanting to lighten the divisions to make them faster in movement. To reinforce the weak binary divisions, a legion of two battalions of the Voluntary Militia for National Security or battalions of Albanian troops was added to the establishment. A relatively minor reinforcement due to the poor training of these divisions and the lack of heavy weaponry among their equipment.

As far as the armament of the Italian soldiers was concerned, it mainly consisted of weapons and equipment dating back to the First World War, especially in the case of the field artillery. Few weapons dated to 1930s designs. Equipping the infantry divisions were the *Carcano* Mod. 91 rifle, the *Breda* Mod. 30 machine gun, the Fiat Mod. 4/35 and *Breda* Mod. 37 machine guns, and the *Brixia* Mod. 35 and Mod. 81 mortars. So far as tanks are concerned, the *Centauro* Division was only equipped with the CV33 light tank, armed only with machine guns, and only when the campaign had begun did a battalion of M13/40 medium tanks arrive to reinforce it. In any case, due to the mountainous and muddy terrain of Epirus, the tanks had little impact on the course of the fighting.

In addition to lacking modern weapons, the Italian soldiers found themselves engaged in a winter campaign in mountainous terrain without adequate mountain equipment, with coats and boots made of shoddy materials and, above all, with an insufficient logistical system: approximately 10,000 tons of supplies were needed daily to supply the campaign, while the two main ports of Durrës and Vlora had a maximum unloading capacity of 3,500 tons per day under optimal conditions. Furthermore, only mules and horses could be relied upon to transport supplies to the frontline units, due to the lack of trucks sent to Albania.

As far as air armament was concerned, Italy could boast a certain superiority. But not all of the aircraft promised by Mussolini were destined for the Greek front, as many had to be engaged in North Africa and the Mediterranean. By 10 November 1940, the *Regia Aeronautica* was able to deploy in Albania, under the command of *Generale* Ferruccio Ranza, eight bombardment squadrons with 31 Savoia-Marchetti S.M.79 and 24 Savoia-Marchetti S.M.81 aircraft, nine fighter squadrons with 47 Fiat G.50, 46 Fiat C.R.42 and 14 Fiat C.R.32 and two reconnaissance squadrons with 25 IMAM Ro.37.

Sixteen bombing squadrons with 60 CANT Z.1007, 18 S.M. 81, 18 Fiat B.R.20 and 23 CANT Z.506 seaplanes were stationed at the air bases in Puglia, two new *Tuffatori* or dive-bomber groups, the 96th and 97th, including the 239th Squadron, with 20 German supplied Junkers Ju 87 'Stuka' aircraft based at Galatina Airport near Lecce, four fighter squadrons with 12 Macchi M.C.200, 33 G.50 and 9 C.R.32.

During the initial stages of the campaign against Greece, the use of aircraft encountered considerable difficulties, mainly due to bad weather and the inadequacy of the airfields in Albania, which the rains turned into veritable swamps. It was therefore not possible to support the troops with aerial bombing, also due to the poor cooperation between the two commanders of the ground and air forces in Albania, Visconti Prasca and Ranza. The possibility of seconding aviation officers to the ground units to coordinate air support missions was not considered.

The *Regia Marina's* role should have been fundamental, especially in the first phase of the campaign, but in the end it proved to be marginal for two reasons: the first, strategic, was the decision not to carry out the landing of troops on the island of Corfu (an action that could have changed the course of the entire campaign) and the second, of a purely logistical nature, the landing capacity of the Albanian ports of Vlora and Durrës was found to be insufficient also there was an insufficient number of transport ships. As the Under-Chief of the General Staff, *Generale* Roatta wrote: The General Staff has never been able to get even one regiment to Albania with all its means of life and action.[1]

Greek Forces

Italy's aggressive policy had forced the Greek Government to initiate a mobilisation that gradually brought about 500,000 men under arms, of whom about 300,000, including elements of the service troops and those in the rear, were committed against the Italians. The Greek General Staff started the war on the basis of the lines of the previously prepared IB plan, which envisaged a defensive war against the joint aggression of Italy and Bulgaria. When it became clear that Bulgaria would not participate in the conflict, *Genikós* Alexandros Papagos, supreme commander of the Greek Army, ordered the transfer of most units from the Thracian front to the Epirus front, thus deploying the most efficient divisions at his disposal on the Albanian front.

At the beginning of the campaign, the Greek Army (*Ellinikós Stratós*) faced the Italian forces in Albania with two groups deployed: the first in Epirus and the second in Macedonia: in Epirus, the 8th Infantry Division (*Genikós* Katsimistrov) was deployed, reinforced by the 3rd brigade, 1 reconnaissance group, with light and heavy artillery (16 batteries), for a total of 15 infantry battalions, with a further 7 battalions deployed as reinforcements in the rear. In Macedonia, there were the 9th infantry Division (*Genikós* Ziguris) and the 4th brigade, with a total of 22 infantry battalions and 22 artillery batteries. As a link between these two groups, a detachment comprising two infantry battalions, an artillery battery and a cavalry squadron was deployed on the Pindus.

Once the campaign had begun, the Greek Command was able to bring in new forces and by 14 November, the number of Greek divisions deployed against the Italians had already risen to seven and by January 1941, to fourteen. The Greek

---

1   AA.VV., *Ottobre 1940: la Campagna di Grecia* (Campobasso: Italia Editrice, 1995), p.70.

divisions had a triangular structure, with three regiments of three battalions each, and were thus individually larger than Italian divisions.[2]

The equipment of the Greek land forces also largely dated back to the First World War: the infantry was equipped with *Mannlicher-Schönauer* rifles and *Saint-Étienne* Mod. 1907, *Hotchkiss* Mod. 1914 and *Schwarzlose* machine guns. Artillery was rather lacking but was compensated for by the availability of a good number of 81mm *Brandt* Mod. 1927 mortars. Tanks and armoured cars were lacking, and the motorisation of the units relied on a few trucks.

The *Ellinikí Vasilikí Aeroporía* (Greek Royal Air Force) was numerically and qualitatively inferior to the *Regia Aeronautica*: according to Greek sources, in 1940 it had 38 fighters, 9 light bombers, 18 heavy bombers and 50 reconnaissance and ground troop cooperation aircraft. According to other sources, however, 44 fighters, 39 bombers and 66 reconnaissance and support aircraft were available. Only a small proportion of the Greek aircraft were modern and competitive aircraft, such as the French Bloch MB 150 fighters and the Polish PZL P.24 and the French Potez 630 bombers, and British Fairey Battle and Bristol Blenheims.

The Royal Hellenic Navy (*Vasilikó Nautikó*) represented a small force: after the sinking of the *Elli*, the fleet comprised the obsolete armoured cruiser *Georgios Averof*, used as a training ship, two old coastal defence ships, ten destroyers of which four were obsolete (*Aetos* class ships) and six modern (four Italian-built *Kountouriotis* class and two British-built *Vasilefs Georgios* class), thirteen obsolete torpedo boats, six relatively modern submarines and other auxiliary units.

The Plan of Attack

Visconti Prasca's plan for the invasion of Epirus was: advance with the main force on the Kalibaki – Gianina – Arta axis and block with the other forces the Metzovo Pass and the southern outlet of Epirus (Filippiade-Arta road junction). In particular, three force groups were to act in Epirus:[3] the *Ciamuria* Army Corps, the *Julia* and the *Littoral* groups, with the possible intervention of the *Piemonte* Division, held in reserve. *Generale* Carlo Rossi's *Ciamuria* Army Corps had at its disposal the *Siena*,

---

2   The assessment of the Italian and Greek forces that clashed, beginning on 28 October 1940, is one of the hottest and most important problems of a reconstruction of the Albanian campaign. Reconstruction is not easy, unfortunately, for different but concomitant reasons, the Italian commander of the first days, Visconti Prasca, and the Greek *Archistrátigos* (Generalissimo/ Commander in Chief) Papagos had the greatest interest in 'inflating' the Italian forces and belittling the Greek forces: Visconti Prasca to mitigate his responsibilities and make less evident the lightness with which he had thrown himself into an offensive action that had no chance of success; Papagos to enhance his merits as commander and valorise the heroism of the Greek soldier. These two coincidental points of view led to only one result: that of placing the blame for the failures not on the political and military leaders, who were either reckless or unsuspecting, but on the Italian soldier, who fought well in spite of everything, and remedied as far as possible the appalling mistakes of those in Rome or Tirana. Mario Cervi, *Storia Della Guerra di Grecia* (Milan: Gruppo Mondadori, 1965), p.127.

3   Mario Montanari, *L'Esercito Italiano nella Campagna di Grecia*, Ufficio Storico Stato Maggiore dell'esercito, p.122.

Ferrara and *Centauro* divisions. According to the plans, it was to break, with the reinforced *Ferrara* Division, the enemy's resistance in the defence of the Kalibaki junction. The advance of this body was to be facilitated with an encircling action from the right (*Siena*) and another from the left (elements of the *Centauro*), and then complete and rapidly exploit the success in the direction of Gianina and Arta.

The *Julia* was to reach the Metzovo junction as quickly and decisively as possible acting in two columns and cover the left flank by occupying the Pindus passes.

The Littoral group had three distinct objectives: Luros for the 3rd *Granatieri*, Preveza for the *Aosta Lancieri* and Arta for the *Milan Lancieri*. Once these objectives had been reached, the group had the task of stopping any influx of Greek units, preparing the outlet to Missolonghi and facilitating the landing of reinforcements at Preveza and Arta.

In Western Macedonia (Korciano sector), was *Generale* Nasci's XXXVI Army Corps, which at that time had only the *Parma* Division and the *Piemonte* Division, a reserve of the High Command. The corps had to secure the border positions by maintaining a dynamic attitude, occupying the sections of the border that were useful for an offensive. At the same time, it had to deceive the enemy by simulating an offensive action simultaneously with the start of operations in Epirus, and finally defend to the utmost the positions of Mali Thatë-Morova-Grammos.

Tanks of the *Centauro* Armoured Division, one of the first units to be transferred to the Greek-Albanian front (USSME).

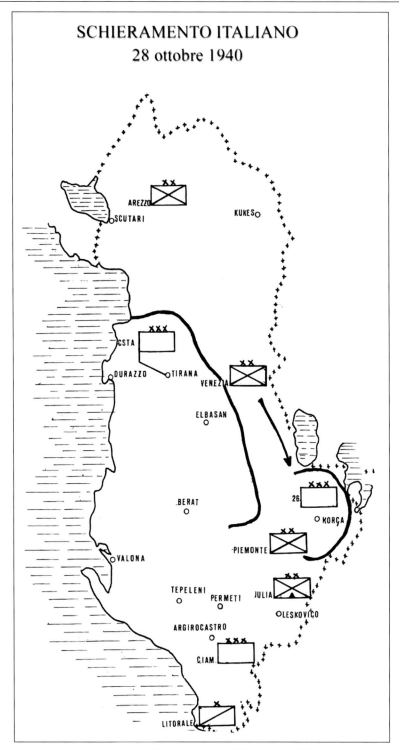

Deployment of Italian forces as of 28 October 1940.

Alpine troops just landed in Albania, September 1940 (USSME).

Generale Gabriele Nasci.

An Alpine soldier with full equipment just arrived on the Greek-Albanian front, October 1940. The Italian soldiers are armed with the *Carcano Mod. 91* rifle (USSME).

Blackshirts lined up during a ceremony on the Greek-Albanian front, autumn 1940 (USSME).

CV35 light tanks and bersaglieri marching on a road in Albania, 1904 (USSME).

An M13/40 tank on the Greek-Albanian front, November 1940 (USSME).

Euzoni, the Greek elite troops, during a parade in special uniform.

Greek soldiers in war move towards the front cheered by the Greek population, October 1940.

A SIAI-Marchetti SM-79 bomber flying over Greek territory, November 1940 (USSME).

The Italian plan of attack (28 October–13 November 1940).

3

The Italian Offensive in Greece

Considering the ongoing autumn season, the beginning of the Italian offensive in Greece took place under disastrous weather conditions. The Italian units moved from the Albanian positions in the pouring rain, which not only made the movement of troops and transport of vehicles difficult, but also hampered the operations of the *Regia Aeronautica*, which could not provide the necessary support to the ground forces.

In the Epirus sector, in the late evening of Sunday, 27 October 1940, the units of the *Ciamuria* Army Corps stood at the border, from the Vojussa Valley to Mount Sarakin, while the corps command moved from Delvino to Frastani, in the Dhrinos Valley, a few kilometres from Kakavia. A few hours later, between 5.30 a.m. and 6 a.m. on 28 October, the troops moved off from their bases.

In the Vojussa-Dhrinos sector, the units moved in four columns, named after the commanders who led them, in an almost concentric fashion around the Kalibaki junction. The two central columns were to penetrate the Greek defences: on the left, the *Trizio* column (*Colonnello* Felice Trizio), comprising the 47th Infantry Regiment, followed the route Lakanokastro – Jeroplatanos (Alizoti) – Mesovouni – height 1090 east of Kalibaki, with the objective of attacking Mount Vigla and possibly also height 1090. On the right, was the *Sapienza* column, commanded by Colonnello Sapienza and comprising the 48th Infantry Regiment, which advanced along the Kakavia – Delvinaki – Kalibaki direction, with the objective of attacking Krioneri and Paliokastro. On the far left, was the *Solinas* column (*Colonnello* Giaocchino Solinas), a grouping of the *Centauro* , which was advancing along the Ponte Perati-Kalibaki road, to support the attack of the 47th regiment.[1] A little further back, a central column was advancing astride the Kakavia-Delvinaki-Kalibaki roadway, comprising the divisional reserve and the bulk of the artillery.

At least initially, weak enemy resistance was expected and the main objective for the Italian troops was to seize the bridges intact. In the end, however, only the bridge at Perati, which was immediately occupied, and another at Burazani were taken before the Greeks blew them up. All others were broken, making the march of the troops even more difficult.

---

1   The column comprised the 5th Bersaglieri command, the XIV/5th Bersaglieri, the III/31st tanks, the II/1st Albanian CC.NN legion, the I/131st artillery, the XIX/26th artillery and other smaller units.

The first real clash with the Greek forces occurred at the Hani Delvinaki Pass in the late morning of the 28th: after a short fight, towards evening the Italian troops reached the Lakanokastro-Krioneri line.

The next day, 29 October, the Jeroplatanos position was taken by the *Trizio* column and the vanguard of the *Solinas* column (in particular the Albanian Bersaglieri and Blackshirts), while the pioneers were busy repairing the numerous roadblocks and building a pontoon bridge over the River Vojussa to allow the passage of artillery and transports. In the meantime, the *Ferrara* Division had reorganised its units, reinforcing the *Sapienza* column with the III/47th, III/48th and the 166th Battalion CC.NN *Piemonte*, for the advance on Paliokastro. The central column had meanwhile arrived at the Grammos River, finding the bridge destroyed: the structure measured some forty metres over four arches. The incessant rain had swollen all the waterways, further complicating the movements of the units.

In any case, *Generale* Rossi, commander of XXV Army Corps of the Ciamuria, considering the breakthrough in the Negrades sector still possible, ordered the continuation of the advance on Gianina after the occupation of the Kalibaki crossroads.

Italian War Bulletin Number 144 of 29 October 1940:

> At dawn yesterday, our troops deployed in Albania crossed the Greek frontier and penetrated enemy territory at various points; the advance continues.

On the morning of 30 October, the vanguard of the *Solinas* column was transferred to the *Ferrara* Division, joining the *Trizio* column. The remaining elements of the *Solinas* column remained stuck on the right bank of the River Vojussa, as the strong current had swept away the bridges built by the pioneers. The bulk of the *Centauro* Division, in a rear position, was also stuck on the Fitoki due to the failure of the pioneers to arrive. In the centre, the position of Doliana had been occupied, while to the south the *Wisdom* column proceeded slowly through the mud and in the rain, between Gormos and Kalamas. The more advanced Greek divisions had meanwhile retreated, avoiding the clash.

Italian War Bulletin Number 145 of 30 October 1940:

> Our troops continued their advance into Greek territory, overcoming resistance from enemy rear guards.

At 10:00 on 31 October, despite the lack of the expected air support, the *Ferrara* Division resumed its march, with two strong central attack columns. The left column, moving from Doliana and passing through Prophet Elias, aimed at the northern slope of the Kalibaki Strait. The right column, on the other hand, was to cross the River Kalamas and reach Paliokastro. Still further to the left, the *Trizio* column, with which the radio link had been broken, was advancing, which according to orders was to continue on to Mesovouni and height 1201. In addition to bad weather, the march was also hindered by Greek artillery fire, whose well-hidden pieces caused many casualties among the attackers.[2] In order to overcome the enemy resistance, it was necessary to widen the front of the attack and therefore the *Centauro* was ordered to carry out a breakthrough manoeuvre along the Hani Dseravinas – Ripitisti route, advancing south of the Kalibaki road.

Italian War Bulletin Number 146 of 31 October 1940:

> Our units, continuing their advance into Epirus, have reached the Kalamas River at various points. The unfavourable weather conditions and the interruptions created by the retreating enemy did not slow down the movement of our troops. Our air force, overcoming the prohibitive atmospheric conditions and the enemy's lively anti-aircraft reaction, bombarded the port of Patras, striking enemy steamships loaded with troops, the Lepanto base, barracks of Greek troops at the Metzovo Pass and important preparations and road junctions in the Kalamas valley. One enemy aircraft attacked by our fighters was shot down. One of our aircraft did not return.

On 1 November, taking advantage of a slight improvement in weather conditions, the armoured vehicles and artillery of the Corps, which had been left behind, were sent forward. The poor state of the roads, the mud and the road interruptions caused by the enemy, made movement difficult. Despite these difficulties, by the morning of 2 November, the units were ready to move forward: the attack should have been launched at 08:00, after a bombardment of the enemy positions by the *Regia Aeronautica*. Instead it started very late and without air support. The units of the *Centauro* moved to attack in three close columns: the passage of the Kalamas near St Attanasio would have allowed the Italian units to envelop the southern slope of Kalibaki and to this end, the *Ferrara* Division was to support the action by continuing its frontal manoeuvre.

In spite of the tenacity and determination of all the divisions, progress was minimal and always for the same reasons: the poor state of the roads and Greek artillery fire, whose position could not be identified and therefore neutralised. By the evening of 2 November, the situation remained virtually unchanged, with the Kalamas not crossed and the enemy positions still in place. For the next day, 3 November, it was decided to concentrate efforts against Kalibaki, committing a strong *Centauro* column. At the same time, further south, other units of the same division would continue to attack towards Negrades and to the north, the *Ferrara* Division would continue its attacks against height 1,090. Once again, despite the efforts of the Italian troops, no results were achieved: there was a lack of artillery and tank support and a river crossing could not be built. It was therefore decided to attempt a new attack the next day, but the High Command intervened to organise the offensive effort

---

2   The greater range of the Greek batteries, which were beyond the range of Italian batteries, could not be countered.

better. The Italian attacks, however, had frightened the command of the 8th Greek Division, which, fearing that it would not be able to hold the Grimbiani positions, decided to withdraw its units to that sub-sector and the neighbouring one on the left of the river.

The Use of *Siena*

The *Siena* Division, reinforced by the *Guide* Regiment and army divisions, was to be engaged on the middle Kalamas. By 28 October, its divisions were deployed between Delvino and Konispoli, in a mountainous area with no viable roads or tracks. It was therefore necessary to prepare the terrain to allow the movement of the divisions, building mule tracks, bridges over the numerous streams and advanced food and ammunition depots. On the other side, near the middle and lower Kalamas course, was the southern part of the Greek resistance position, the Granitsopoulo and Vrusine subsectors of the Kalamas sector and the Thesprotia sector that extended from Mount Ambelia to the sea. Further south, in the Ambrakis region, there was also a Preveza-Filippiade sector with an infantry battalion and a machine gun company. These units, however, when hostilities began and the area towards Kalamas appeared more threatened, were moved to reinforce the Thesprotia sector.

At 6.15 a.m. on 28 October, hidden by thick fog, the *Siena* Division moved from its starting positions. After some clashes with isolated enemy elements, towards evening the Italian units reached Raveni with the 31st Infantry Regiment and Filiates with the 32nd Regiment.

During the fighting for Povla, *Sergente* Felice la Sala, born in 1919 in Contursi (Salerno), serving with the 31st Infantry Regiment fell in combat. For his valour in combat, he was decorated with the *Medaglia d'Oro al Valor Militare alla Memoria*, with the citation:

> He took part with a squad of brave soldiers in the capture of an enemy stronghold. During the action, seeing that any further advance was hindered by the accurate and precise fire of an automatic weapon placed in a small hut, with absolute disregard for any danger, he threw himself against the enemy stronghold to reduce it. Hit a first time in the right hand by a shot that knocked his rifle to the ground, he did not stop in his dash. When he reached under the redoubt, he threw all his bombs into it, using only his left hand. Hit a second time severely, on the position he had taken, he incited his infantrymen to proceed on fast, and led them until he fell exhausted, consecrating with the sacrifice of his life the full success he had achieved. [Povla (Greek front), 28 October 1940]

The following day, at 08:00, the units resumed their march, but the vehicles and most of the artillery had to be left at Konispoli, while waiting for the pioneers to make the mule track to Sajada passable for them. This caused considerable logistical problems for the marching units, which ended up stopping at Kalamas, where the enemy had blown up all the bridges and along which the Greek line of resistance ran. The Italian divisions could not cross the river, which was in heavy flood at the time, because the pioneers lacked the proper materials to build a possible crossing. Between 1 and 4 November, attempts to cross the Kalamas continued, considerably delaying the march of the divisions. Since it was not possible to get the *Carloni* column the materials needed for the construction of a bridge,[3] *Generale* Gabutti decided to leave one infantry battalion and one Albanian battalion at Raveni, transferring the bulk of the 31st Infantry Regiment southwards to support the offensive in the Vrisela area. In the meantime, the opening of the Konispoli-Filiates roadway in the evening of 2 November, thanks to the work of hundreds of workers, allowed the transit of horse drawn artillery and light vehicles. However, the barges were not transported to the river area until the evening of 4 November and so that night, a footbridge was built. It was then decided to force the Kalamas on 5 November, after a heavy bombardment by the *Regia Aeronautica* and at the same time as the passage over the lower Kalamas by the *Littoral* group. On 3 November, the Division had transferred its command to Filiates. On 4 November, Visconti Prasca issued directives for action along the entire Epirus front:

> The *Regia Aeronautica* was to attack the close targets from 9 a.m. to 10 a.m. and on the rearmost targets from 10 a.m. to 1 p.m. The Navy was to act with gunfire to assist the *Littoral* group from 11 a.m. to 1 p.m. on the positions of Igoumenitsa and then, if possible, on the Paramithia node.[4]

Attacks Resume

On 5 November, the attacks along the entire Epirus front resumed. To this end, *Generale* Rossi had changed the tasks and positions of the divisions: the *Centauro* Division was to break through between Kalibaki and Paliokastro, moving along the road to Gianina. On its right, a column was to advance, moving from Paliokastro to Negrades via the St Attanasio bridge. In reserve was the reconstituted *Solinas* column, which was however left at the disposal of the army corps command. The *Ferrara* Divisions were to support the breakthrough action of the *Centauro* Division and secure the flanks of the subsequent breakthrough: on the left, the 47th infantry regiment was to occupy height 1,090 and continue on to Kato Sudenia and height 1,134. On the right, the 48th Infantry Regiment, meanwhile, was to target Mount Vurtopa to eliminate the northern front of the Kalibaki defences and then continue north of the road to Gianina. Further south, a tactical group also of the 48th regiment was to pass over St Attanasio bridge (after the *Centauro* units had passed), garrison it and continue towards Ligopsa. The *Guide* Regiment was to protect the Division's right flank from possible attacks from the south, staying in the Goritsa area. On the other side, the Greeks were firmly determined to hold the Kalamas line.

---

3   The first divisional column consisted of the 31st Infantry under the orders of *Colonnello* Mario Carloni, reinforced by artillery (III/51st) and divisional mortar units (1st Cp.).

4   Mario Montanari, *L'Esercito Italiano Nella Campagna di Grecia*, Ufficio Storico Stato Maggiore dell'esercito, p.163.

At 10 a.m. on 5 November, the Italian columns moved forward without the expected air support. The march was hampered by a massive barrage of Greek artillery. The units of the *Centauro* in particular were blocked by numerous obstacles: the left column, comprising tanks and bersaglieri, was stuck in front of a large ditch protected by iron barricades, while the right column, due to misdirection, found itself bogged down on the banks of the Kalamas. Losses continued to mount: between 28 October and 5 November, the *Ferrara* and *Centauro with* their corps supports, suffered a total loss of 645 men (147 killed, 438 wounded and 40 missing). Losses in vehicles were also heavy: the 31st Tank Regiment had one battalion reduced to 40 percent of its tanks and another to 70 percent. Despite the meagre successes, *Generale* Rossi, after consulting with Visconti Prasca and noticing a decrease in enemy resistance on the right of their deployment, decided to resume the attacks the next day.

The units of the two divisions then returned to the attack on the morning of 6 November, poorly supported by the *Regia Aeronautica*, which was unable to make a decisive contribution. Once again, the advance of the Italian forces was strongly resisted by enemy automatic weapons fire. It was only towards evening, thanks to a decrease in Greek artillery and machine gun fire, that some positions were reached. This convinced *Generale* Rossi to make a last attempt to conquer the 1,090 height and, pivoting on this, to carry out with other forces the bypassing of the Kalibaki junction and then continue towards Gianina. At the same time, other divisions were to conquer the positions at point 790 east of Gianina, which were already under bombardment by the *Regia Aeronautica*.

At dawn on 7 November, the attack resumed. The Italian columns moved forward under enemy artillery fire, which increased considerably in intensity around 11:00. At 13:00, the divisions had to stop at the positions they had reached. The *Ferrara* Division had occupied height 1201 and the northern slopes of height 1,090 but was stuck under the slopes of Vurtopa, while the *Centauro was* stuck on Kalamas at the St Attanasio bridge.

During the fighting on 7 November, *Tenente Colonnello* Adalgiso Ferrucci, born in Pico (Frosinone) on 10 May 1891, in command of the 47th Infantry Regiment of *Ferrara*, fell in combat. He was awarded the *Medaglia d'Oro al Valor Militare alla Memoria* with the citation:

> Commander of a column, daring and enthusiastic, always at the head of the advanced units that he animated with his faith and youthful enthusiasm, always present where the danger was greatest, he daringly led his troops through several days of fierce fighting, taking important positions that were firmly fortified. During an extremely violent action, countered by an intense reaction from the enemy, who had managed to halt the battalion's movement, he took the lead of his men on his own initiative and preceded them in the attack, succeeding, with the example of his indomitable valour and magnificent disregard for danger, in giving new impetus to the offensive movement. In the course of this heroic action he was shot dead. A superb figure of an infantryman and a daring and dashing commander. [Delvinaki – Doliana – Prophet Elias (Greek front), 28 October – 7 November 1940]

The Battle Continues

On the other side, *Genikós* Katsimitros, commander of the 8th Greek Division, was receiving reinforcements, so he was ordered by the Supreme Command to continue to hold the position of Elea (Kalibaki) – Kalamas. However, a possible retreat into the Thesprotia sector, where Italian pressure had become stronger, was considered. And in fact further south, *Siena's* units, after continuous attempts, had succeeded in throwing a crossing with boats, in the early afternoon of 5 November. Immediately, two battalions of the 32nd regiment crossed the river and after overwhelming the Greek positions, captured the heights of Varfani at 18:30. In the course of the night, the bridgehead was firmly consolidated. The next day, the construction of a bridge was completed, thus allowing more troops to cross the river. In the evening of 6 November, Riziani was occupied, but the same night, the order came to halt the advance and to hold on to the positions that had been reached.

On the same day, 5 November, the *Littoral* group also succeeded in forcing the River Kalamas in the course of the morning, thanks to a bridge thrown over at dawn, a footbridge, and little Greek resistance. Around noon, a solid bridgehead was established. The three columns of the group began to descend southwards, overwhelming the resistance of four enemy battalions from the Thesprotia sector, whose remnants began to fall back. Soon after, *Genikós* Katsimitros ordered the planned retreat of the entire Thesprotia sector along the left bank of the Acheron. In the meantime, however, the Italian offensive had come to a halt: as early as the morning of 7 November, the Albanian High Command had in fact ordered *Generale* Rivolta to halt the advance of the 3rd *Granatieri* at Plataria and to send a forward scouting regiment only. At the same time, the *Aosta* and *Milan* Regiments, which had reached Murtos and Margarition, had to fall back.

The Use of the *Julia* on the Pindus

The main objective of the *Julia* was to occupy the mountain passes of Metzovo and Drisko in order to prevent the possible joining of the Greek forces of Thessaly with those of Epirus. The orders for the Division were to cross the Perati Bridge over the Sarantaporos Stream, occupy Konitza and continue along the course of the River Vojussa towards Metzovo behind the Pindus mountain range. The Pindus mountain range extends from Mount Grammos to the Metzovo plain, and the only road connecting Epirus with Thessaly and Macedonia crossed the Pindus via the Metzovo Pass, moving from Filiates along the coast. By interrupting this road, the two largest regions of northern Greece, Epirus and Macedonia, were completely isolated. The taking of the Metzovo Pass was the final objective of the *Julia* Division. The Italian divisions found themselves engaged in a mountainous area, on impassable terrain with few passable tracks that offered numerous logistical problems to the attacking forces.

In that sector, the Greek forces had in the front line a detachment comprising two infantry battalions, a frontier company and a cavalry squadron, while in the second line there were several other units ready for action.

The units of the *Julia* were organised into two groups.

The 8th *Alpini*, under the orders of *Colonnello* Vincenzo Dapino, was in three columns: the *Tolmezzo* Battalion, initially protecting the outer flank and then in the rearguard; the *Gemona* Battalion with the *Conegliano* Group (minus one battery); the *Cividale* Battalion with a battery from *Conegliano*. The regimental command was with the *Gemona*, while the divisional command was with the *Cividale*. The objective of the attack was the conquest of Zygos di Metzovo.

The 9th *Alpini* regiment, under the orders of *Colonnello* Gaetano Tavoni, was in two columns: L'Aquila Battalion with a battery from the *Udine* Group and the *Vicenza* Battalion with another battery. The regimental command was with L'Aquila Battalion. The objective of the attack was the positions of Plaka (elevation 1593) – Peristeri (elevation 2294).

On the right flank of the Division, was the 5th Albanian Volunteer Battalion, reinforced by a few Alpine squads, with orders to occupy the Konitsa Basin and then secure the flank as far as Metzovo.

At dawn on 28 October, the Alpine troops crossed the border, easily overrunning the enemy's frontier positions, also managing to capture considerable quantities of weapons and ammunition. The columns of the *Julia* reached as far as Sarantaporos and at sunset the *Gemona* and *Cividale* occupied Mount Stavros. The next day, 29 October, the advance resumed under torrential rain that swelled the Sarantaporos and turned the paths into rivers of mud. The Alpine troops managed to cross the river at the ford, despite a multitude of difficulties. The resistance put up by the Greek units was overwhelmed with strength and determination. By 31 October, the 8th Alpini firmly held the Furka Junction, with the *Gemona* to the south-east, the *Cividale* to the south and the *Tolmezzo* to the north-east. The 9th *Alpini*, on the other hand, had reached the northern slopes of Smolika. The bad weather had slowed down the march of the units considerably and therefore it was necessary to speed up the march to Metzovo.

On the other side, the Greek Supreme Command, seeing the rapid occupation of Stavros and foreseeing the threat of the separation of the forces of Pindos from those of Western Macedonia, ordered a concentration on Pindos of all the closest units, defining their main task as the defence against the invasion of Thessaly along the Gianina – Metsovo – Trikkala route. In particular, *Genikós* Vrahnos' 1st Division was ordered to contain the Italian breakthrough and then eliminate it by counterattacks. The Pindus sector had in the meantime passed to *Genikós* Papadopoulos' 2nd Army Corps, which was ordered to prepare a counter-offensive to recapture Mount Stavros.

On 1 November, the Greeks attacked Likorrachi and the Furka knot: at Likorrachi, there was still a company from *Tolmezzo* that, after repelling the enemy attack, fell back and re-joined the battalion engaged in the rearguard. The attack at the Furka Junction was repulsed by the *Gemona* Alpine troops and at the same time the *Cividale* Alpine troops attacked and reached Samarina late in the evening. Thus, the 8th *Alpini* regrouped and continued in a single column across the eastern slope of Smolika to reach Distraton.

After crossing the western slope of the Smolika, the 9th *Alpini* Regiment had reached the River Aoo in the Elefterion – Pades section, but was unable to cross the river due to both the strong current and the heavy enemy fire coming from the opposite bank. *Generale* Girotti then decided that if during the night the Alpine troops of the 9th regiment did not manage to cross the river; they should re-join those of the 8th regiment in the Distraton area. The new attempt to cross the river failed, and in the end, the two regiments could not even be reunited because the Pades-Distraton section was under fire from automatic weapons and Greek artillery stationed on the left bank of the river. Thus, on the evening of 3 November, the 9th *Alpini* found itself grouped between Paleoselio and Pades and the 8th *Alpini* was at Distraton, except for the *Cividale*, which had almost reached Vovusa. The *Julia* was now on the verge of being surrounded by Greek units and perhaps even more serious, it had been fighting for a week and the Alpine troops had only received food for five days. There was also a shortage of fodder for the transport animals. After receiving assurance of air resupply for the next day, *Generale* Girotti sent the following message to High Command Albania:

> …Enemy is to the rear, on the flank and ahead stop to proceed in any direction supplies are needed stop I would like to know about the command's intentions and possibilities stop sent Konitsa column for supplies as it appears that the enemy descends Sarandaporos stop enemy planes fly over and act daily on our units stop[5]

From the High Command came the following reply:

> …contain the enemy, mass in the Bryaza [Distraton] area and secure the communication route to Konitsa.

On 5 November, the *Gemona* Battalion, which was stationed in positions on Mount Smiliani (height 1991) and Mount Kergoli (height 1609), was attacked by two Greek battalions and the 1st cavalry regiment.

The Alpine troops defended themselves fiercely, however the enemy managed to occupy height 1609 and immediately tried to force into the village of Distraton, but was driven back thanks to a fierce counterattack launched by the battalion's command company. The objective of the Greeks was to penetrate between the two Alpine regiments to separate them, and to ward off this threat *L'Aquila* Battalion was ordered to move to the eastern slopes of Smolika and attack the units facing the *Gemona* on the flank. At the same time, the *Vicenza* Battalion was sent to Mount Kleftis to protect the lines of communication. Hard fighting followed that lasted for at least seven hours without succeeding in driving the enemy divisions away. The losses were very high, 691 men in total: 126 killed (including 3 officers), 259 wounded (including 12 officers), 306 missing (including 3 officers). The Greek cavalry units attacked Vovusa, defended by the *Cividale* Alpine troops, on 5 November but were repulsed with heavy losses. After being reinforced by an infantry battalion, the

---

5   Mario Montanari, *L'Esercito Italiano Nella Campagna di Grecia*, Ufficio Storico Stato Maggiore dell'Esercito, p.179.

Greeks returned to the attack, but the Alpine troops had meanwhile fallen back to Distraton.

On 6 November, the *Tolmezzo* Alpine troops, stationed on Mount Gomara, repelled new enemy attacks of at least two infantry battalions, while those of *Cividale*, stationed on the southern slopes of Mount Valisitsa, repelled attacks by two more Greek battalions. However, the enemy pressure continued to intensify, thanks to the continuous influx of their reinforcements, and so the *Gemona*'s Alpine troops, still on the heights of Mount Smiliani and Mount Kersoli, after fighting tenaciously, were forced to retreat. The presence of *L'Aquila* Battalion on the eastern slope of Smolika, slowed down the progress of the Greeks, who were concerned about an Italian counterattack on the flank.

During the course of the night, it was decided that the 8th *Alpini* troops would fall back to the Pades-Elefterion area. The *Tolmezzo* Alpini, after launching a fierce counterattack to put the Greek units that were surrounding them to flight, managed to fall back to the heights to the north-west of Distraton, eliminating the Greek forces present. *Cividale* continued to fight tenaciously but lost ground, while the presence of *L'Aquila* on Smolika prevented the collapse of the entire front. The other two Alpine battalions stood on the Smiliani – Kiura line. During the night, the *Cividale*, surrounded and under attack, managed to break through and join the rest of the regiment.

The retreat continued over the next three days, with the units marching in the rain and snow, under continuous enemy attacks, all repulsed by the Alpine troops. On the afternoon of 7 November, *Generale* Girotti received a telegram from Visconti Prasca in which he sanctioned the end of the Pindus offensive. On 8 November, divisional command moved to Konitsa and then to Ponte Perati, finding the situation uncertain. The retreating divisions were threatened with being overrun by the pursuing Greek troops. In the course of the morning, while the Alpine troops of *Cividale* resumed their march to remain united with the other battalions, they were attacked by Greek units on the ridge south of Bryaza. Thanks to an immediate counterattack, the Alpine troops managed to reach the village and, engaging in fierce hand-to-hand combat, fought their way through the enemy lines with dagger and bayonet. The other battalions of the 8th Alpini, the *Tolmezzo* and the *Gemona*, after having been engaged throughout the day in repelling the enemy attacks, managed to fall back during the night, following different routes, to Pades and Eleutero. At the same time, the 9th Alpini also continued its retreat, under strong enemy pressure from both the north and east.

> The weather conditions are getting worse. Swirls of snow envelop the units, which make their movements slowly and with difficulty. The retreat march is exhausting. Tattered, exhausted, dirty, the survivors of the 'Julia' advance, but all of them, without distinction, even the wounded who are dragging themselves groggily and the stretcher-bearers, have their weapon in hand, a rifle, a musket, a pistol, a machine gun. They advance without a look, without words, some without shoes, others without clothing, wrapped in a tent tarp or a camp blanket, but all with the worn-out alpine hat on their heads, even if with a worn-out stub of a feather. Along the trail was a

monstrous spectacle: mules' carrion, crates, empty crates, sacks, shoes, the remains of clothing, abandoned materials, unburied corpses…⁶

On 9 November, the *Vicenza* Battalion found itself deployed on the Cristobasileus Saddle, while the *L'Aquila* and the *Udine* Group were on the Sant'Attanasio Saddle to be engaged against the Greek divisions that, after having reached the ridge north of Piclati, were obstructing the 8th *Alpini*'s retreat. The retreat of the units continued slowly under the continuous fire of the Greeks: the columns that crossed the Eleutero Basin were attacked by units coming down from Smolika.

Right in the Eleutheros basin, the *Conegliano* group, which was marching with the commander of the 8th *Alpini* and two Alpine companies, to reach Konitsa, was suddenly surrounded by strong Greek units. Fierce fighting ensued, which increased in intensity around 13:00. The *Conegliano* pieces fired for six consecutive hours at enemy soldiers only a few hundred metres away. The machine guns of the batteries were also particularly busy, the artillerymen of the *Julia* continued to fight valiantly. Towards evening, the few Alpine soldiers and artillerymen still alive led the way in withdrawing while continuing to fight at close range, taking most of the artillery equipment with them. During the difficult retreat, most of the surviving mules were lost, killed by Greek mortar fire.

The *Sottotenente* Joâo Turolla, born on 26 July 1915 in Ariano nel Polesine (province of Rovigo), of the 13th battery of the *Conegliano* group, distinguished himself during these last battles. During the retreat of the Alpine troops, he continued to fire his machine gun to the last to cover the repositioning of his comrades. For his valour shown in combat, he was awarded the *Medaglia d'Oro al Valor Militare alla Memoria*, with the citation:

> Officer of an Alpine battery, in a succession of numerous and bitter battles he gave shining proof of the highest military virtues. Several times a volunteer in risky tasks, he carried them out with daring and skill. When his group was surrounded by a preponderant adversary force, he decisively moved to a dominant position, beaten by deadly fire, to carry out a strenuous defence of the batteries with a machine gun. Seriously wounded and aware of the imminent end, he continued to keep the fighting ardour and faith in victory alive in his men, until he fell heroically on the weapon with which he had fired until the last moment. [Eleuthero (Greek front), 9 November 1940].

It was the *Julia*'s first *Medaglia d'Oro*. On 10 November, the bulk of the 8th Alpini finally managed to escape the enemy's grip and regroup at Konitsa. The 9th *Alpini*, on the other hand, was ordered to continue defending the Cristobasileus Saddle. Towards evening, the sector came under the control of the *Bari* Division, under the orders of *Generale* Matteo Negro, while the divisions of the *Julia* were transferred to Premeti to be reorganised, with the exception of the 9th Alpini and the *Udine*

---

6   Aldo Rasero, *Alpini della Julia: Storia della Divisione Miracolo* (Milan: Ugo Mursia Editore, 2018), p.153.

Group, which remained in the front line for a few more days under the command of the *Bari* Division.

Another *Medaglia d'Oro* was awarded to Staff Sergeant Silvio di Giacomo, who served with the *Vicenza* Alpini Battalion. Born in Acciano, province of L'Aquila, on 1 January 1915, he enlisted in the Royal Army in April 1935 and was assigned to *L'Aquila Alpini* Battalion of the 9th Alpini Regiment. In June of the same year, he began attending the non-commissioned officer cadet course at the Central Mountaineering School. Promoted to *caporale* in September 1936, he was put on leave in 1938. On 30 April 1939, he left for Albania where he was promoted to *Sergente Maggiore* in June of the same year and assigned to the *Vicenza Alpini* Battalion. On 11 November 1940, despite being assigned to the unit's corps, he did not hesitate to take up a machine gun to repel enemy attacks. After being wounded several times during the fighting, he fell on the saddle of Cristobasileus. He was then awarded the *Medaglia d'Oro al Valor Militare alla Memoria*, with the following citation:

> A non-commissioned officer endowed with special military virtues and a magnificent ascendancy towards his inferiors, whom he had animated with every fervid enthusiasm, he rushed, as the unit's corpsman, into the line to guard, with his drivers, a particularly threatened position. Wielding a machine gun, he stood and inflicted heavy casualties on the enemy, who attacked in overwhelming force. Badly hit in several places, he refused to abandon the position and still found the extreme energy to direct the defence. He died shortly afterwards to the cry of 'Long live Italy' among his Alpine soldiers, who, animated by the heroic example of their commander, fought strenuously and succeeded in maintaining firm possession of the position. [Kristobasileo (Greek front), 11 November 1940].

Operations in the Korça Sector

The fighting in the sector of the XXVI Army Corps was initially characterised by small clashes between frontier units, particularly in the Bilishti area. Between the Bilishti Basin and the Korça Plain was the Morova Massif, a real natural obstacle. In fact, communication between the two plains was only possible by bypassing the Morova. *Generale* Nasci, who had just arrived in the sector at the end of October, had decided to hold out on the Mali i Thatë – Morova – Grammos line and at the same time attempt a few local offensives with the most advanced units, mainly to occupy some border areas to improve the tactical situation. At his disposal were the *Piemonte* Division, the *Parma* Division and some elements of the Army Corps. The defence of the sector was provided by the *Parma* Division alone, comprising two regiments, each of which had only two battalions in line, with the other two in reserve. The *Venezia* regiments were also arriving and between 28 and 30 October, the bulk of the 83rd Infantry had already regrouped in Korça. *Generale* Nasci intended to deploy the *Venezia* on the left of the *Parma* and, by moving the latter southwards, to be able to transfer part of the *Piemonte* to the Korça plain and thus have a larger reserve. He therefore began to modify the defensive deployment by organising a stronger line between little Prespa and Trsteniku near the Kapestica gap, where the Greeks had already made their presence felt.

On 1 November, the Greeks attacked in the Treni sector, forcing the *Venezia* units to retreat. Counterattacks were immediately launched and some positions were regained. In the following days, only local actions occurred, in order to better organise the disposition of the divisions on the ground.

At dawn on 5 November, after a massive artillery barrage, the Greeks attacked the Vipiakut – Bilishti mountain section, where the 109th CC.NN. battalion and the II/83rd infantry were stationed. After several hours of furious fighting, the Blackshirts were forced to retreat while the II/83rd continued to hold its positions firmly. The regimental commander attempted to close the breach by extending his lines towards Mount Vipiakut, but a new massive enemy attack prevented the manoeuvre: they fought for a few more hours with the Italian units still in their positions. Considering the high losses suffered and the strong pressure exerted by the enemy, *Generale* Nasci decided around 8 p.m. to withdraw all the divisions to positions further back. During the fighting at Bilishti, the Albanian volunteers of the *Tomori* Battalion, attached to the 83rd Infantry, behaved badly in front of the enemy, convincing *Generale* Nasci to avoid their redeployment into the front line.[7]

Capitano Alfredo Longo, of the 84th Infantry Regiment of the *Venezia* Division, fell in the course of the last fighting on the heights of Bilishti. Born in 1899 in San Lorenzo del Vallo (Cosenza), he had taken part in the First World War and in the campaign in East Africa. On 5 November 1940, during a heavy firefight with the enemy, *Capitano* Alfredo Longo was hit in the chest by a machine gun burst and died. He was decorated with the *Medaglia d'Oro al Valor Militare alla Memoria* with the following citation:

> During a bloody fight, he walked several times along the line beaten by intense enemy fire to animate the soldiers and personally direct the action of his accompanying weapons decentralised to the rifle companies. He then voluntarily took command of a unit without an officer, quickly reorganised it and impetuously led it several times to the counterattack, succeeding in arresting the enemy and inflicting heavy losses. In the impetuosity of the last attack, while solidly asserting himself on the enemy's difficult position, he was struck down by enemy machine gun fire and met a glorious death. [Bilishti Heights (Albania), 5 November 1940].

On the morning of 6 November, *Generale* Ubaldo Soddu, Under-Secretary of War and Chief of the General Staff, who had been sent to Albania by Mussolini to verify the situation, flew to Korça. After being informed of the state of affairs, he recommended that Nasci hold out for another five or six days, while awaiting

---

7 At dawn on 4 November 1940, the *Tomori* Battalion was ordered to attack and recapture the positions on Mount Lapishtit. The attack was stopped by automatic weapon and artillery fire, forcing the battalion to fall back in great disorder and completely disperse. In the confusion of the moment, some Albanian volunteers opened fire on the Italian troops themselves. The bulk of the battalion, after being regrouped, was disarmed and moved to the rear.

reinforcements. When he left for Tirana a few hours later, Soddu agreed with Nasci to continue the defensive attack and avoid moving back west of Bilishti. The next day, the first elements of the *Arezzo* Division arrived. Between 28 October and 5 November, the XXVI Army Corps had suffered a total loss of 760 men: 85 killed (including 4 officers), 365 wounded (including 16 officers) and 310 missing, mostly from the Albanian *Tomori* Battalion.

Reorganisation of Forces

On the same day, 6 November 1940, having finally ascertained the numerical inferiority of the Italian forces along the entire Greek-Albanian front, the General Staff decided to reorganise the forces and set up the Albania Army Group, sending new divisions from Italy. On 7 November, Visconti Prasca himself was forced to admit the end of the offensive with the following telegram: 'Our attack can be considered halted by enemy resistance and it is useless to hope to reach the objective until other divisions arrive...' The order came from the General Staff to halt the offensive for good and to hold the positions reached, securing the Konitsa area. For his part, *Generale* Soddu, from Tirana transmitted the following directive to Visconti Prasca:

> ...Epirus sector strengthen on achieved positions and facilitate Julia concentration on Konitsa area to be held firmly. Reinforce on current positions. Central sector confirm reinforcement with second Bersaglieri. Accelerate the inflow of the Bari Division in the Perati area.... I will assume command at zero hours on the 9th.

On 9 November 1940, *Generale* Soddu was appointed Senior Commander of the Albanian Armed Forces. The Albania Army Group was organised into two armies:

The 9th Army of *Generale* Mario Vercellino committed to defending the Coriza sector with the *Piemonte, Parma, Venezia* and *Arezzo* Divisions and the Pindus sector with the *Julia, Bari* and 2nd *Tridentine Alpini* Divisions arriving.

The 11th Army of *Generale* Carlo Geloso, which was to continue the offensive in Epirus with the *Siena, Ferrara* and *Centauro* Divisions plus another four divisions in the inflow phase; three more divisions were to be concentrated in Apulia as a reserve.

Generale Visconti Prasca was side-lined, on 9 November he was temporarily placed in command of the 11th Army, but was replaced as early as 11 November by Geloso and on 30 November was placed on indefinite leave.

Italian soldiers and light L tanks penetrate Greek territory, encountering considerable difficulties because of the muddy and impassable terrain. (USSME)

Italian soldiers ready to cross the Greek border. (USSME)

The vanguard of the *Centauro* Armoured Division, stopped by mud, waited for the road to be opened up by the engineer corps. (USSME)

Italian troops cross a watercourse over a bridge repaired by the engineer corps, 28 October 1940. (USSME)

A SIAI-Marchetti SM-79 bomber flying over Greek territory, late October 1940. (USSME)

Sergente Felice la Sala (www.movm.it).

Tenente Colonnello Adalgiso Ferrucci (www. movm.it).

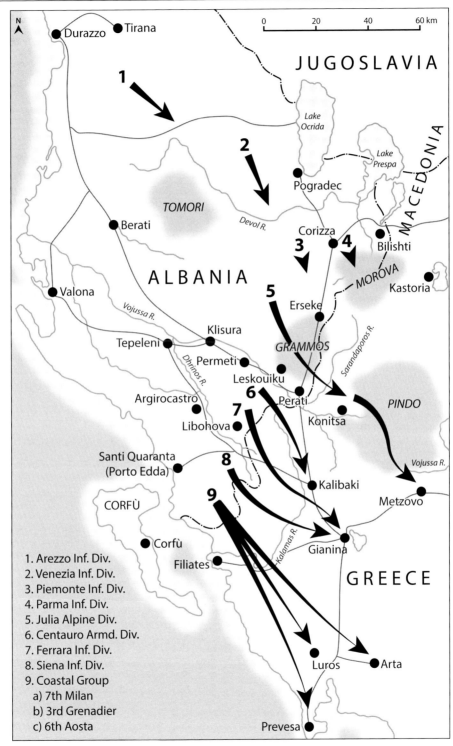

The attack directions of the Italian divisions, October-November 1940.

FELICE LA SALA

Giovane Fascista di anni 21, sergente, da Contursi (Salerno), alla memoria.

• Partecipava con una squadra di arditi alla conquista di un munito caposaldo nemico. Durante l'azione, visto che ogni ulteriore avanzata era ostacolata dal fuoco nutrito e preciso di un'arma automatica posta in un ridottino, con assoluto sprezzo di ogni pericolo si lanciava da solo contro l'apprestamento nemico per ridurlo al silenzio. Colpito una prima volta alla mano destra da una raffica che gli faceva cadere a terra il moschetto, non si fermava nel suo scatto. Giunto sotto il ridottino vi lanciava dentro, servendosi della sola mano sinistra, tutte le sue bombe. Colpito una seconda volta gravemente sulla posizione conquistata; incitava i suoi fanti a procedere sollecitamente oltre e li guidava fino a quando cadeva esausto, consacrando col sacrificio della vita il pieno successo ottenuto. •

(Povle, fronte greco, 28 ottobre 1940-XVIII)

Contemporary postcard commemorating the awarding of the *Medaglia d'Oro al Valor Militare* to Squad *Sergente* Felice la Sala.

Bersaglieri pull an anti-tank piece by hand, November 1940. (USSME)

Centauro tanks and bersaglieri engaged in an attack, November 1940. (USSME)

Italian column in the Vojussa River area, November 1940. (USSME)

The rugged Pindus mountain range in Greece in November 1940, where the Alpine troops of the *Julia* fought with great valour. (USSME)

Alpine units penetrate Greek territory, 28 October 1940. (USSME)

Transporting materials on mules, moving with great difficulty over muddy terrain, October 1940. (USSME)

The complementary Joâo Turolla (www.movm.it).

Capitano Alfredo Longo. (www.movm.it)

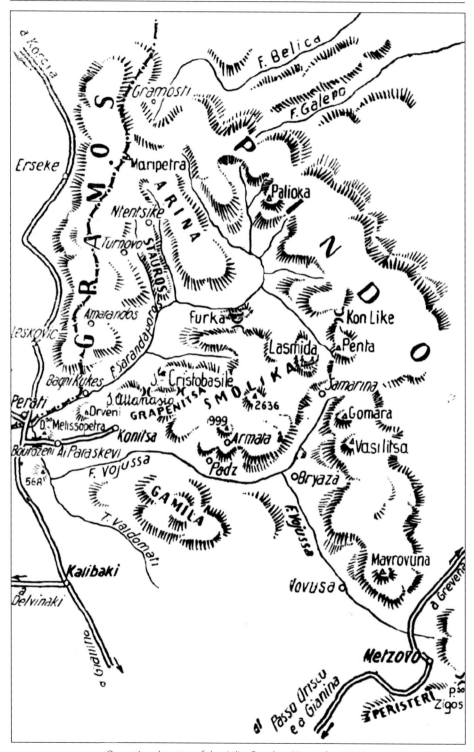

Operational sector of the *Julia*, October-November 1940.

JOAO TUROLLA

Sottotenente 3° Regg. artiglieria alpina, da Ariano Polesine (Rovigo), alla memoria.

«Ufficiale di una batteria alpina, in un seguito di numerosi ed aspri combattimenti dava fulgida prova delle più alte virtù militari. Più volte volontario in compiti rischiosi, li portava a compimento con ardimento e perizia. Accerchiato il suo gruppo da preponderanti forze avversarie, si portava decisamente su una posizione dominante, battuta da fuoco micidiale, per effettuare con una mitragliatrice una più strenua difesa delle batterie. Gravemente ferito e conscio della fine imminente, continuava a tener vivo nei suoi dipendenti l'ardore combattivo e la fede nella vittoria finchè si abbatteva da eroe sull'arma con cui aveva fatto fuoco sino all'ultimo istante.»

(Eleutero, fronte greco, 9 novembre 1940-XIX)

Contemporary postcard commemorating the awarding of the *Medaglia d'Oro al Valor Militare* to *Sottotenente* Joâo Turolla.

SILVIO DI GIACOMO

Sergente magg. 9° Regg. alpini, da Acciano (L'Aquila), alla memoria.

«Sottufficiale dotato di spiccate virtù militari e di magnifico ascendente verso i suoi inferiori che aveva animato di ogni fervido entusiasmo, accorreva - per quanto addetto alle salmerie del reparto - in linea per presidiare, con i suoi conducenti, una posizione particolarmente delicata. Imbracciato un fucile mitragliatore, in piedi, arrecava gravi perdite al nemico che attaccava in forze soverchianti. Colpito gravemente in più parti, rifiutava di abbandonare la posizione e trovava ancora l'estrema energia per dirigerne la difesa. Spirava poco dopo, al grido di "Viva l'Italia" fra i suoi alpini che animati dall'eroico esempio del loro comandante, si battevano strenuamente, e riuscivano a mantenere il saldo possesso della posizione.»

(Kristobasileo, fronte greco, 11 novembre 1940-XIX)

Contemporary postcard commemorating the award of the *Medaglia d'Oro al Valor Militare* to *Sergente Maggiore* Silvio di Giacomo

Italian soldiers engaged in combat on the Greek-Albanian front, November 1940, (USSME)

Generale Ubaldo Soddu, Under-Secretary of War and Vice-Chief of the General Staff

4

The Greek Counter-Offensive

With the offensive halted, the Italian troops on the entire Greek-Albanian front assumed a defensive posture, while waiting for new orders. *Generale* Soddu was therefore mainly engaged in organising a solid Italian defensive line. New troops were arriving from Italy, but slowly: the transport of men and vehicles was hindered by the British submarines in the Adriatic Sea and by air by the Royal Air Force whose planes were now taking off from Greek territory. *Generale* Soddu issued his first directive mainly to reorganise the deployment of forces: the 11th Army was to defend the bridgehead of Igoumenitsa and the Konitsa area. At the same time, the 9th Army was to recapture the heights north of Devoli between the two lakes of Prespa, in order to have a good base to strike the enemy's right flank, and to the south, it was to repel the Greek attacks aiming at the Ersekë road.

In the meantime, reinforcements from Italy were continuing to arrive in a disorderly manner: the 1st *Valle* Alpine Group was in Valona with the *Val Fella*, *Val Tagliamento* and *Val Natisone* Battalions, but without mules and materials because they had been airlifted. Some elements of the *Tridentine* Alpine Division had also arrived, partly landed in Durrës and partly flown to Tirana. Some elements of the *Modena* Division had also arrived, landed in Valona, while the bulk of the division was concentrating in Bari. An armoured battalion equipped with M 13/40 tanks had landed in Durrës.

Order of Battle of the Italian Forces, 16 November 1940

Commander-in-Chief F. A. Albania (*Generale* U. Soddu)
9th Army (*Generale* Vercellino)
III Army Corps (*Generale* Arisio)
    Venezia Infantry Division (*Generale* Bonini)
    Arezzo Infantry Division (*Generale* Ferone)
    Support and services
XXVI Army Corps (*Generale* Nasci)
    Parma Infantry Division (*Generale* Grattarola)
    Piemont Infantry Division (*Generale* Naldi)
    Support and services
11th Army (*Generale* Geloso)
VIII Army Corps (*Generale* Bancale)

> *Bari* Infantry Division (*Generale* Zaccone, later *Generale* D'Havet)
> *Julia* Alpine Division (*Generale* Girotti)
> Support and services
XXV Army Corps (*Generale* Rossi)
> *Ferrara* Infantry Division (*Generale* Zannini)
> *Siena* Infantry Division (*Generale* Gabutti)
> *Centauro* Armoured Division (*Generale* Magli)
> Support and services

The Greek forces had been similarly considerably reinforced and by mid-November, they had some 80,000 men and 198 artillery pieces in the Korça sector in Western Macedonia (against 45,000 men and 200 pieces in the Italian forces), 32,000 men and 114 artillery pieces (against 23,000 men and 112 pieces in the Italian forces) in the central Grammos sector, and 80,000 men and 184 pieces (against 47,000 men and 248 pieces in the Italian forces) in Epirus. In reserve, the Greek Command had another 40,000 men and 60 artillery pieces. On the Italian side there was no reserve, but new troops were expected to be landed in Albania.

Greek Counterattacks Begin

On 14 November, able to count on the superiority of their forces in the field, the Greeks launched a counter-offensive in the Macedonian sector, engaging *Genikós* Tsolakoglou's III Corps, reinforced by two more infantry divisions. The Greeks first attacked on Devoli, then outflanked the Italian positions on the Morova massif from both the south and the north, in the area of Ersekë: the main purpose of the action was to divide the Italian forces of the 9th Army from those of the 11th Army. The frontal attack of the Greek units against Mount Ivanit in the lake region, a key position for both contenders, was unsuccessful. However, towards evening, along the Morova front, units of the 15th Greek Division reached Devoli, while those of the 9th Division overran it in the southern part of the sector. *Generale* Nasci hastened to ask Soddu for reinforcements, as he had already had to transfer troops to reinforce the isolated garrison at Ersekë. The next day, the *Venezia* Division launched some counterattacks to stem the pressure of the 15th Greek Division, while in the Bilishti-Kapestica area, attacks by the 13th Greek Division took place.

On the afternoon of 15 November, *Generale* Soddu gathered the commanders and chiefs of staff of the two armies in Tirana to discuss the situation. While waiting for reinforcements from Italy, it was decided to maintain a defensive attitude and continue to face the enemy counter-offensive. At the same time, a general retreat to a stronger defensive line was also planned, in order to improve logistics and optimise the limited resources available. On the morning of 16 November, the High Command issued the new directives, following the decisions made at the meeting the previous day. The 9th Army was to receive the motorised *Trieste* Division and the *Pusteria* Alpine Division as reinforcements.

On the Greek side, the poor initial successes achieved during the counter-offensive, both due to the difficulties of the terrain and the strong resistance put up by the

THE GREEK COUNTER-OFFENSIVE 71

Italian units, pushed the Greek Command to commit new forces, putting the 11th Division on alert and transferring the 13th Division to the III Corps.

At around midnight on 16 November, *Colonnello* Giuseppe Azzaro, commander of the garrison at Ersekë, reported that he had repulsed numerous strong attacks by Greek troops, but at the same time he expressed doubts as to whether he could hold out much longer. *Generale* Nasci therefore authorised the retreat of the garrison to the Qarrit Pass.[1]

On 17 November, the units of the Greek III Corps returned to attack near the Devoli narrows, but without being able to make much progress, except that the Greek 9th Division managed to occupy Mount Propas and some positions in the southern section of the Morova. At the same time, the Greek 10th Division managed with great efforts and after suffering heavy losses to approach Mount Lofka. Given the poor results, the Greek Command sent new forces to increase the pressure.

On 18 November, the Greeks attacked again, but still failed to achieve any significant results. In particular, the 13th Division had been ordered to insert itself between the Italian 15th and 9th Divisions, to advance directly on Zemblaku. Its divisions marched at two o'clock in the morning, in torrential rain, and during the advance the columns completely lost touch with each other, coming under Italian artillery fire. Eventually, the Greek units were forced to retreat. In the course of the night, however, a few patrols of the 9th Division crossed the Morova ridge and started to descend towards Drenova, in the Korça basin. The defection of an Albanian rifle division allowed the Greek units to take control of the mule tracks leading to Drenova-Borijë and then to Korça. In order to cope with this critical situation, the XXVI Corps was ordered to transfer a battalion of the 4th Bersaglieri Regiment from Qarrit Pass to establish a defensive line east of Korça, together with a battalion of the 1st Bersaglieri. At the same time, the *Verona* Battalion was to move to its flank and launch a counterattack to stem the enemy breakthrough. On the same day, *Generale* Vercellino, commander of the 9th Army, took the decision to withdraw his forces. To this end, he ordered a series of counterattacks at various points on the following day, 19 November, in order to ease enemy pressure and prevent enemy troops from pressing hard on the Italian units. The beginning of the retreat was set for the night of 20 November.

In the evening of 20 November, Soddu sent the order for the 9th Army to retreat to the Pogradec – Valamare – Velusches line. However, *Generale* Vercellino decided to postpone the action for 24 hours, in order to launch the planned lightning counterattacks. So in the afternoon of 21 November, the retreat of the majority of the

---

1 According to other sources, the withdrawal of the garrison at Ersekë created a dangerous gap on the left of the *Bari* Division, whose command had not been alerted to the manoeuvre. A 30km gap was thus created between the two Italian armies, which was fortunately not exploited by the enemy. An enquiry was opened into Azzaro's behaviour: the *colonnello* claimed to have received the order to retreat from Nasci. The latter, when questioned, explained that in a conversation with Azzaro he may well have hinted at the opportunity of a retreat to better positions, but he was not authorised to give instructions because the 1st Bersaglieri depended on the 11th Army and not on him. In the end no action was taken against Azzaro. Mario Cervi, *Storia Della Guerra di Grecia* (Milan: Gruppo Mondadori, 1965), pp.190–191.

units began, without much interference from the enemy. At dawn on 22 November, the last units of the 4th Bersaglieri deployed at the Qarrit Pass and passed through Korça, after which the commander of the XXVI Corps' engineers blew up the abandoned ammunition. A company of light tanks remained in the basin until 9 a.m. to cover the retreat of the last units. The disengagement manoeuvre was then successfully completed, countered only by Greek artillery fire and a few attacks by the *Ellinikí Vasilikí Aeroporía*, which caused no casualties.

The war bulletin number 168 of 22 November, sounded like a defeat for all Italians, also because the Italian General Staff reported that Greeks had crossed the Albanian border:

> Our covering troops, consisting of two divisions, which had been on the defensive on the Greek-Albanian border of Korça since the beginning of hostilities, withdrew, after 11 days of fighting, to a line west of the town, which was evacuated. During this period, bitter fighting took place. Our losses are considerable. Equally, and perhaps more serious, were those of the enemy. Our reinforcements are concentrated on the new line. Despite the prohibitive weather conditions, our aviation cooperated with the troops by bombing some enemy targets.

In the afternoon of 22 November, the units of the Greek 9th Division entered Korça, while those of the 15th Division moved on Ivanit and the north-western slopes of Morova. The entry of the Greek troops into Albanian territory was a severe blow to the local populations:

> The retreat was sufficiently orderly, although much material was abandoned and the soldiers had scattered supplies and worn-out equipment. The battalions passed through desolate and deserted villages, the Albanian battalions had all disbanded, on the faces of the rare Albanians who made themselves seen as the Italians left one could read a sort of resentment against this army, believed to be so mighty, which was backing down in front of the Greeks...[2]

And to think that a few days earlier, on 18 November, in the control room of Palazzo Venezia in Rome, Mussolini had delivered a speech to the leaders of the provincial headquarters of the Fascist Party:

> The rugged valleys of Epirus and their muddy roads do not lend themselves to *blitzkrieg* wars as the incorrigible who practice the convenient strategy of pins on paper would claim.... Does anyone among you comrades remember the unpublished Eboli speech, delivered in July 1935, before the Ethiopian war? I said we would break the Negus' kidneys. Now, with the same absolute, I repeat absolute, certainty, I tell you that we will break the

---

2   Mario Cervi, *Storia Della Guerra di Grecia* (Milan: Gruppo Mondadori, 1965), pp.194–195.

kidneys of Greece. In two or twelve months, it doesn't matter. The war has just begun. We have sufficient men and means to crush all Greek resistance. English aid will not be able to prevent the fulfilment of this very firm intention of ours, nor prevent the Hellenes from the catastrophe they have wished for and proved to deserve. To think or doubt otherwise is not to know me. Once I get going I do not let up until the end. I have already proved it and whatever happens, or may happen, I will prove it again. The 372 killed, 1,081 wounded, and 650 missing in the first 10 days of fighting on Epirus will be avenged…

Without Respite

At dawn on 24 November, with the units of the 9th Army settling on the new Pogradec – Valamare – Velusches line, the following message from *Generale* Geloso, commander of the 11th Army, arrived in Elbasan, the new headquarters of the army command:

> Today on the front of the VIII C.A. the *Bari* Division succumbed to a strong enemy attack, retreating to the bottom of the Vojussa Valley and leaving a gap between Q.Martës and Frasheri. The VIII C.A. Command is sending a few available units to block the threat on the bottom of the Osum Valley. The Higher Command is requested to send truck units to Cerevodë. Yesterday an Alpine company was sent to Q. Martës and another to Q.Calibarit, and it is still not known whether they have arrived. The *Bari* Division is no longer efficient, lacking automatic weapons and with little artillery, it will not be usable for a long time.[3]

While the Italian command was busy dealing with the many critical situations as a result of the retreat, *Genikós* Papagos, instead of taking advantage of the success and pressing the retreating Italian troops, preferred to wait, afraid to stretch his supply lines too far and fall into a trap himself. Being a military man of the old school, he preferred to always advance with his flanks and shoulders solidly protected. However, he kept receiving orders from the general command to resume the offensive and give the Italians no respite. *Genikós* Tsolakoglou, commander of the Greek III Corps, which was engaged in the extreme Western Macedonia sector near the Yugoslav border, then intervened. Tsolakoglou proposed to launch an attack towards Pogradec, a key position on the new Italian defensive line, with a combat group, comprising four infantry battalions supported by scout units and some artillery batteries. Its fall would have made it possible to outflank the Italian 9th Army on the left, to secure control of part of the coast of Lake Ohrid and to make landings behind the front possible.

3   Mario Montanari, *L'Esercito Italiano Nella Campagna di Grecia*, Ufficio Storico Stato Maggiore dell'esercito, p.257.

On 24 November, the Greek battalion group moved in the direction of Pogdarec. The next day, more units arrived to bolster the offensive. On 26 November, the Greek units launched their first attacks in the sector of Italian III Corps: the Greek 13th Division attacked the positions of Pogradec, but without gaining ground. It was only thanks to the action of a group of Greek mountaineers, who managed to infiltrate a narrow valley crossed by a small stream, the Tseravas, that the Greeks managed to penetrate through the Italian positions. Hard fighting followed, which saw the soldiers of the *Venezia* Division engaged. The attacks of the Greek 9th Division, launched against the Kamia, at the junction between the positions of the *Arezzo* and *Venezia* Divisions, were also more successful. On 28 November, after hard fighting a Greek division captured the key positions of Bregu Bari Kuqit and Guri Kamias, on the Kamia mountain range. On 30 November, the Pogdarec position was also conquered by the Greeks after strong resistance by the Italian soldiers.

There had been many episodes of bravery, including that of Private Benedetto Citriniti; born in 1911 in Simeri Crichi (Catanzaro), serving in the 207th infantry regiment of the *Taro* Infantry Division, at that time attached to the *Venezia* Division,[4] who fell in combat and was decorated with the *Medaglia d'Oro al Valor Militare alla Memoria*, with the following citation:

During a violent attack by a preponderant enemy force, on his own initiative and contemptuous of the intense fire, he leapt from the trench and went to an advanced and uncovered position, from which he held the adversaries in check for a long time with very effective shooting. Having exhausted his ammunition, he twice returned to the lines to resupply and return to his post, resuming the deadly fire with serene courage. Finally, realising that the weapon would remain ineffective because the circle of assailants was tightening, he repeated the daring gesture for the third time, twice managing to repel the enemy, until he fell valiantly. [Stropka – Pogradec (Greek front), 29 November 1940].

Generale Arisio, commander of the Italian III Corps, was forced to order the retreat of the *Venezia* Division during the night of 30 November/1 December. On 30 November, the units of the Greek 9th Division launched a massive new attack, preceded by artillery fire, in the Bregu Kemerit – Guri Regianit sector, in fog and thick snow. The Greek soldiers managed to get as far as the slopes of the high altitudes, but were repulsed by the fire of the well posted and well positioned Italians. In the meantime, another attack by the 13th Infantry Division led by Beragozhda, allowed the Greeks to take height 1244, from which they dominated the entire Pogradec Basin, and this forced the Italians to abandon all positions east of the city. In the afternoon, following the retreat of the *Venezia* units, the Greeks moved on Staroba and Remeni.

---

4   On 10 June 1940, the *Taro* Division was stationed in the Civitavecchia area. On 19 November 1940, it was transferred to Bari to be embarked for Durrës in Albania, where it arrived between 27 and 30 of the same month and was immediately sent to the Greek-Albanian front. The Division's units, due to the delicate situation on the Greek-Albanian border, were transferred to the front line as they disembarked. At the end of November, the 207th Infantry Regiment under the *Venezia* Division and the 208th Infantry Regiment with the *Arezzo* Division found themselves deployed in the Pogradec area.

After managing to contain the Greek attacks in the Pogradec area, the command of the 9th Army was engaged repelling attacks on the right wing. From 25 November, the *Tridentine* units had rushed to the front line, and were immediately engaged in repelling Greek cavalry and infantry patrols.

During the night of 1 December, the command of the 11th Army reported that the Alpine company of the *Val Fella* Battalion, detached from the VII Corps at Q. Martës, had been forced to fall back, after having been attacked in force, to Mount Faqiakuqit, at the southern end of Ostravicë, leaving a dangerous gap open between the two Italian armies. In an attempt to deal with the threat, it was decided to use a tactical formation group comprising the best elements of the *Parma* Division to stop any enemy breakthroughs.

At the same time, *Generale* Vercellino ordered the withdrawal from the front line of all units already severely tired from the previous fighting in order to reorganise them: the units of the *Parma* Division were transferred to the Devoli Valley, north of Gramshi and those of the *Piemonte* Division to the Kukës – Librazhd area.

On 3 December, the Greeks (units of the 9th Division and the 17th Division) attacked along the entire sector of the Italian III Corps, but mainly concentrating against the positions of the *Arezzo* Division, with the aim of penetrating the front between Bregu Brezavet and Pleu i Kieve, in order to take Guri Regjanit, open a gap and overwhelm the left flank of the Italian deployment. After a series of attacks and counterattacks, the latter launched by the *Venezia* and *Arezzo* Divisions, the Greeks were temporarily repulsed.

In the afternoon, the Greeks returned to the attack and at 15:00, the position of Pleu i Kieve fell into their hands, and soon afterwards, the position of Guri Regjanit also fell. Counterattacks were launched with the *Venezia* reserves, but without success. Around 17:00, the positions of Bregu Dragotin and Mount Sareces were also captured by the Greeks. Thanks to some counterattacks launched by the last available units late in the evening, it was possible to stop the Greeks on the Macikak – Brumbulinit line. *Generale* Arisio summarised the events thus:

> … the situation as it presents itself in the evening is undoubtedly serious: troops worn out from fighting and bad weather, with few officers, are fighting well and contesting the opponent's ground. But how long can this last? It obviously depends on imponderables and how far the enemy will go.[5]

Generale Vercellino in turn reported to the Higher Command:

> It is my duty as commander to point out that the divisions and indi-viduals of the *Arezzo* and *Venezia* Divisions only surrendered in the face of the enemy's overwhelming strength, but had heroically marked the way with blood.[6]

---

5   Mario Montanari, *L'Eesercito Italiano Nella Campagna di Grecia*, Ufficio Storico Stato Maggiore dell'esercito, p.267.
6   DS Headquarters 9th Army, tele situation 8 p.m. 3.12.1940.

The fighting on Kamia was indeed very hard, characterised by numerous hand-to-hand combats, between snow, caves and overhangs.

Fighting on the Border with Epirus

On the Epirus front, after offensive actions had ended, the units of the *Ciamuria* Army Corps had succeeded in establishing a new defensive front. By 14 November 1940, the following sectors had been established, from the Voidomati River to the sea:

Sector I (*Colonnello* Solinas), with the XXIV/5th and XXVII/2nd Bersaglieri, a light tank company and two 149/13 batteries. The orders were to secure the left flank of the army corps and to establish a connection with both the *Bari* and *Ferrara* Divisions by engaging mobile elements. It was also to defend a position west of the Perati-Kalibaki road.

Sector II (*Generale* Zannini), with *Ferrara* reinforced and with orders to defend the Kalibaki – Kakavia line.

Sector III (*Maggiore* Campini) with the II/2nd Bersaglieri and the 4th Albanian Volunteer Battalion of *Maggiore* Grandi, who were engaged in protecting the right wing of *Ferrara* and establishing the connection with Siena.

Sector IV (*Generale* Gabutti) with *Siena*, engaged in defending the lower Kalamas.

In reserve of the army corps were the II/31st Tank, XXII/5th and IV/2nd Bersaglieri and I *Guide* Squadron Group.

The new defensive line presented some difficulties, especially in the section between Konitsa and Ersekë, where the units of the *Bari* were after the *Julia*'s retreat from Pindos. When the *Julia* returned, the 8th Alpini and the *Conegliano* group were transferred to Premeti to be reorganised. Then the Konitsa positions passed to the 9th *Alpini* and the *Udine* Group, units subordinate to the *Bari*. Other elements of the *Bari* stood in defence of the Sarandaporos Valley. Between 11 and 14 November, the Greeks launched several attacks, but were always repulsed. The Italians' positions held, but losses continued to mount. The Greeks were mainly aiming to recapture Konitsa. On the flanks, however, the situation appeared more difficult, with the Greek 1st Cavalry Division attacking the positions of the Solinas Group and the left wing of *Ferrara*. The *Bari* Division was also struggling to defend the Leskoviku area, so *Generale* Bancale decided to reinforce it with the *Tolmezzo Alpini* Battalion.

On 15 November, the fighting resumed with greater intensity, in particular the attacks against the positions on the extreme right held by the 108th Company of *L'Aquila* battalion. The Greeks attacked throughout the day, but were always repulsed by the fierce Alpine troops, who continually launched counterattacks. Height 1640 was lost and recaptured three times by the Alpine soldiers of a platoon of the 108th Company, under the orders of *Tenente* Guido Rodorigo. On the third counterattack, only seven men remained. Rodorigo's Alpine troops managed to regain the height thanks also to the outflanking manoeuvre carried out on the left by the platoon under the orders of *Sottotenente* Vincenzo Rossi sent as a reinforcement. In the course of the action, *Sottotenente* Rossi himself fell at the head of his Alpine men. *Tenente* Rodorigo's Alpine troops, who were left with only a single machine gun and little ammunition, repelled a new assault by two Greek patrols by rolling rocks, using the fallen men's rifles as levers to move them. Towards evening, the situation was re-established along the entire front.

The Bridgehead of Perati

New enemy attacks were brought against the positions of the I/139th Infantry, which was forced to retreat. In this way, the positions of the 9th *Alpini* and the *Udine* Group, which remained with eight operational pieces, were threatened with being outflanked. In the evening of 15 November, the *Julia* took control of the Perati-Konitsa sector and then moved to the Perati Bridge. It then passed to the 8th Army Corps of *Generale* Bancale, who in those same hours ordered a retreat during the night to defend the Perati Bridgehead along an arched line: Kukës baths, Mount Derveni, Aj Paraskevi up to a height of 568 to the left of the Vojussa – a fairly wide front. Since the 8th *Alpini* regiment, which was being rebuilt, had been assigned to the *Bari* Division, the *Julia* command asked for at least the attachment of a battalion from this regiment. The *Cividale* Battalion was therefore assigned to it, which was initially engaged in the protection of Ponte Perati and then transferred to the front line. At Ponte Perati, meanwhile, the batteries of the *Udine* Group continued to fire relentlessly on the advancing enemy columns.

While the Alpine troops were holding out on the Perati Bridgehead, since it was clear that in the 11th Army sector, the Greek objectives were Berat and Vlora, it was decided to fall back to positions that would allow these two key positions to be held, the loss of which would certainly have put the Italian deployment in Albania into a crisis. Thus, on 16 November, *Generale* Geloso officially assumed command of the army, immediately finding himself committed to stabilising the front along a defensive line further to the rear to counter Greek counterattacks.

The sector defended by the *Bari* and the *Julia*, in the central area of the deployment, along the Ersekë – Leskoviku – Perati line, was particularly critical, since it not only acted as a link between the 9th and the 11th Armies, but also included the Perati road junction, a key communication route to Berat and Durrës.

Also on 16 November, the position of Konitsa was attacked and captured by the Greeks, and the *Julia* battalions fell back to Perati. After Ersekë had also fallen, only the 9th Alpini and the 140th Infantry of the *Bari* remained deployed between the latter town and Ponte Perati.

By 18 November, the *Bari*, under the orders of *Generale* Achille D'Havet, was defending the sector from Q. Barmash to Bagni di Kukës, with the 140th infantry, the 8th Alpini (except for one battalion) and the III/4th Bersaglieri. The *Julia*, meanwhile was defending the Perati Bridgehead with the 139th infantry, the 9th Alpini, the *Cividale* Battalion, the I/1st Bersaglieri and a tank battalion. *Generale* Girotti ordered a shortening of the front, maintaining the two bridges of Perati and

Bourozeni. *Generale* Bancale also decided to transfer the *Val Tagliamento* Battalion to Perati in support of the *Julia*. At 22:00, *Generale* Geloso arrived in Premeti to personally assess the situation: Bancale told him that the resistance on the positions occupied at that moment could not last long, both because of the lack of fresh troops and because of the insufficient means, and proposed a new retreat. The High Command for its part had already planned a retreat on the line P. Edda – Jerguçat – Suhes and Lengatica valleys – Q. Dellenjës – Q. Martës – Devoli narrows between Kosnicë and Suhagora – M. Kamia – Pogradec.

On 19 November, *Generale* Geloso issued the directives for the retreat. In order to contain possible enemy breakthroughs into the Osum and Tomorrecës sides, a tactical group comprising the 3rd Battalion of the *Guardia di Finanza* and two hundred Albanian Blackshirts was organised. The manoeuvre was to be carried out in stages and, above all, it was to re-establish the connection with the 9th Army, which, after the loss of Korça, was also falling back.

In the XXV Corps' sector, the fighting with the Greek troops continued under pressure, and with the Italians engaged in rearguard actions, clinging to the terrain features. On the *Ferrara* front, the situation was most critical: *Generale* Zannini telephoned the army corps to ask for reinforcements: '…*Ferrara* is exhausted. It has a huge front. If at least two reinforcement battalions do not arrive by tonight, the line can no longer be held.'

Late in the evening, the 47th Infantry fell back, having suffered heavy losses, while to the north-east of Lakanokastro, the Solinas Group continued to hold out for a whole day and then also fell back to Vesane, west of Gormos. At dawn on 20 November, the fighting resumed with greater intensity, and with the retreating *Ferrara* Divisions still engaged. At 10:00, the Vesane-Delvinaki track became completely clogged with retreating units. At 11:00, the commander of the 48th Infantry reported that Greek units were on the verge of overrunning the left of the III/48th and he had no means of stopping them. Shortly after noon, *Generale* Zannini ordered the 14th Artillery to withdraw their pieces and reported to the corps that he had ordered the *Ferrara* remnants to fall back to the Delvinaki – Kakavia line: the 48th infantry was reduced to two battalions as was the 47th infantry. The 166th Blackshirts Battalion still had 240 men, but shortly afterwards, the Albanian *Dajti* Battalion deserted to the enemy with all of their weapons and equipment.

The 14th Artillery continued its staggered retreat, continuing to counter Greek pressure on the infantry units. Several times the Greeks managed to get close to the batteries, but were always repulsed by desperate bayonet counterattacks launched by the artillerymen.

The Retreat Continues

On 21 November, *Generale* Geloso issued directives for the retreat, ordering the inner wings of the corps to fall back last. By the morning of that same day, the Greek II Corps had resumed its forward movement with the 5th Brigade and the 1st Infantry Division, aiming mainly to seize control of the Perati-Korça road. The position of Perati remained a key objective, with its road junction and bridge. Against it, the

Greeks launched the 1st Cavalry Division, managing to make some breakthroughs. In the afternoon, around 4 p.m., *Generale* Girotti was forced to request to be allowed to blow up the bridge. *Generale* Bancale authorised the destruction, informing the army command. In fact, the destruction of the bridge was not immediately authorised, as the High Command considered it indispensable for their imminent offensive! Had it fallen intact into the hands of the Greeks, however, they would have had a clear path to Premeti, Tepeleni and Vlora. The words of Alpine soldier Arturo Gazzini of the *Cividale* Battalion on the destruction of the bridge are worth considering:

> We were soon at the Perati Bridge. I found myself in the midst of that furious battle: it was 21 November, trampling on the dead, climbing over the wounded, the forest was burning; infantrymen up in the hollow were overwhelmed and mangled by grenades; the bersaglieri abandoned their vehicles to improvise as alpine artillerymen; from above I saw the bridge blow up. The Alpine soldiers and artillerymen fought furiously to contain the enemy and save what could be saved.

At 19:00, *Generale* Geloso ordered the retreat: the VIII Corps immediately encountered difficulties, because as soon as the movement began, the connections with the unis of the *Bari* Division were broken. Even the following day, the situation remained uncertain and the *Alpini* battalions retreating from Perati, the *Cividale* and *Val Tagliamento* were transferred to secure the Lengatica sector, while the Vojussa sector was assigned to the 41st *Modena* Infantry. On the extreme left, the *Salvoni* tactical group was engaged in protecting the gap in the high Osum and Tomorrecës valleys.

On the afternoon of 23 November, bad news came from *Bari*, whose regiments had been overwhelmed by the new Greek attacks and had run out of ammunition. On the other hand, there was no news from the *Gemona*, the *Tolmezzo* and the VII/1st Bersaglieri. Thus, on the night of 24 November, the Lengatica sector was defended by only a few units and the Vojussa Valley by an incomplete regiment that had just arrived from Italy. The Army Command therefore decided to send the 3rd *Granatieri* (minus one battalion) to secure the passages from the Osum Valley to Klisura. Fortunately, the Greeks had missed the collapse of the *Bari* units and this gave the Italian command time to take countermeasures.

During the 24th, the situation of the 8th Army Corps at Bancale improved when, in the afternoon, the 3rd *Granatieri* arrived. Shortly afterwards, the 8th Alpini was able to communicate that, after being isolated north of Leskoviku, it had finally managed to disengage, reaching Frasheri, disengaging the *Tolmezzo* and *Gemona* Battalions from Q. Martës to Q. Dellenjës. With the 8th *Alpini* was the III/47th Artillery (with its remaining six pieces) and the surviving battery of the *Conegliano* Group. The *Julia* Division, very tired from the latest fighting and after having suffered a heavy bombardment in the Premeti area on 20 November that had caused considerable losses (8 officers and 387 non-commissioned officers and soldiers, dead and wounded), stood in three sectors: the 8th *Alpini* of four battalions (its three plus the *Val Tagliamento*); the 9th *Alpini* of three battalions (its two plus the *Val Fella*); and the *De Martino* tactical Group of two battalions – the I and VII/1st Bersaglieri.

Following an attempted landing of Greek troops in the Bays of Butrint and Filia on 23 November, which was repulsed and which had led to the capture of the entire enemy contingent, from 25 November the army command decided to reconstitute the Littoral Regiment with the *Siena*, the *Milan Lancieri* and a battalion of the 3rd *Granatieri*, placed under the direct command of the army.

In the meantime, the Greeks attacked in three directions: in the upper Suhes Valley, where they had overrun the Panaja Pass with a strong group; on the southern slopes of Makrikambos, where they were, however, stopped by the strong resistance of the 48th infantry of the *Ferrara*; and at Kakavia, where the bulk of the Greek 8th Division was unable to overcome the Italian defences in the Dhrinos sector. The XXV Corps was able to concentrate the few forces at its disposal at two large strongholds: the *Ferrara* was ordered to resist at all costs and the *Centaur*, reinforced by a grenadier battalion and the 42nd infantry, was ordered to hold the positions reached at Kakavia – Katuna, stemming any breakthrough towards the valley floor by night and day.

Capitano Bernardino Biagini, of the 5th Bersaglieri Regiment of the *Centauro* , born in 1898 in Serre di Rapolano in the province of Siena, distinguished himself during these battles. He was seriously wounded by machine gun fire at Pontikates on 24 November 1940 and died the following day at Field Hospital No.472. He was decorated with the *Medaglia d'Oro al Valor Militare alla Memoria* with the following citation:

> Commander of a rifle company during 27 days of epic battle, he gave contin-uous proof of ardent enthusiasm, heroic valour, always the leader among his bersaglieri. In the defence of important positions attacked by over-whelming forces, he contested the enemy's impetus for entire days, with tenacious resistance and overwhelming counterattacks. Seriously wounded by machine gun fire, he refused all help and continued to direct the action, until, having fallen in the strenuous effort and exhausted, he was taken to hospital. He died peacefully the next day, after expressing his satisfaction with the duty performed. [Pontikates (Greek front), 24 November 1940].

For their part, the Greeks regrouped forces to attack at the junction between the two Italian armies with the aim of reaching Berat. For this purpose, *Generale* Soddu assigned the *Pusteria* Division to the 11th Army: of this Alpine Division, only the 7th *Alpini* command and the *Feltre* and *Cadore* Battalions had arrived in Albania. With these new reinforcements, the III Corps was to bar the Osum line and link with the 9th Army. At the same time, *Generale* Bancale had to pass the 3rd *Granatieri*, the 41st Infantry and other elements of the *Modena* to join the rest of the Division in the Dhrinos Valley and the *Bari*, already withdrawn from the front line, which had to move north of Klisura to reorganise. The army eventually found itself organ-ised as follows: the XXV Corps, with the *Ferrara* and *Modena* Infantry Divisions and the *Centauro* Armoured Division; the VIII Corps, with the *Julia* and *Pusteria* Alpini Divisions; the *Siena* Division under direct command of the army; and the *Bari* Division in reserve.

The weakest point in the army's defensive front remained the juncture between its two corps, between the Vojussa and Dhrinos valleys. And it was precisely here that the Greeks concentrated their efforts. On 24 November, the Greeks had penetrated the upper Suhes Valley, overwhelming the Albanian *Grammos* Battalion. On 27 November, they occupied height 900 and other heights dominating the Bidan Narrows. *Generale* Geloso, after considering a counterattack by committing elements of the two army corps, decided to opt for a new retreat on the Vojussa – Kurvelesh – right line Vojussa – Klisura – Kjarista – Potomit – Q. Kualibardhë. But from Tirana, fearing serious political repercussions, Soddu ordered Geloso to limit the retreat to the Premeti – Argirocastro – Delvino – Santi Quaranta line. Geloso's further requests to accept his decision were to no avail.

On the front line, the situation continued to worsen, with the VIII Corps in great difficulty and the XXV Corps busy defending its foothold on the Bureto, on whose southern slopes the *Ferrara* units were fighting hard. *Generale* Rossi had changed the deployment of his troops, with the *Ferrara* to the north of Dhrinos and the *Centauro* to the south, with a containment position near Derviçani. The *Modena* units were to gradually replace the exhausted *Ferrara* units, which were to regroup behind the containment position and reorganise with new battalions arriving from Italy. The *Centauro continued* to defend the right sector with the support of a machine gun company and the 68th Blackshirts Battalion and at the same time maintained links with the *Siena*, which was falling back to reorganise the defensive front. This manoeuvre could in the event not be completed due to both the Greek attacks on Mount Bureto and the wounding of *Generale* Gloria, commander of the *Modena*. After the Greek breakthrough into the Suhes Valley and the fall of Makrikambos, the Greek attacks were concentrated against Bureto, the conquest of which would have allowed the enemy to descend on Libohovo, to the rear of the army corps. Defending Bureto were the remnants of the *Ferrara* Division, which was only joined by the *Bolzano* battalion on 30 November.

Along the coastline, no Greek attacks had yet occurred, so on 28 November the Siena units were able to retreat without any problems, reaching the Pavla creek.

The situation as of the evening of 29 November was as follows:

> …on the front of the VIII Corps the Greeks with another violent effort had managed to seize Viniahu and the Malibardhë Ridge, but had been repelled by the hard assaults of the Julia in the area of m. Qelqës-Frasheri; in the Suhes Valley the Battalion *Val Natisone* was unable to prevent the enemy from asserting itself in the area of 900 sq. metres; in the Dhrinos Valley an important point of m. Bureto fell, thus causing a particularly serious situation on the left flank of Ferrara, such as to threaten the entire XXV Corps deployment from behind.[7]

Under these conditions, the execution of the retreat manoeuvre planned by Geloso appeared complicated, with the Greeks continuing to attack. In the evening of 30 November, the VIII Corps reported that the *Val Fella Alpini* Company stationed at Q. Martës, after being attacked by superior enemy forces was forced to retreat to

---

7   Mario Montanari, *LEesercito Italiano Nella Campagna di Grecia*, Ufficio Storico Stato Maggiore dell'Esercito, p.303.

Mount Faqiakuqit during a blizzard. At the same time, the 41st *Modena* Infantry was overwhelmed, but then managed to return to the abandoned positions. In the Zagorias Valley, the *Val Natisone* was also forced to abandon its positions, but soon afterwards, thanks to the support of the *Belluno* Battalion, the situation was stabilised. Further west, the *Siena* units had moved to the right bank of the Vistritsa. Geloso informed the High Command of his decision to fall back, despite calls to remain in place. Hard fighting followed in the upper Dhrinos Valley. The Solinas Group and the 47th Infantry Regiment were particularly busy, while the 42nd *Modena* Infantry moved along the border positions and behind it, the 48th Infantry, the *Centauro* and the II/3rd *Granatieri* regrouped.

On 30 November, there was a massive attack against the positions of the 47th Infantry Regiment: *Colonnello* Felice Trizio, born in 1899 in Altamura in the province of Bari, in command of the Regiment, regrouped all the men still available and launched them in a desperate counterattack, falling almost immediately, mortally hit by mortar fire, but his action temporarily halted the enemy offensive. He was awarded the *Medaglia d'Oro al Valor Militare alla Memoria*, with the citation:

> In thirty days of continuous and bitter fighting, he repeatedly led his regiment to attack and counterattack. Always at the head of the battalions forged by him and brought to the highest spiritual level, he imposed himself on the enemy. A shining example of a bold and capable commander, in a final strenuous counterattack, infantryman among infantrymen, brave among the brave, he fell heroically on the field. [Drino Valley (Albania), 1 December 1940].

The next day, 1 December, the *Bolzano Alpini* troops were hard at work fighting in the rain and snow. Thanks to their action, the situation on the Bureto was re-established in the afternoon. On 2 December, the 11th Army issued further orders for the retreat of the XXV Corps and the coastal group, which was carried out on the night of 5/6 December.

Arrival of *Alpine* in Albania transported by air, November 1940. (USSME)

Italian artillerymen with a field artillery piece on the Greek-Albanian front in the Devol Valley sector.

FELICE TRIZIO

Colonnello comandante 47° Regg. fanteria, da Altamura (Bari), alla memoria.

« In trenta giorni di continua ed aspra lotta conduceva ripetutamente il suo reggimento all'attacco ed al contrattacco. Sempre alla testa dei battaglioni da lui forgiati e portati alla massima elevazione spirituale, si imponeva al nemico. Esempio fulgido di comandante ardito e capace, in un ultimo strenuo contrattacco, fante tra i fanti, valoroso tra i valorosi, cadeva eroicamente sul campo. »

(Valle Drino, Albania, 1° dicembre 1940-xix)

Contemporary Postcard commemorating the awarding of the *Medaglia d'Oro al Valor Militare* to *Colonnello* Felice Trizio.

Medium M13/40 tanks marching on a road in Albania, November 1940. (USSME)

Generale Mario Vercellino, commander of the
9th Army. (USSME)

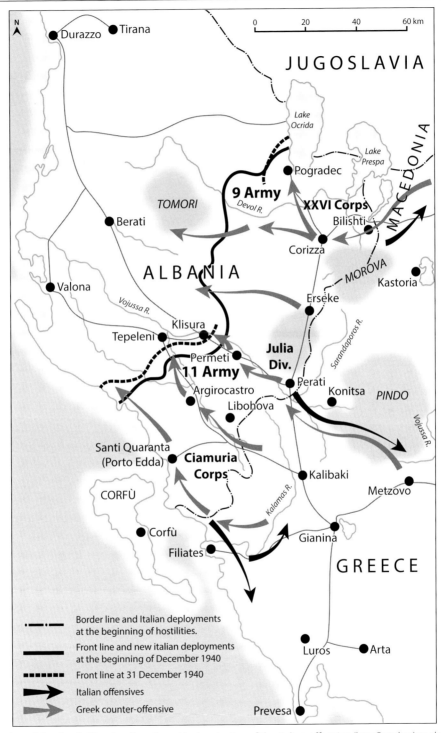

Map of the Greek-Albanian front from the beginning of the Italian offensive (late October) to the Greek counter-offensive (November–December 1940).

Greek artillery on the move. The towed piece is a *Canon de 155 Grande Puissance Filloux modèle 1917* of WW1 vintage. The gun on the shoulder of the Greek artilleryman is a 6.5mm *Mannlicher-Schönauer*.

Greek soldiers carry a *St Etienne* machine gun during the counter-offensive against Italian positions in Albania.

Italian soldiers with a *Breda* machine gun in a defensive position, November 1940. (USSME)

Greek artillerymen with a *Schneider-Dahlgren* mountain piece on the Albanian front,
late November 1940.

Benedetto Citriniti, serving in the 207th Infantry Regiment of the *Taro* Infantry Division (www.movm.it).

Generale Mario Arisio, commander of the Italian III Corps (USSME).

An Italian mortar team on a defensive position on the Albanian front, November 1940. (USSME)

Greek soldiers exult after capturing an Italian artillery piece, December 1940.

Alpini della Julia during a
blizzard, December 1940.
(USSME)

The Perati Bridge over the Sarandaporos River, where the *Alpini* divisions of the *Julia* Division fought hard to halt the enemy offensive.

Italian troops, including of the motorcycle bersaglieri units, on the move in the high mountains, November 1940.

Italian artillerymen engaged in moving a piece to counter enemy attacks, November 1940.
(USSME)

Italian artillery emplacement, November 1940. (USSME)

Italian soldiers in a defensive position high in the mountains repel an enemy attack with rifle fire and hand grenades. (USSME)

Alpini della Julia during a retreat, stopped by muddy terrain, December 1940. (USSME)

Capitano Bernardino Biagini of the 5th *Centauro* Bersaglieri Regiment. (www.movm.it)

Colonnello Felice Trizio (www.movm.it).

A *Centauro* tank driver on the Greek-Albanian front, December 1940. (USSME)

5

Containment Battle

With the Greeks pushing the Italians in Albania towards the shores of the Adriatic, it was normal for a few senior military officials in Rome to be held responsible and in the face of this serious military defeat, Chief of Staff Badoglio was replaced by *Generale* Ugo Cavallero. King Victor Emmanuel III himself congratulated Mussolini on the replacement. On 4 December, Cavallero arrived in Albania to meet with Soddu and to plan military operations. Soddu presented him with a frightening memo: the troops lacked food, equipment and ammunition. As soon as he returned to Tirana, Cavallero immediately telephoned Mussolini to inform him of the situation and request the immediate dispatch of men, weapons, ammunition, parts and food.

The Situation on the Front of the 9th Army

Greek attacks in the Pogradec sector on 3 December had led to the fall of Mount Sareces and this forced the III Corps commander, *Generale* Arisio, to change the defensive line. Agreeing with his decision, *Generale* Vercellino, commander of the 9th Army, decided to move the defence north of the confluence of the two Skumbini, Llëngë and Dunica, to the point where the Skumbi Valley narrowed, thus being better able to face the enemy superiority in numbers. The *Arezzo* and *Venezia* Divisions were told to retreat in good order. However, the situation of the *Tridentina* remained critical, called to face the Greek troops that were about to descend the Skumbini. Furthermore, in order to prevent the left wing of the *Tridentine* from being exposed, it was necessary for the division to change its deployment. But from Cavallero came the order to Vercellino to cancel any retreat and maintain the existing positions.

On 9 December, the Greek 17th Infantry Division attacked the left wing of the *Venezia*, the positions on Mount Kalaze and the join between the *Venezia* and the *Arezzo*. On Mount Kalaze the fighting was particularly hard, but in the end the enemy attacks were contained. On Mount Kosica, on the other hand, after the initial dispersal of the Italian units, the situation was re-established thanks to a decisive counterattack launched with two battalions of Blackshirts and the elements of the *Arezzo* Division that Generale Ernesto Ferone managed to rally. However, the losses were heavy and *Generale* Arisio reported in alarm: 'I only have a single battalion of Blackshirts available, and our losses were significant'. From *Generale* Vercellino came the reply to hold the positions at all costs. However, the Greek III Corps forces

were also exhausted by the hard attacks and counterattacks and especially demor-
alised by the tenacity of the Italian units. Considering the poor weather conditions
Genikós Tsolakoglou ordered the 17th Division to suspend their attacks and hold on
to their positions.

While the III Corps was repelling enemy attacks, in the XXVI Corps sector, the
retreat of the units was proceeding smoothly, with the exception of the right wing,
where the *Scrugli* Group, under the orders of *Colonnello* Napoleon Scrugli, of the
Piemonte Division was in great difficulty, because of the Greek attacks. In addition,
the River Devoli had become unpassable due to heavy rains. Numerous cases of
frostbite began to effect the *Piemonte* divisions.

In the southern sector of the army, the situation appeared just as critical: the
commander of the 3rd Guard Battalion, threatened with encirclement, asked if
he could regroup all his remaining forces on Gostanghës and then fall back on Q.
Devris, further north. The next day, *Colonnello* Scrugli reported that the battalion
was dispersed and only a few men had managed to join his forces, and thus, the
connection with the 11th Army could be considered as broken.

At the time, the 9th Army still had the following forces ready: III Corps with
about 16,000 men, XXVI Corps with 8,800 men, army troops about 1,500 men, in
all about 27,000 troops spread over a front of about 70km. After the loss of the Mali
i Cipes – Gostanghës section, the right wing of the 9th Army was forced to regroup
northwards on the Varr i Lamit ridge, while the left wing of the 11th Army had
fallen back into the Osum Valley, forming a defensive flank in front of Cerevodë.
Subsequent Greek attacks continued to particularly threaten the right wing of XXVI
Corps, in the Mali Mietës salient, with the *Edolo* Battalion reduced to 180 men and
the units of the 3rd Infantry in no condition to face further fighting.

On 13 December, the *Edolo* Battalion of the *Tridentine* Division under the orders
of *Tenente Colonnello* Adolfo Rivoir, born in Vallecrosia on 7 October 1895, fought
hard in the Dushar Basin: the Italian command had ordered resistance to the bitter
end on height 1822 with all available forces. The *Edolo Alpini* soldiers, little more
than a hundred in number, due to losses suffered in previous battles, were up against
three Greek battalions, resisting their attacks for three days. In the end, the Greeks
managed to conquer height 1822, but were subsequently hit by the cannon fire of
the 31st *Alpini* battery, having to abandon the positions they had reached after bitter
fighting. The survivors of the *Edolo*, five officers and 23 *Alpini* men and *Guardia di
Finanza*, were later able to re-join the other units.

Tenente Colonnello Adolfo Rivoir, while commanding his men in the defence of
the positions on Varri Lamit, was seriously wounded in the chest. For the valour
shown in battle, he was awarded the *Medaglia d'Oro al Valor Militare*, with the
following citation:

> Commander of an Alpine battalion, in a month of uninterrupted opera-
> tions, he gave glowing proof of his leadership skills, shrewdness of leader-
> ship, spirit of sacrifice and disregard for danger, always facing delicate and
> difficult situations with virility and offensive spirit, from which he repeat-
> edly emerged victorious, inflicting on several occasions serious losses of
> men and material to the adversary. In the end, at the head of a hundred or

so survivors of his battalion, already decimated by the continuous fighting, he calmly and decisively faced the renewed violent enemy attack and was seriously wounded in the chest by machine gun fire while, standing up, he animated the few groups of Alpine soldiers left almost without officers, with his voice and heroic example, leading them to the counterattack. [Corciana Region (Greek front), 14 December 1940].

Enemy attacks were also launched in the north against the 6th *Alpini* and in the centre against the 5th *Alpini*. On 15 December, reinforcements arrived for the 5th *Alpini*, but the regiment could not be contacted because of the breakdown of the radio link. At the same time, the 1st *Guardia di Finanza* Battalion, having lost most of its officers in the initial fighting, fell back from Çuka and Liqerit, the *Edolo* Battalion was isolated and the 3rd *Guardia di Finanza* Battalion was overwhelmed. As there was no longer a continuous front and no troops to counterattack, *Generale* Nasci decided to set up a new defensive position, from Çuka and Grevës to Q. Kulmakës, moving the 2nd Battalion of the *Guardia di Finanza* and two battalions of the *Parma*. Immediately afterwards, Nasci himself went to Han, to the *Tridentine* command, to discuss the situation with *Generale* Santovito. The latter had recently inspected the 5th *Alpini*'s sector and found a disastrous situation.

Soddu for his part issued directives for the start of work to the rear of the first line, to allow the units to retreat in good order, with the creation of the Librazhd defensive position (Skumbi Valley) and the Devoli-Tomorrecës confluence (Devoli Valley) for the 9th Army, Q. Dardhës (north of Tomori), Cerevodë (Osum Valley), Klisura (Deschniçës valley), Tepeleni (Vojussa Valley) and Porto Palermo for the 11th Army. The formation of the Librazhd position was entrusted to the *Piemonte* Division and that of the Devoli-Tomorrecës confluence to the XXVI Corps.

The retreat of the right wing of the 9th Army had widened the gap between the two armies, so it was necessary to take immediate action to re-establish connections and particularly avoid the outflanking of the 11th Army in the Osum Valley. Soddu relied on the arrival of new troops to immediately establish connections at Q. Kulmakës, especially by committing the first available battalions of the *Cuneense*. It was precisely the arrival of the first elements of the *Cuneense*, the relief of the 5th *Alpini* and the withdrawal of the *Piemonte*, that served to re-establish the situation between 18 and 19 December and restore morale to the troops in the front line. On 20 December, *Generale* Cavallero returned to Albania and held a meeting in Rrogozhinë with the army commanders, announcing the arrival of reinforcements and reporting the information on the enemy provided by the S.I.M., which showed that the Greek troops were also severely tired.

Meanwhile, the attacks against the southern wing of the 9th Army continued, especially in the section from Mali Pupapit to Mali i Komjanit, defended by the 6th *Alpini*. On the morning of 23 December, *Generale* Soddu went to Gramshi to personally assess the situation, meeting with *Generale* Nasci: the lack of reserves forced the continuous transfer of forces from one sector to another, in order to face crisis situations. The *Parma* Division had to be regrouped, recovering its divisions assigned to other divisions and had to be resupplied and re-equipped with weapons and material. Of the *Cuneense*, only the 1st *Alpini* was present at that moment and it was necessary for the rest of the divisions to join in order to withdraw the exhausted *Tridentina* Division from the front line. *Generale* Soddu promised the immediate dispatch of at least two Alpine battalions.

In the meantime, the Greek offensive continued, both against the northern wing of the *Pusteria* and on the ridge between Devoli and Tomorrecës: furious hand-to-hand fighting ensued, which saw the battalions of the 1st and 6th *Alpini* engaged. Despite the fact that many enemy breakthroughs were stemmed with rapid counter-attacks, it was not possible to completely stop the Greek advance. On 29 December, the positions of Çuka and Gjatë were taken by the enemy and the next day Maja and Korbiet. *Generale* Nasci was forced to ask to be allowed to retreat to a holding position, in order to avoid the envelopment of the entire Tomorrecës Valley. But Vercellino could not authorise the manoeuvre without first hearing from the High Command and asking for reinforcements. Cavallero had no troops to send and therefore left him free to decide:

> Listen, Vercellino: you are the judge. But before you decide on a retreat, see that it is unavoidable..'[1]

At 17:00, Vercellino in turn told Nasci:

> I authorise you to do as the situation requires. In relation to the meagre forces you have at your disposal, if you decide to fall back to a line of defence, you are authorised to do so.[2]

And so at 8 p.m., the XXVI Corps command issued the order to fall back. On that same day, *Generale* Cavallero took command of all armed forces in Albania, but maintaining the position of Chief of the General Staff.

The Situation on the Front of 11th Armoured

On 5 December 1940, *Generale* Geloso, commander of the 11th Army, ordered the continuation of the manoeuvre to occupy the new defence positions Porto Palermo – Kurvelesh – Dhëmbel – Qarishta – Mali Velushes, stipulating that it should be completed by the night of 7/8 December. Although the troops were completely exhausted, the retreat was carried out in an orderly manner and according to the marching schedules. The state of the troops had been fully explained by Geloso to Cavallero on the morning of 6 December:

> To the left is the *Pusteria* with four brigades without the *Carloni* (it does, however, use those of the *Bari*). The *Pusteria*'s Corps are arriving in Valona. The 5th *Alpini* Artillery Regiment has the materials but does not yet have the mules. It will take five to six days before it is complete and can arrive

---

1   Cavallero diary, 30.12.1940.
2   DS Command XXVI Army Corps, dated 30.12.1940.

in position. The *Bari* has lost everything. The 8th Alpini lost 80 percent, the 9th Alpini lost less. The *Vicenza* and *L'Aquila* behaved heroically. They kissed the ground they stood on. The *Julia* is shrunken but continues to fight. Three valley battalions are not yet completely worn out, but they have no troopers. The 41st and 42nd infantry regiments are tired, especially the 41st.[3]

Considering the state of the units and the lack of ammunition, the 11th army could hold out for a maximum of eight more days. The northern wing, from Tomori to Klisura, represented the weakest sector. On the eve of the Greek offensive, the 11th army was thus deployed, from left to right, with the VIII Corps in three divisions and an Alpine group between Q. Devris and the Zagorias Valley, with the XXV Corps in three divisions and some Alpine battalions from the Zagorias Valley itself to the Sushiça Valley excluded. The *Siena* Division and some Blackshirts battalions were deployed from the Sushiça Valley to the sea. There were actually only six divisions in the front line, as the *Centauro* had been moved to the second line, continuing as part of the XXV Army Corps. The new defensive positions had been set up in a hurry, so the troops had to work to improve them at least at the most important points, because in addition to facing the enemy, it was also necessary for the Army to endure the cold weather.

The Greek offensive within Albanian territory developed along four different routes: the Osum-Tomorrecës route, at the junction between the 9th Army and the 11th Army; the Vojussa-Deshnicës route, with Klisura as the first target; the Dhrinos-Vojussa route, with Tepeleni as the immediate target; the Sushiça Valley, to bypass the Kurvelesh and Logora defences and breakthrough towards lower Vojussa. By attacking along all four lines, however, the Greeks divided their forces and allowed the Italians to offer a more effective resistance.[4]

On 8 December, the Greek 11th Division attacked in the Osum Valley, committing its three regiments. Extremely hard fighting ensued, which involved the *Pusteria* Divisions, which, with about 2,500 men, held a 25-kilometre-wide front line, and under pouring rain that made all movement difficult. The *Cadore* Battalion was located on the ridge of Galina el Ciaf, an important high ground on the right side of the valley, where there were trenches and shelters. In the afternoon of 8 December, the Greek infantry attacked, covered by mortar bombardment and machine gun fire. *Tenente* Luzzatto took some Alpine men with him and attempted a counterattack, but enemy fire stopped his action and cut short the officer's life. The Greek infantry tried several times to break through, but were always repulsed. The enemy artillery began to hit the Italian positions, resulting in numerous casualties, including that of *Capitano* Tarabini.

The commander of the 7th regiment, Colonnello Rodolfo Psaro, born on 7 November 1892 in La Spezia, arrived on the front line, muddy and with a long beard. He continued to inspect the outposts under enemy fire and to observe the attack

---

3   Cavallero diary, 6.12.1940.
4   At the start of the halting battle, the force ratio was 2 to 1 in favour of the Greeks, 26 attacking infantry regiments against 13 Italians.

through his binoculars. During a fresh attack by Greek infantry, under fire from Greek mortars and artillery, Colonnello Psaro was hit and seriously wounded. He was immediately transferred to a field hospital, where he died shortly afterwards. He was decorated with the *Medaglia d'Oro al Valor Militare alla Memoria*, with the citation:

> With his *Feltre* and *Cadore* Battalions he bravely and victoriously with-
> stood the impact of overwhelming enemy forces. In the immediate coun-
> terattack, which he launched and led with skill and audacity to crush the
> enemy's boldness, he was mortally wounded at the head of his magnificent
> Alpini troops. A superb figure of a soldier and heroic commander, a shining
> example of daring, contempt for danger and obedience to the holy law of
> the Fatherland. [Albania – Ciafa Gallina December 1940].

In addition to the loss of *Colonnello* Psaro and *Tenente* Luzzatto, two other company commanders also fell in combat. In the course of the fighting, the two bodies of gunners were also dispersed. Around midnight on 9 December, *Generale* Amedeo De Cia, commander of the *Pusteria*, informed the command that he had been forced to retreat. *Generale* Bancale ordered the holding of Cerevodë at all costs, while the *Julia* reported that it was itself engaged at the Osum – Ambum confluence. For his part, *Generale* Geloso ordered: 'The ground must be held in hand-to-hand. We need to gain time while waiting for reinforcements to arrive...'

The need to hold Cerevodë, had caused the loss of contact between the *Pusteria* and *Julia* Divisions, so that on the afternoon of 11 December, *Generale* De Cia reported numerous enemy breakthroughs some 10 kilometres south of Cerevodë itself. Fortunately, the Greek forces suffered heavy losses and from 12 December, the enemy pressure decreased considerably across the entire front. As early as 10 December, the Greek units had launched a first attack towards Shës i Mal and Strakavec, but were repulsed by the *Pizzi* Group, under the orders of *Colonnello* Enrico Pizzi and comprising the *Belluno* and *Val Natisone Alpini* battalions and a machine gun company. In the afternoon of 12 December, the Greeks managed to occupy height 623, allowing the possibility of advancing along the left bank of the Vojussa. In the course of the night, thanks to a counterattack, the height was recaptured by the Italians.

On 13 December, the Greeks attacked the positions of the *Bari* Division, concentrating on the two pillars of the Zagorias Valley. Fighting also raged on Shës i Mal, where an *Alpini* company and one of the 140th were engaged. Despite the dispatch of some reinforcements, the situation became critical and the Greeks managed to penetrate deeply, even in the Zagorias Valley.

On 16 December, *Generale* Bancale, commander of the VIII Corps, ordered a retreat to a more rearward line, with the left wing on Vojussa and the right wing on Brezhanit, a sort of bridgehead in defence of Klisura, which was already under fire from Greek artillery. On 17 December, Bancale himself ordered the commander of the *Bari*, Generale D'Havet, to '...hold on to the positions at all costs and to gather men however they found themselves in the rear and lead them to the defence points on horseback.'

In this critical situation, *Generale* Geloso decided to transfer two complement battalions of the 9th *Alpini* and the I/17th Infantry *Acqui*, which had just landed, to the VIII Corps: the latter unit was transferred to the Tolari area to counterattack should the Greeks penetrate the front south of Qarishta and Fratarit. At the same time, since the group had fallen back as far as Golico-Brezhanit and no longer had any connection with *Bari*, it was decided to transfer it to the XXV Corps, moving the boundary between the two corps to the ridge of the Trebeshines.[5]

For a few days, the situation remained stable, characterised only by attacking patrols and distant clashes between the opposing artillery. It was only in the north, in the Osum sector, that some major clashes took place: on 20 December, the *Feltre* Battalion captured the northern spur of Gostanghës and defended it for two days. When it was on the verge of being surrounded by the enemy, it fell back to the west of Q. Devris.

Fighting in the XXV Corps Sector

As of 10 December 1940, the forces of the XXV Corps were arranged as follows: the *Ferrara* Division straddling the Dhrinos, with the 48th infantry in two battalions east of the river, the 47th with three battalions with reduced staffs to the west, and the 166th Blackshirts Battalion in reserve. The *Modena* Division was stationed on the Kurvelesh, with the 3rd *Granatieri* in two battalions from Bus Devrit to Mali Shpat; the 42nd infantry in three battalions to Mali Thät; the *Bolzano* Battalion isolated on the far right and the 36th Blackshirts battalion in reserve. The *Centauro* was the reserve Corps reserve, reassembled west of Tepeleni, together with the 2nd Bersaglieri stationed at Dragoti.

On 12 December, the Greeks launched an attack against the *Modena* positions, defended at that time only by the 42nd Infantry (1,500 men), the 36th Blackshirts Battalion (450 men) and two groups of the 29th Field Artillery. The 41st Infantry had been sent to reinforce *Bari* while the rest of the units were still in Italy awaiting transfer.

At 9:45 a.m., two Greek infantry battalions, under the cover of fog, attacked the sector defended by the II/42nd, in the direction of Golem-Progonat, and succeeded in making some headway. Thanks to the intervention of the 36th Blackshirts Battalion and the I/42nd, the situation was re-established. Numerous losses were suffered, including all four company commanders of the II/42nd. In the afternoon of 13 December, the Greeks attacked again against the positions of Sella di Golem (Golemi), on the right wing of the *Modena*. The soldiers of the I/42nd were overwhelmed within hours and subsequent counterattacks launched by the divisional reserve were to no avail. Another enemy attack on Mali Shpat was repulsed by the III/42nd. Towards evening, the 14th and XXIV/5th Bersaglieri arrived to reinforce Lekdushaj and the defensive line was somewhat restored.

---

5   Mario Montanari, *LEesercito Italiano Nella Campagna di Grecia*, Ufficio Storico Stato Maggiore dell'Esercito, p.373.

The situation remained serious, however, due to the loss of the Golemi Saddle and was aggravated on the morning of the 15th, when Greek divisions penetrated towards Progonat. The breakthrough was stemmed at the last moment thanks to the arrival of a complement battalion of the 47th Infantry. On that same day, command of the Division was taken over by *Generale* Luigi Trionfi, replacing *Colonnello* Francesco Sclavo, chief of staff of the *Modena*, in command of the unit after the wounding and hospitalisation of *Generale* Gloria on 29 November. The II/2nd Bersaglieri, comprising about 300 men, also arrived at *Modena*'s positions as reinforcements. In total, the division fielded about 1,400–1,500 men in the front line, while the attackers, the Greek 4th Infantry Division, fielded about 4,500 men. Intense cold and a sudden blizzard temporarily halted the fighting. But by 17 December, the Greeks had resumed their infiltrations, engaging numerous patrols. When these breakthroughs came within a few hundred metres of Progontat, *Generale* Trionfi was forced to ask the army corps command for permission to fall back on Gusmara and Lekdushaj, which they did on 18 December, as confirmed in the following message sent by Trionfi:

> Enemy overwhelmed our defence front sector 42nd infantry points in the direction of the Bencia valley and Gusmara stop ordered to retreat to the line of strongholds 28–10 and on high ground south Gusmara stop I will try to transfer command to Lekdushaj.[6]

Modena's retreat created serious problems for the XXV Corps and consequently for the entire army. The defence of the sector found itself split into two sections with no connection between them and the Greek formations took advantage of this to wedge themselves between the two divisions, attacking the supply columns. To meet the threat against Tepeleni, the corps had already sent two battalions of the 18th *Aqui* Infantry to the most threatened sectors. At the same time, the remnants of *Bolzano*, isolated on Mali Thät, were ordered to continue to resist at all costs.

On 19 December, the line of strongholds was occupied and turned into a defensive line from Lekdushaj to the Mali Palciës ridge. The remnants of the 82nd Blackshirts Battalion were sent to occupy the massif north of Progonat, between the branches of the Bençës. Other elements of the Division were entrenched at Gusmara. On the night of 20 December, the two battalions of the 18th Infantry finally arrived.

On 15 December, the Greeks attacked the *Ferrara* positions on the left side of the Dhrinos up to Bus Devrit. The units of the 47th Infantry Regiment suddenly found the Greek soldiers upon them. The toughest fighting took place on height 1381, located between Mali Terzorit and Bus Devrit, and it was the arrival, and example, of *Colonnello* Francesco Imbriani, commander of the regiment, that saved the day. After realising the gravity of the situation, Imbriani moved towards Bus Devrit. On his way up the mule track, he came across some 70 stragglers, stopped them and, after encouraging and motivating them, led them to counterattack. Fierce fighting ensued, which grew in intensity in the evening of the 15th but lasted until

---

6   Mario Montanari, *LEesercito Italiano Nella Campagna di Grecia*, Ufficio Storico Stato Maggiore dell'Esercito, p.385.

the afternoon of the following day. The enemy attack was stopped, but the III/47th, comprising about 250 men, suffered the loss of two-thirds of its men, dead and wounded.

Among the fallen was Corporal Felice Di Nicolantonio, born in Barren Island (United States) in 1916, serving with the 47th Infantry Regiment. He was decorated with the *Medaglia d'Oro al Valor Militare alla Memoria*, with the citation:

> As part of a battalion already tired from bloody fighting and in a critical situation, he was charged with a few daring men to reach and urgently occupy a height in order to prevent and hold back the enemy, made bold by their unexpected success. With determination and reckless disregard for danger, he was the first to reach the objective and with the calm and precise fire of his machine gun, he stopped the enemy, encouraging his comrades with his words and inflaming them with the example of his own bravery. Seriously wounded, he remained heroically at his fighting post for three days, until he was mortally wounded in the chest and fell to his weapon, offering his life to his country to the cry of 'Long live Italy'. A shining example of military valour and heroic devotion to duty. [Mali Terzorit (Q. 1381), 14–16 December 1940]

The Greeks also suffered such heavy losses that they were forced to cease their attacks for some days, but on 18 December, the Greeks returned to attack, mainly to stop any Italian counterattacks. At the same time, the *Modena* Division reported that it was on the verge of being surrounded, but with the arrival of the 18th *Aqui* Infantry, it was possible to reorganise *Modena*'s units in the rear strongholds and repel the new Greek attacks. Between 20 and 21 December, a counterattack on Progonat was launched by the units of the *Modena*, but the defence of Lekdushaj at Gusmara could not be consolidated. At the same time, new Greek attacks towards the Salarije Valley were repulsed.

Fighting in the Coastal Sector

The retreat of the *Siena* Division from Bistriva took place in two phases, the first at the height of Gjirokastra and the second on positions west of the Borshi stream. The Greek attacks began on 15 December, along two lines: one towards the passes of Vestes and Drass and the other towards Qeparoj and Mali and Varit. The attack along the first direction was initially repulsed by the *Siena* units, but after three days of hard fighting, the Division's right wing was overwhelmed. On the morning of 17 December, the I/3rd *Granatieri*, having suffered under yet another enemy attack, fell back. Towards midday, it was the turn of the III/32nd, which had been busy trying to close the breach. Only the II/32nd, with its reduced numbers, continued to hold its positions although at great cost.

Generale Giulio Perugi, who took over command of the division on 9 December 1940, then attempted to establish a link from Mali and Qeparojt to Varit by withdrawing the III/31st from the northern sector, but the breach remained open.

Fighting raged on until nightfall, with heavy losses inflicted on the attackers. On 18 December, *Generale* Perugi asked the Army Command for urgent reinforcements, most especially to shore up his right wing. The situation got worse shortly afterwards when, at 11.40 a.m., the commander of the 32nd Infantry reported that during the previous night his regiment had been forced to fall back with the remains of its battalions, including the I/32nd defending the position of Mali Corajt. And so, while the *Siena* command decided to fall back its right wing from the Limana Gulf to Mount Gjemit to then link up with Mali Qishes, and the *Modena* Division fell back on Gusmara and Lekdushaj, both *Generale* Geloso and *Generale* Soddu ordered the recapture of the positions of Mali and Varit and Mali and Qeparojt at any cost.

At dawn on 19 December, the Greeks attacked again, first against Q. Drass and then against Q. Vestes. The fighting soon afterwards extended to the whole front. The Italian units remained in their positions until the evening, then collapses began to occur that allowed the Greeks to take the positions of Maja and Gjemit, Q. Drass and Kuçi. The position on Mai Papathia, defended by a battalion of Blackshirts, held out for another two days, then with no more supplies and ammunition, and surrounded, it was forced to surrender.

To stem the Greek offensive thrust in the coastal sector, a Special Army Corps was formed and placed under the orders of *Generale* Giovanni Messe. The army corps had been in Albania since November 1940, without troops, at the disposal of the High Command. On 19 December, it was placed under the 11th Army to 'guarantee the absolute integrity of Vlora and its hinterland,'[7] along the line Mali Thät – Mureve – Q. Pisces – Cipini – Smokthina and the sea. It was joined by:[8]

> *Generale* Mariotti's *Aqui* Division: 17th Infantry, 18th Blackshirts Legion in two battalions, two Bersaglieri companies of the 5th (already reinforcing the *Siena*) and support units.
> *Generale* Piazzoni's Special Alpine Division: 2nd *Alpini* in two battalions, a dismounted cavalry regiment (in three groups), two position machine gun companies and support units.
> Army Corps troops: various units, including two tank battalions and later the *Siena* Division.

In an attempt to relieve the enemy pressure, it was decided by the High Command, pressed also by Mussolini, to carry out offensive actions to take the initiative away from the Greek forces, who were also exhausted and tired by the fighting of the previous weeks. And so, *Generale* Geloso issued new directives, according to which, by 25 December at the latest, counterattacks were to be carried out along the most suitable lines, also employing armoured units. In the meantime, while the arrival of the Special Army Corps units had not yet been completed, the Greeks attacked again, aiming to break through towards Vlora or Berat. The Greek attacks along the Valona route hit the positions of *Siena* on 22 December 1940. Then between 26 and

---

7   On the night of 19/20 December, the Greeks carried out a naval raid on Vlora.
8   Mario Montanari, *L'Esercito Italiano Nella Campagna di Grecia*, Ufficio Storico Stato Maggiore dell'Esercito, page 396.

28 December, more attacks were launched in the Sushiça Valley and between 28 and 30 December, on the Littoral. For a few days, the *Siena* with about 700 men in the Sushiça Valley, near Vranishta, and another thousand north of Himara, managed to hold its positions, thanks also to reinforcements that had just arrived from Italy. Meanwhile, the Special Alpine Division was regrouping its units.

The Greek attacks in the Sushiça Valley continued and it was necessary to send troops to stop them. Considering that some units of the *Aqui* had already been transferred to the Littoral and that the 31st Infantry, no longer able to face the enemy, had been replaced with the 2nd *Alpini*, it was decided to commit the units of the *Cuneo* Division, arriving from Italy. The objective was to push the enemy forces back from the Sushiça Valley, bring back the line of resistance to between Thmonit and M. Lëpietres and remove the threat from Vlora. *Generale* Geloso therefore issued new directives, transferring the *Cuneo* Division to the Special Army Corps, except for a couple of battalions sent to Klisura and the *Galbiati* Group, comprising three battalions of Blackshirts, under the orders of MVSN *Tenente Generale* Enzo Emilio Galbiati.

On 28 December, Cavallero asked *Generale* Messe for a report on the situation in the Sushiça Valley: the 2nd *Alpini* was in line with its three battalions, *Saluzzo*, *Dronero* and *Borgo St Dalmazzo*, firmly in its positions and even on the coast, where the 32nd infantry had been engaged in hard defensive fighting, the situation appeared stabilised. For the launching of a possible counter-offensive, Messe reported that another 4 to 5 days were needed, therefore for 2–3 January 1941.

As of 27 December 1940, the situation of the 11th Army was as follows: on the right wing, where the Special Army Corps was located, continuous Greek attacks posed a threat in the direction of Vlora. That left the defensive position south of Brataj, only some forty kilometres away, as a last defence. In the centre, where the XXV Corps was, the Tepeleni-Klisura route remained under threat due to enemy attacks on Qarishta and Fratarit and against Progonat-Gusmara. On the left wing, where the VIII Corps was, the threat was through the Osum Valley, where the *Pusteria*, having been attacked frontally and on the flank from the Tomorreçës Valley to Mali Kulmakës, had been forced to retreat to Q. Sirakut, establishing a connection with the Cerevodë positions, protected by the tumultuous waters of the River Osum.

The Kurvelesh Situation

In addition to the threat hanging over Vlora, *Generale* Geloso was also very concerned about the situation in Kurvelesh: the retreat of the *Siena* had made Mali Thät indefensible, where a group of Alpine troops still remained completely isolated, so the junction between the Special Army Corps and the XXV Corps was established from 22 December on Thmonit. The attacks of the Greek 4th Infantry Division towards the Vojussa Valley resumed on 25 December. Facing them in the Salarije Valley sector, were the remnants of the I and II/42nd, II/47th, *Bolzano* and the II/18th *Aqui* Infantry. In the *Modena* sector, there were 200 men of the II and III/3rd *Granatieri*, 140 men of the III/42nd, 90 men of the III/29th artillery, 250 soldiers of the 36th and 82nd Blackshirts battalions, about 250 men of the XIV and XXIV Bersaglieri battalions, and another 800 men of the I and III/18th infantry.

After occupying the line of the strongholds with elements of the 18th Infantry, *Modena* withdrew the other unit to the town of Lekdushaj to reorganise them into formed units and reconstitute the divisional reserve. However, an incident had occurred during the retreat, when stronghold 38 on the spur of Mali Palciës had not been immediately occupied during the night of 19 December, and this allowed the units of the Greek 2nd Infantry Division to capture it, along with the height 1430, and descend to Mali Palciës. In the morning of the 21st, the III/18th was sent to occupy the stronghold, but the Italian battalion was engaged in fierce fighting until late into the night to recapture the height, and the next day had to repel new enemy attacks. In the afternoon of the 22nd, the battalion moved north to drive the Greeks out of Mali Palciës, but was stopped by enemy fire.

Three days later, at dawn on 25 December, a reinforced company of the 18th Infantry succeeded in occupying Mali Palciës, but in the afternoon, a new Greek attack overwhelmed the same company, which was forced to retreat. During the night, *Generale* Giovanni Magli, commander of the *Centauro*, took command of the Bençës Valley sector. In the following days, the fighting continued: the village of Bençë was strenuously defended, while height 1430 was recaptured by the Greeks on 27 December. Further furious fighting broke out around stronghold 38 and stronghold 10. By the evening of 30 December, the situation continued to remain critical: the I/18th Infantry defending stronghold 10 had suffered heavy losses as had the 3rd *Granatieri*. In the meantime, two companies of complements from the 5th Bersaglieri had arrived and the XXV Corps Command reported that the first two battalions of the 232nd Infantry of the *Brenner* Division were moving up the Bençës Valley to reinforce the *Modena* Division.

In the Salarije Valley, the Greeks attacked Mureve, on the far right of the sector, and occupied the summit. The objective was to envelop the Italian positions on Kurvelesh from the west. On 30 December, the Nivice position fell and on the 31st, the Greeks also occupied M. Beikes. Thanks to the arrival of the first elements of the 231st *Brenner* Infantry, it proved possible to stem the enemy attacks.

The defence of Tepeleni was entrusted to the *Ferrara* Division and that of Klisura to the *Bari*. The Dhrinos Valley was barricaded near the Mali Terzorit – Golico line. The main objective of the Greek forces was the elimination of the bridgehead that the *Ferrara* had established south of Tepeleni. The attacks began on 28 December, but were stopped on the Bus Dervit as well as in the Dhrinos Valley. In the Zagorias Valley, the Greek attacks were stopped at Pesclani and on Brezhanit: at this last position were the remains of the *Val Natisone* Battalion, about seventy Alpini soldiers, who resisted the enemy assaults.

At the end of December, the main concern for the XXV Corps Command remained the reinforcement of the defensive line on the northern edge of the Kurvelesh plateau. To this end, *Generale* Paolo Berardi's *Brenner* Division was engaged, and was called upon to gradually replace the units in the two sectors defended by *Modena* and to stabilise the defensive front with the retaking of strongholds 38, 39 (Mali Palciës) and 9 (Progonat settlement). The relieved units were to regroup in the rear and then return to their divisions, except for the *Bolzano* and 18th Infantry, which were placed under the *Brenner*.

The Fighting on the Front of the 8th Corps

Since 18 December, the 2nd Greek Corps had ordered the resumption of an offensive and decided to attack the entire sector of the 8th Italian Corps, particularly along the Mali Qarishta ridge. The Greek 15th Infantry Division, supported by the 5th brigade and other units, was to penetrate the *Julia*'s front and to continue towards the Mali Trebeshines range. On the flanks was the 11th Division, which was to advance on the right of the Osum to reach Dobrusha and the 1st Division, which was to take Klisura. The attack began in the morning of 23 December, under snow and a cloudy sky. The Greek 15th Division advanced on an attack front of about three kilometres against Qarishta and Fratarit: the main effort was carried out at the junction point between the positions of the *Julia* (Fratarit) and the *Bari* (southern slopes of Fratarit) Divisions. A good seven hours of attacks and counterattacks followed, which severely tested the resistance of the Italian units. When it was evening, the 9th *Alpini* was still firmly established on Qarishta and Fratarit, while the southern ridge had given way and the *Bari* units had been forced to retreat, leaving a gap on the right of the *Julia*.

There were many episodes of heroism and numerous *Medaglia d'Oro* were awarded. Among them, was the award to *Tenente* Pietro Chiampo of the 9th *Alpini* Regiment, born in 1914 in Perosa Argentina (Turin), and decorated with the *Medaglia d'Oro al Valor Militare alla Memoria* with the citation:

> On a day of hard and bloody fighting, when the company was left without officers, he took command, reorganised the survivors and led them to attack the positions that the enemy, much superior in strength, had managed to occupy. Three times, he led his men to the counterattack with élan and daring, three times the adversary pushed back, renewing their furious counterattacks. In the course of the bitter and alternating events, during which he succeeded in capturing several automatic weapons, although wounded, he remained with his Alpine troops, keeping their fighting ardour intact by his example, and then led them, for the fourth time, to a last desperate counterattack, during which he was mortally wounded. While being carried to the dressing station, with stoic steadfastness, he pronounced lofty words of faith in victory, regretting only that he had to abandon the fight [Monte Chiarista – Fratarit (Greek front), 23 December 1940].

Another man decorated man was Tenente Bruno Ranieri, of the 4th *Alpini* Artillery Regiment, born in Ivrea, province of Aosta, in 1915. After effectively countering no less than seven enemy attacks, he was wounded along with the others serving his piece, and launched himself into the attack with a machine gun in an attempt to repel the enemy. He thus managed to save his battery, but due to the serious wounds he sustained, he lost consciousness and died there. He was awarded the *Medaglia d'Oro al Valor Militare alla Memoria* with the citation:

> Commander of an advanced gun, in line with the Alpine troops, in an advanced and delicate position, contemptuous of any danger, he generously

used his weapon and succeeded, firing continuously at zero range, in containing repeated and violent enemy attacks. Wounded along with several men during the seventh enemy attack, he refused treatment and, in the raging battle near him, daringly threw himself forward, and with his machine gun and hand grenades, drove back the attackers and saved the gun. Exhausted by the amount of blood lost, he died shortly afterwards. An example of courage and high military virtues. [Chiarist and Fratarit (Greek front), 23 December 1940].

Also decorated was *Capitano* Franco Bughetti, commander of the 2nd Company of the LXVIII Blackshirts Assault Battalion, born in 1909 in Imola. During the fighting on 23 December 1940, he was seriously wounded and was decorated with the *Medaglia d'Oro al Valor Militare*, with the citation:

Company commander, already distinguished for his courage, during an attack by an overwhelming enemy force against the position held by his unit, he strenuously sustained the defence despite the heavy losses suffered and led his men to the counterattack several times. Hit by a hand grenade that wounded him in the chest and removed both his hands, in a supreme burst of dedication, shaking his bleeding stumps, he led the few brave survivors back to the top of the contested position, where he was the first to arrive. The impetus of his men encouraged by his heroic example annihilated the enemy defenders on the conquered position [Alto del Chiarista – Fratarit (Albania), 23 December 1940].

The next day, the Greeks attacked Fratarit again, four times, but were always repulsed, with heavy losses. Further north, elements of the Greek 11th Infantry Division managed, after furious hand-to-hand fighting, to penetrate into the town of Mollasi, where they were stopped by Italian units. Further south, the Greek 1st Infantry Division failed to capture the Varibodi Ridge, defended by the left wing of the *Bari*. In the afternoon of 24 December, *Genikós* Papadopoulos ordered the cessation of the attacks.

In the evening, *Generale* Bancale received reports from the three sectors of the front: the *Pusteria* command reported that there had been a retreat of its left wing, but the position of Cerevodë and the Kulmakës and Sirakut passes had been held. From the *Julia*, a message arrived from the commander of the 9th Alpini: 'The positions are still in our possession, but the conditions of the troops, severely tried by the fighting and bad weather, have reached the limits of human possibility and, aware of the responsibility I have, I ask that everything possible be done so that reinforcements will invariably arrive tomorrow morning.' The *Bari* guards found themselves with the left wing on Qarishta and Fratarit and the right wing on Klisura. The main problem, however, concerned the closing of the gap opened on the southern slopes of Qarishta and Fratarit. Three attempts had been made, involving the *Julia*'s supplementary battalion, under the orders of *Maggiore* Guindani, supported by elements of *L'Aquila* from the north and the *Bari* from the south, but without success. The attack was launched again and once again the Alpine men of the *Julia*, with their officers in the lead, moved forward. But the defensive positions of the Greeks also stopped this attempt and so the breach between the *Julia* and *Bari* remained.

During these attacks, *Tenente* Aldo Zanotta, commander of the 2nd Company of the *Julia's* supplementary battalion, born on 2 February 1903 in Novi Ligure (Alessandria), distinguished himself. He fell in combat while leading his Alpine troops and was decorated with the *Medaglia d'Oro al Valor Militare*, with the citation:

> Commander of an Alpine company, he was first to counterattack a strong enemy position. Twice wounded, he returned to take command and again counterattacked the superior adversary in force, managing, by example and with prodigies of valour, to repel him and maintain the contested position until, mortally wounded, he donated his youth to the Homeland on the positions he had conquered. [Q. 1067 Chiarist and Fratarit (Greek front), 27 December 1940].

On 29 December, the *Val Tagliamento* Battalion was transferred to the 9th Alpine to try to resume the attacks with new forces, but on the morning of the 30th it was the Greeks who went on the attack, with the II Corps. Before sending the infantry units forward, a massive artillery and mortar bombardment was unleashed. The Italian positions were overwhelmed and Qarishta and Fratarit were captured by the enemy. Soon afterwards, Sevranit also fell, while the remnants of the 9th *Alpini* and the *Udine*, *Conegliano* and *Val Tanaro* Groups regrouped on Topajanit, which was already threatened with encirclement.

Almost all of the unit commanders had fallen in combat, either dead or wounded. Among them was *Maggiore* Francesco Confalonieri, born in Milan in 1896, commander of the *Vicenza Alpini* Battalion. For the courage he showed in the face of the enemy, he was awarded the *Medaglia d'Oro al Valor Militare*, with the citation:

> A superb commander, a magnificent soldier, in a long period of combat conducted through the most arduous trials, against an insidious and preponderant enemy, in a harsh terrain and climate, amidst hardships of all kinds, he showed that he possessed exceptional qualities of an organiser, a driving force and a valiant fighter. He was always the first where the danger was most serious and his work as a commander was the most necessary. In a combat of exceptional importance, with his personal leadership and heroic behaviour, he succeeded with a few survivors of the battalion in maintaining an important position attacked by overwhelming enemy forces. Seriously wounded, he repeatedly refused to abandon his Alpine soldiers, continuing to encourage them to resistance. Exhausted by the abundant blood lost, he died shortly afterwards. [Epirus – Pindus – Monte Chiarista (Greek front), 28 October –30 December 1940].

The vanguard of the *Val Tagliamento* arrived as a reinforcement and Topajanit was held despite repeated Greek attacks. Further south, the Greek 1st Infantry Division succeeded in taking the Variboldi Ridge, forcing the 41st Infantry to retreat to the Tolari Spur.

Generale Ugo Cavallero. (USSME)

Tenente Colonnello Adolfo Rivoir. (USSME)

Soldiers engaged in transporting a dismantled artillery piece, during a retreat, December 1940.
(USSME)

Situation in the sector of the 9th Army between 9 and 17 December 1940. (USSME)

Alpini della Julia on a defensive position, December 1940. (USSME)

Colonnello Rodolfo Psaro. (www.movm.it)

An Alpine artillery piece in the high mountains, December 1940. (USSME)

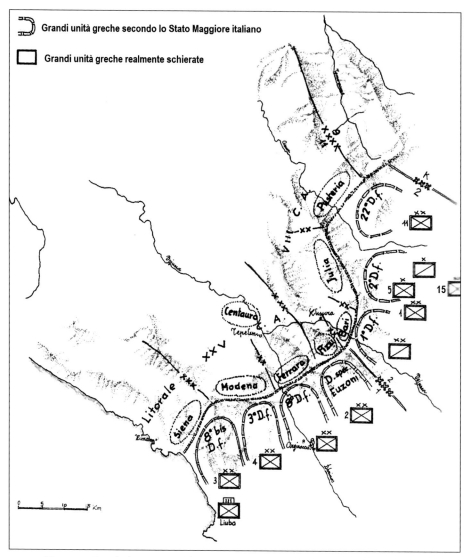

The opposing deployments in the 11th Army sector on 8 December 1940. (USSME)

MEDAGLIA D'ORO ALLA MEMORIA « CON I SUOI BATTAGLIONI "FEL-TRE" E "CADORE" SOSTENEVA VA-LOROSAMENTE E VITTORIOSA-MENTE L'URTO DI PREPONDERAN-TI FORZE NEMICHE. NELL'IMME-DIATA AZIONE DI CONTRATTACCO DA LUI SFERRATO E GUIDATO CON PERIZIA E AUDACIA PER STRONCARE LA BAL-DANZA NEMICA, CADEVA COLPITO MORTALMEN-TE, ALLA TESTA DEI SUOI MAGNIFICI ALPINI. SUPERBA FIGURA DI SOLDATO E DI EROICO CO-MANDANTE, ESEMPIO FULGIDISSIMO DI ARDI-MENTO, DI SPREZZO DEL PERICOLO E DI OBBE-DIENZA ALLA SANTA LEGGE DELLA PATRIA. »

(*Albania - Ciafa Gallina, 8 dicembre 1940*-XIX)

RODOLFO PSARO

Colonnello 7° Reggimento alpini, da La Spezia

Contemporary postcard commemorating the awarding of the *Medaglia d'Oro al Valor Militare* to *Colonnello* Rodolfo Psaro.

An Italian machine gun emplacement dug into the snow, December 1940. (USSME)

An Italian light mortar team in a defensive position, engaged in repelling an enemy attack, December 1940. (USSME)

A Greek mortar team providing supporting fire to infantry units, December 1940.

Generale Luigi Trionfi, commander of the *Modena* Division from 15 December 1940.

Caporale Felice Di Nicolantonio. (www.movm.it)

**F E L I C E
DINICOLANTONIO**

*Caporale 47° Reggim. fanteria, da Barren
(Stati Uniti d'America), alla memoria.*

« Facente parte di un battaglione già provato da sanguinosi combattimenti ed in critica situazione, veniva incaricato con pochi arditmentosi di raggiungere ed occupare di urgenza una quota allo scopo di prevenire e trattenere il nemico reso baldanzoso da un inaspettato successo. Con decisione e sprezzo del pericolo giungeva primo sull'obiettivo e col tiro calmo e preciso della sua mitragliatrice, fulminava l'avversario, incitando con la voce i camerati ed infiammandoli con l'esempio del proprio ardimento. Gravemente ferito, rimaneva eroicamente al suo posto di combattimento per tre giorni, finché mortalmente colpito al petto si abbatteva sull'arma, offrendo la sua vita alla Patria al grido di " Viva l'Italia! " Fulgido esempio di valore militare e di eroico attaccamento al dovere. »

(Mai Terzorit, quota 1 381, 1 4-16 dic. 1940-XIX)

Contemporary postcard commemorating the awarding of the *Medaglia d'Oro al Valor Militare* to *Caporale* Felice Di Nicolantonio.

Italian soldiers during an attack on an enemy strongpoint in the high mountains, December 1940.
(USSME)

Greek troops move to attack Italian positions, December 1940.

Generale Giovanni Messe. (USSME)

MVSN *Tenente Generale* Enzo Emilio Galbiati.

Italian soldiers on a high mountain defence post, December 1940. (USSME)

The southern part of Albania, affected by the Greek attacks in late December 1940.

Tenente Pietro Chiampo of the 9th *Alpini*
Regiment. (www.movm.it)

Tenente Bruno Ranieri, 4th *Alpini* Artillery
Regiment. (www.movm.it)

Left: *Tenente*
Aldo Zanotta,
commander of the
2nd Company of the
Julia Complement
Battalion. (www.
movm.it)

Right: *Maggiore*
Francesco
Confalonieri,
commander of
the *Vicenza Alpini*
Battalion. (www.
movm.it)

6

New Greek Offensive

On 31 December 1940, *Generale* Cavallero and *Generale* Geloso met to discuss the serious military situation on the Albanian front: by this time, the Greeks had taken the Sushiça Headland, the positions on the Kurvelesch Plateau were threatened, and the pressure on Valona had become untenable. The two generals agreed that a large-scale counter-offensive was necessary to relieve enemy pressure and, above all, to remove the threat from Vlora. However, time and forces were needed to prepare and plan it properly, so it was decided in the meantime to conduct some counterattacks immediately, especially in the sector of the 11th Army, in the most threatened sectors. But while the Italian command was planning, the Greeks went on the attack first.

The Offensive on Berat

After the fighting at the end of December, the line of the VIII Italian Corps started from the south-eastern slopes of the Tomori (Q. Sirakut), bent westwards, moved up the left bank of the Osum to the confluence with the Ambum, then ascended the Mali Topajanit, the centre of the new resistance position and finally descended to Klisura. From Tomori to Mali Qarishta (excluded) the *Pusteria* Division was deployed, while Mali Qarishta was defended by the *Julia* and the Vojussa Furrow by the *Bari*.

In the meantime, the formation near Berat of the IV Army Corps, under the orders of *Generale* Mercalli, had begun, comprising the *Lupi di Toscana* Division arriving from Italy, the reconstituted *Siena* Division (only the 31st infantry), the 21st artillery *Trieste*, a carabinieri battalion and two cavalry squadrons. On 2 January 1941, it was decided to transfer *Pusteria* to the new corps, which, however, remained in its positions, while the entire IV Army Corps, whose sector corresponded to the *Pusteria* front, was assigned a static defence task to form a mass of manoeuvre to control the outlets from the Tomorreçës, Osum and Vojussa Valleys.

On 1 January 1941, the Greek forces had attacked with two companies *Chiaf* and *Sposit*, but were repulsed. In the afternoon, Mali Topojanit positions were attacked, but to no effect. On 2 January, a new attack was launched by the enemy, preceded by preparatory artillery fire, but which was also repulsed by the *Val Tagliamento Alpini* troops. During this action *Sergente* Ugo Giavitto, born on 13 August 1920 in Tarcento (Udine), was killed at the head of the 278th Company of the *Val Tagliamento* on the

Mali Topojanit Massif, after having been the highest ranking officer left and having taken command of his unit. He was decorated with the *Medaglia d'Oro al Valor Militare alla Memoria*, with the citation:

> Commanded to a rearward base, he insistently asked and obtained permission to join his unit on the line, where he voluntarily carried out daring scouting tasks several times. When he realised that a house used as a shelter for wounded members of his company had been hit by enemy mortar fire, he rushed to the scene and managed to rescue the soldiers. Then, at the head of a platoon, he launched himself against a fortified position and, after a bloody fight with hand grenades, made a valuable contribution to the recapture of the position. In the violent fighting of the following day, when the only surviving officer of the company was wounded, he took command and, animating his men, tenaciously resisted the onrush of overwhelming forces. Seriously wounded in his thigh, he refused all help so as not to leave the hard-pressed unit, and after superficial medical treatment, he resumed the fight, which was made more bloody by repeated enemy attacks. After the crew of a machine gun fell, he reached the weapon that had been left idle, and alone ensured the continuity of fire, mowing down the advancing enemy units with precise shots. Hit again in the arm, he still remained at his post, firing until a machine gun burst brought him down on the weapon he had so valiantly employed. [Mali Topojanit (Greek front), 2 January 1941].

Between 3 and 6 January, a supplementary battalion of the 139th Infantry arrived to reinforce the *Julia*. The units continued to reinforce their positions, despite continuous Greek artillery and mortar fire. At 7.30 a.m. on 8 January 1941, after a massive artillery barrage and aerial bombardment, the forces of the Greek II Corps attacked, concentrating particularly in the Mali Qarishta sector, defended by the remnants of the *Julia* and *Bari* Divisions. During the furious hand-to-hand fighting on the summit of Topojanit, *Tenente Colonnello* Umberto Tinivella, born in Lucca on 7 October 1891, commander of the *Val Tagliamento* Battalion, was mortally wounded, while *Colonnello* Gaetano Tavoni, commander of the 9th *Alpini* troops, born in Vignola on 6 February 1889, was seriously wounded in the legs and head.[1]

Tenente Colonnello Umberto Tinivella was decorated with the *Medaglia d'Oro al Valor Militare alla Memoria*, with the citation:

> Intrepid battalion commander, arousing a great enthusiasm, sent to operate in the sector of another regiment that was strongly committed, he learned, while on a transfer march, that a section of the front had given way and that the defenders, pressed by the dominant enemy, were retreating. He then promptly gathered his units and counterattacked the enemy, immobilising

---

1   Brought to safety in the immediate rear, along almost impassable paths, where he sank in knee-deep mud, with a makeshift stretcher made of tent cloths and ornello poles, he was then taken, almost dying, to the hospital in Berat. Later transferred to the Celio military hospital in Rome, *Colonnello* Gaetano Tavoni died on 16 March 1941.

him. Having secured his position, he held it with indomitable valour for eight days, under heavy bombardment and against repeated, stubborn attacks. In the end, overwhelmed by the impetuosity of the attacking forces, he threw himself with the survivors into the counterattack to re-establish the situation. Severely wounded, while being transported to the dressing station, he encouraged those present to carry on the fight. Surrounded by the enemy, he continued to incite his Alpine troops, until a machine gun volley, fired at point-blank range, mortally wounded him. [Mali Topojanit (Greek front), 30 December 1940 – 8 January 1941].

Colonnello Gaetano Tavoni, was also decorated with the *Medaglia d'Oro al Valor Militare*, with the citation:

> Commander of an Alpine regiment that had already been severely tried in a long and arduous period of glorious battles in harsh terrain and against a fierce enemy, he guided his regiment to brilliant successes, also so that other units that were surrounded by overwhelming enemy forces, could thus disengage. Fearless, indefatigable, constantly serene in the face of major enemy offensives during uninterrupted hard fighting, he instilled in his units, through his personal example, his ardent faith and his outstanding commanding virtues, an ever-increasing spirit of struggle and resistance. He was severely wounded and, regardless of the wounds he sustained, which later led to his death, he continued, with his heroic behaviour and personal ascendancy under violent enemy fire, to strengthen the action of his units aimed at breaking the stubborn attacks of the enemy who was forced to retreat in disorder. Heroic leader figure, superb example of faith and sacrifice. [Pindus (Greece), Mount Chiarista, 28 October–31 December 1940 – Mali Topojanit, 8 January 1941].

The Alpini divisions were then forced to retreat to Mali Hiroche about a kilometre north-west of Mali Topajanit, where they resisted new enemy attacks, protecting the retreating artillery. The advance of the Greek divisions was fiercely resisted, but the fall of Mali Topajanit had allowed the enemy to threaten, from behind, the *Val Fella*, *Cividale* and *Tolmezzo* battalions, deployed towards Ambum and already engaged in repelling attacks to the front of their positions. These three battalions were therefore ordered to fall back to Mali Taronine to establish an initial defence, while the *Gemona* Battalion was ordered to maintain links with *Trento*, which was stationed on the extreme right of the IV Army Corps. At around 11:00, the attacks extended into the area south-west of Mali Topajanit, opening a dangerous breach in the Italian line. *Generale* Cavallero arrived at the VIII Corps headquarters, while the *Bari* reinforcements were busy making defences on the valley floor. He immediately reported to *Generale* Bancale that the *Siena* was busy reorganising and that the *Lupi di Toscana* had been transferred to his charge to re-establish the situation in the *Julia* sector. Over the course of the night, the remnants of the *Julia* had regrouped on Mali Taronine: 1,000 men, with 12 machine guns, 25 submachine guns and 5 mortars. According to *Generale* Bancale's orders, the *Lupi di Toscana* units were to pass through those of the *Julia* and move on Mali Topajanit, then on Qarishta and Fratarit. Only later would the *Julia* move forward to reoccupy the positions of Mali Topajanit. For its part, the *Bari* was to move its left wing to link up with the southern slopes of Qarishta and Fratarit. While the units of the *Lupi di Toscana* moved to reach Kajca and Çuka Fecit, a new enemy attack repulsed the *Julia* on Mali Tabajan and at the same time Greek patrols arrived on the Suka – Klisura road.

Aldo Spagnolo, of the CLV *Battaglione CC.NN. d'Assalto Matera*, born on 15 May 1920 in Brindisi, was killed in combat in the Klisura area on 9 January 1941. He was awarded the *Medaglia d'Oro al Valor Militare alla Memoria*, with the citation:

> University student, exempt from military obligations, a volunteer in a CC.NN. battalion, in every contingency he showed great ardour as a fighter, unwavering faith and indomitable courage in Albanian territory. When the enemy, with an overwhelming force, was pressing on one side of the battalion and the intense fire was claiming numerous victims among our ranks, he jumped out of the trench, alone and with his haversack full of bombs. Having exhausted them and returned unharmed to the lines, resupplying himself with bombs under deadly fire, he returned again to face the oncoming enemy. Disregarding all warnings, he stood on the trench and, with supreme disregard for the impending danger, he wreaked havoc with his bombs until, hit by a volley of fire, he was mortally wounded. Aware of the imminent end, he refused all help so as not to take men away from the fight. In his last moments, he encouraged his comrades to resist in order to hold their position, turning his thoughts to the Homeland and *Il Duce*. A glittering expression of Italian youth and superb example of legendary bravery. [Klisura zone – Caposaldo 25 (Greek front), 9 January 1941].

At dawn on the 10th, the counterattack was launched by the *Lupi di Toscana*, with the 77th infantry (without an accompanying battery), the 78th infantry (without a mortar company or accompanying battery) and the 3rd *Alpini* Artillery of the *Julia*.[2] According to the plan, the attack was to be conducted in successive waves, each made up of two battalions. However, the Italian units had to face an attack by the Greek 15th Infantry Division, launched at the same time. After managing to stop the enemy attack, the two battalions of the first wave came under enemy fire and then suffered attacks from Greek infantry. One of the battalions was surrounded and almost annihilated, while the other found itself under enemy attack, waiting for the battalions of the second wave to arrive.

Among the many who distinguished themselves in battle was *Tenente* Igino Urli, of the 78th Infantry, born in 1913 in Tarcento (Udine), who was decorated with the *Medaglia d'Oro al Valor Militare alla Memoria*, with the citation:

> Having taken command of a rifle company, replacing the *capitano* who had fallen in the fight, and remaining the only officer in the unit, at the head of a

---

2   The 3rd Alpine Artillery comprised the *Udine*, *Lanzo* and *Val Tanaro* groups and the III/47th, with a total of 28 pieces.

handful of infantry, personally operating a machine gun, he successively took two fiercely held enemy positions. Wounded a first time in the knee, after quick, cursory medication, he immediately resumed command of the company. Wounded a second time in the shoulder, he refused all help and, brandishing the machine gun by the handle, persisted in the hand-to-hand fight. Wounded for the third time and mortally, he expired in the arms of his infantrymen to the cry of: 'Long live my wolves'. A shining example of high military virtues, he crowned with the supreme sacrifice the life of a heroic fighter that he had begun as a volunteer in Spain. [Mali Tabaian (Greek front), 10 January 1941].

Also during 10 January, *Generale* Cavallero went to Fieri to discuss the possibility of withdrawing VIII Corps command in order to transfer control of the left wing of 11th Army to IV Corps. *Generale* Geloso agreed and immediately ordered *Generale* Mercalli to move with his staff to Rehova, taking over the VIII Corps command, which was to move to Berat, as a reserve.

The situation on the front line continued to remain critical, especially after the collapse of the *Lupi di Toscana* units. By the morning of 11 January, the Division's fighting capacity had been greatly reduced and towards evening, the units returned to their home bases without having achieved anything.[3]

The Fall of Klisura

On the evening of 10 January, *Colonnello* Vincenzo Carlà, commander of the 140th Infantry, despite having received peremptory orders to hold on to his positions at all costs, retreated with his 1,000 men for six kilometres from Klisura towards the valley floor, to escape the encirclement.[4] On 11 January 1941, Galeazzo Ciano noted in his diary:

> From Cavallero we have not good news about the progress of things in Albania. Klisura is lost. In itself it is nothing: a pile of more or less ruined hovels, but it is a name and the Anglo-Greek propaganda is already blowing all the trumpets of the press and radio. Then it proves that the wall, the famous wall that we have been waiting for in vain for seventy days, is not yet built.

With the fall of Klisura, the Greeks had inserted a dangerous salient in the Italian lines, forcing the Italian commands to run for cover. The units of the *Julia* had been assigned the defence of the positions of Çuka Fecit and height 817, between the *Bari*

---

3   The division had been hastily transferred to Albania, incomplete and arrived in the area of operations practically exhausted after a gruelling march in the rain and snow. Furthermore, *Lupi*'s units had arrived on the line with no mortars, no artillery, and no engineers.

4   Carlà was placed under disciplinary investigation but was acquitted. Instead, *Generale* d'Havet, commander of *Bari* paid for the loss of Klisura and was dismissed a few weeks later by *Generale* Matteo Negro (officially from 16 February 1941).

Division on the right and the *Lupi di Toscana* on the left. Between 11 and 13 January, strong enemy attacks occurred in this sector, all of which were repulsed thanks to some counterattacks launched by the 31st Infantry Regiment.

On 14 January, fresh Greek attacks managed to penetrate the Desnizza Valley, at the juncture between the *Julia* Division and the *Bari* Division, forcing the Italian units to retreat to the ridge east of Hani Bubesit. On 15 January, *Maggiore* Giuseppe Perrot, received the order to regroup all the survivors of the *Julia* still capable of fighting and to descend into the Desnizza Valley to make themselves available to *Colonnello* Achille Billia, who was engaged in reconstituting a new temporary defensive line to allow the divisions of the *Cacciatori delle Alpi* Division (under the orders of *Generale* Giovanni Pivano), which was arriving in the sector, to establish a solid defensive position at the head of the valley. The remnants of the *Julia*, a few hundred men, were divided into three groups:

8th *Alpini* Group, under the orders of *Maggiore* Lorenzo Savoré
9th *Alpini* Group, under the orders of *Maggiore* Giuseppe Perrot
Val Fella Group, under the orders of *Maggiore* Angelo Zancanaro

While the 8th *Alpini* Group and *Val Fella* Group were sent to Spi Bechiarem to establish the defensive position, the 9th *Alpini* Group was ordered to recapture the ridge southwest of Ciaf and Sofiut: the Group consisted of 8 officers and 200 *Alpini* soldiers, ragged, hungry and exhausted. Raking the terrain, they managed to recover two machine guns, a submachine gun, an 81mm mortar and a large quantity of ammunition and hand grenades, material that would prove extremely useful in repelling the subsequent Greek attacks.

In the meantime, the artillerymen of the 3rd *Alpini* artillery, with their few remaining pieces, supported the defensive fighting of the *Lupi di Toscana* Division, during which *Maggiore* Mario Ceccaroni, born in Recanati (Macerata) in 1897, of the 3rd artillery, distinguished himself. He was awarded the *Medaglia d'Oro al Valor Militare alla Memoria*, with the citation:

Attached to a command of an Alpine artillery regiment, during two days of fierce and bloody fighting, he remained in an improvised observatory in the most advanced and exposed area, to better observe and direct the firing. Returning to his command, exhausted by fatigue, he still found the strength to offer to return immediately to the line and deliver and illustrate to an infantry regiment commander an order of great importance and urgency. Having completed his mission, seeing the outline of a violent enemy attack, and realising the need for the prompt intervention of our artillery, instead of going back, he had a radio set delivered to him and with this he left our lines to reach an advanced and intensely beaten position from which he could better observe and direct the shots. While, after taking cover to operate the radio, he carried out the task he had spontaneously imposed on himself, with no regard for the grave danger, he was shot dead. A shining and living example of sacrifice and complete dedication to duty. [Mali Tabajani – Dras and Cais (Greek front) 14–16 January 1941].

New Directives

On 19 January, the Higher Command of the Armed Forces Albania issued new directives, assigning the 11th Army, the *Pinerolo* Division, the reconstituted *Siena* Division, the *Cacciatori delle Alpi* Division and the *Monte Cervino* Battalion[5] Thanks to these reinforcements, the 11th Army was to not only secure the existing defensive line but also to advance it forward as quickly as possible. The first step was to withdraw the remnants of the *Julia*, *Bari* and *Lupi di Toscana* Divisions and other minor units from the front line, in order to give greater compactness to the deployment and begin the reorganisation of the large units that had become exhausted.

By 21 January 1941, the defensive front had the units of Mercalli's IV Corps and those of Bancale's VIII Corps intermingled. The IV Corps, comprising the *Pusteria*, *Cacciatori delle Alpi*, *Julia* and *Lupi di Toscana* Divisions, effectively had only the *Pusteria* in the front line to hold the entire front, with the 7th Alpini attached from Tomori to Osum and with the 11th Alpini (battalions *Bassano*, *Trento* and *Val Chiese*, one of the complements of the 139th infantry and one of the formations of the 78th infantry) from Osum to Chiaf and Sofiut. The *Alpini Cacciatori* Division had the 52nd infantry on Mali Trepelit and the 51st infantry still in the Paraboar area. The *Julia* Division, now reduced to the numbers of one regiment of three small battalions, was regrouping at Hani Bubesit. The *Lupi di Toscana* Division, in addition to the 78th Infantry's formation battalion on the line, had also regrouped its remnants, some 800 men, at Hani Bubesit.

The VIII Corps comprised the *Bari*, the *Siena* and the *Pinerolo* Divisions but the defensive front was effectively manned by a mixture of units of various origins under the orders of the *Bari* Command. Starting from the extreme left, there was a formation battalion of the 8th *Cuneo* Infantry, the *De Renzi* Group (under the orders of *Colonnello* Edmondo De Renzi, based on the 41st *Modena* Infantry), the *Carloni* Group (based on the 31st *Siena* Infantry) and the 32nd *Siena* Infantry (except for one battalion). In reserve were the 140th infantry *Bari*, a battalion of the 139th infantry *Bari*, a battalion of the 32nd infantry and a light tank battalion. The *Pinerolo* Division was stationed in a defensive position behind, with the 13th Infantry in the IV Corps sector from Bregu Gliulei to Chiaf and Bubesit, and the 14th Infantry further south in the Chiaf Chiciocut sector.

The Use of the Matterhorn

Having disembarked in Durrës on 18 January 1941, the *Mount Cervino's Alpini* troops went directly from the ship to the trucks that took them to Tepeleni, from where they immediately reached their assigned position on Mali Trebescines, in

---

5   This elite unit was formed with personnel from the Alpine Military School in Aosta and members of the 4th *Alpini* Regiment recruited in the Piemonte Mountains, and was named after a glorious battalion of the Great War, the *Monte Cervino*, formed in 1915 as part of the 4th Regiment and disbanded in 1919. All the members of the newly formed battalion were ski instructors and/or mountain guides.

Dragoti, on foot. On 21 January 1941, the *Matterhorn* had its first casualties on the Greek front caused by mortar fire from the Greek lines. The battalion at that time had 340 men in two companies, plus a command platoon. The position assigned to *Matterhorn* was a then undefended point, in the junction of two large units. Against this weak point, the enemy's effort was exhaustive and for three days the *Matterhorn* fought without supplies. In the account of a surviving officer, *Tenente* Cossard: 'We did not have time to get to know our men: when an attempt was made to summarise events in writing, only exceptionally was it possible to give a name to the alpine soldier we had seen fall beside us.'

Between 23 and 24 January, the two companies of the battalion, fighting separately, had 14 dead, 37 wounded and 21 missing. In the first days, the companies almost immediately lost their commanders: the two commanders, *Capitano* Brillarelli and *Capitano* Mautino, were killed in combat. *Aiutante* Astorri, who had wanted to go out with a patrol, was also killed. The battalion had no changes, no rest shifts, rarely did the rations arrive hot in the front line, when they arrived at all. The losses among the officers were such that for a few days the command of the battalion was held by two *sottotenenti*. A month after its arrival in Albania, the *Matterhorn* had practically ceased to exist as an organic unit; it had fought a single, continuous battle, but was unable to be used for the purposes for which it had been created: infiltration, hand-to-hand combat, nor could it use skis due to the particular climatic conditions that alternated between snow and mud without interruption.[6]

The Greeks Return to Attack

On the evening of 22 January, the Greek troops, after pushing back the *Bari* forces, arrived near the three strongholds that barred Chiaf and Chiciocut. In short, from Mount Groppa (south-eastern slopes of the Trebeshines) to Osum, fighting raged. This was not a general offensive, but a series of attacks against some key positions – the Chiaf Sofiut position and the Calà ridge, in the IV Corps sector, were particularly fiercely contested, but the Italian defences held. On the Trebeshines, however, the Greek 1st Infantry Division succeeded in taking Chaif Lusit and height 1308 after many attacks, breaking the connection between VIII Corps and IV Corps.

---

6   On 5 March 1941, what remained of the battalion, reduced to the strength of one platoon, was sent to Mali Scindeli, where it remained until 10 April. The losses on the Greek front were 14 officers killed or wounded out of 19 (including eight replacements), 8 non-commissioned officers killed or wounded out of 13, and 153 Alpine men killed or wounded out of 208. The *Monte Cervino* battalion was awarded the *Medaglia d'Argento al Valor Militare* with the citation:

> During three months and in a particularly delicate situation, with admirable spirit of sacrifice and unwavering faith, overcoming the rigours of a harsh winter, it maintained possession of a wide high mountain front, bitterly contested by overwhelming forces. Present everywhere, daring in mountain blizzards and storms of fire, with indomitable valour he put up a tenacious resistance, crushing the enemy's impetus in bloody attacks and swooping down on the flanks and rear of the adversary, breaking up formations. It thus proved that more than number and weapon, courage counts. [Greek front, 10 January 1941 – 23 April 1941].

A counterattack was then immediately launched to retake the summit of the Trebeshines, height 1308, committing the I/14th with two companies. The action was successful, but the Greeks counterattacked soon afterwards and, in turn, forced the Italians to fall back.

In the course of the fighting, the commander of the I/14th, *Maggiore* Umberto Saracini, born in Ancona in 1900, was killed. He was awarded the *Medaglia d'Oro al Valor Militare alla Memoria*, with the citation:

> Battalion commander, launched towards the retaking of a difficult position in near impenetrable terrain and heavily beaten by the enemy, he was the first to assault the position, leading his men under intense machine gun fire and violent mortar fire. Wounded for the first time in the arm, he refused all treatment and, without allowing himself to rest, advanced towards the enemy, locking him and his units in an ever tighter grip. Wounded a second time, he still found the strength to leap forward, until, mortally wounded, he fell to the ground, gathering his last energies in a final cry to his soldiers: 'Forward! Forward!' An example of fighting virtues carried to the sublime momentum of self-denial and of supreme devotion to duty. [Height 1308 Mali Trebescines (Greek front), 23 January 1941].

To re-establish the situation, everything was postponed to the counter-manoeuvre of Klisura by the XXV Corps, which was set to begin at dawn on 25 January. At the same time, *Generale* Geloso had ordered his left wing to conduct offensive actions and carry out intensive artillery activity. But once again, it was the Greeks who attacked first, destroying the Italian plans. The Greek 15th Infantry Division attacked on Bregu Gliulei-Mali Spadarit, forcing the 52nd Infantry to abandon Bregu Gliulei, but retaining Chiaf Bubesit. At the same time, the 11th *Alpini* held out tenaciously at Mali Spadarit. The planned counterattack by the 51st Infantry also failed to materialise because of the continuous Greek attacks.

The Pinerolo Attack

In the VIII Corps sector, the *Pinerolo* Division's attack was to be carried out in two columns: on the left, under the orders of *Colonnello* De Renzi, were the remains of the De Renzi tactical group, the II/14th and the III/13th. On the right, under the orders of Colonnello Barone, were the 141st, the 136th Blackshirts Battalion and other accompanying units. In addition, a tactical group comprising two companies, with the support of an *Alpini* company from another direction, was to recapture height 1308 Mali Trebeshines. The *Siena* Division was to remain in the rear. The start of the attack was set for 7 a.m. on 25 January. However, nothing went according to plan: the right column did not move because the 136th Blackshirts Battalion did not reach the starting positions until the afternoon of the 25th. The left column managed to make little headway because of radio connection problems and enemy fire. The action against height 1308 also met with a new Greek attack, which was repulsed but did not allow the position to be wrested from the enemy. The Greek

Capitano, Firenze Infantry Division, Albania 1941.
(Artwork by Renato Dalmaso © Helion & Company)

Motorcyclist, 5th Bersaglieri Regiment, *Centauro* Armoured Division, Yugoslavia, 1941.
(Artwork by Renato Dalmaso © Helion & Company)

Soldato, 77th Infantry Regiment, *Lupi di Toscana* Infantry Division.
(Artwork by Renato Dalmaso © Helion & Company)

Capitano 'Edolo' Alpine Battalion, 5th Alpine Regiment, *Tridentina* Alpine Division.
(Artwork by Renato Dalmaso © Helion & Company)

Maggiore, 54th Infantry Regiment, *Sforzesca* Infantry Division.
(Artwork by Renato Dalmaso © Helion & Company)

Tenente, Centauro Armoured Division.
(Artwork by Renato Dalmaso © Helion & Company)

Carro veloce CV35, armed with 20mm Solothurn antitank rifle. (Artwork by and © David Bocquelet)

Carro Armato M13/40 of the IV Battaglione carri in the Balkans, 1941. (Artwork by and © David Bocquelet)

breakthrough at Bregu Gliulei aggravated the situation allowing the enemy to attack the Bubesi stronghold from the east and north-east. The Italian defenders held the position firmly.

At the end of January, while on the Trebeshines the XXV Corps reinforced its defensive flank by establishing the connection with the VIII Corps at Arza, *Generale* Bancale reorganised his forces by dividing them into two sectors: to the north, the *Pinerolo* on the line of strongholds and to the south, the *Siena*.

Klisura's Counter-Manoeuvre

For the action against Klisura, set for 26 January, the divisions of the *Legnano* Division (*Generale* Vittorio Ruggero) were engaged, organised in three columns: on the left, the 68th infantry with the support of elements from the *Val Cismon*, on the right, the 67th infantry, and in the centre, the XXVI Blackshirts Legion was to aim directly at Klisura, overrun it and establish a bridgehead facing east. Right from the start, things went badly: the *Legnano* units reached their starting positions for the attack on the night of 26 January in freezing weather, which slowed down the movements considerably. In particular, it took the left column 12 hours to cross the Mezgorani mule track leading to the Trebeshines Ridge in the pouring rain. *Generale* Ruggero suffered a fractured leg and was replaced in command of the division by *Generale* De Cia. In the meantime, the *Val Cismon*, after a short but intense fight, managed to take Mount Groppa. The units of the *Pizzi* group, on the other hand, encountered strong resistance on the summit of Brezhanit, engaging in fierce fighting that lasted for the entire day, but it did not manage to overcome the pass. The left column managed to advance as far as Frashtani, while the right column did not make much headway. On 27 January, at 4.30 a.m., a new attack was launched against the summit of Brezhanit, which was taken and lost several times during the course of the day, only to remain in the hands of the Greeks at the end of the day. In the meantime, the central column with tanks in the lead had reached the first houses of Klisura, having to stop in front of an anti-tank defence built with walls and iron girders: some medium tanks initially managed to get through, only to fall back, while the light tanks did not manage to overcome the obstacle. Further north, the 68th Infantry managed to reach its objective, but due to a strong enemy counterattack, it was forced to fall back.

From the Albanian High Command came new directives, mainly addressed to the 11th Army: continue the attacks in the Klisura sector and continue to defend the Berat and Tepeleni sectors at all costs. Therefore, the *Sforzesca* Division (*Generale* Ollearo) was assigned to the army, while the *Cagliari* Division (*Generale* Gianni) was kept in reserve. The *Legnano* units, after reorganising and being resupplied, returned to attack: the Greeks attacked in turn, triggering furious clashes throughout the sector from the Trebeshines to the Brezhanit, on both sides of the Vojussa. The Italian units firmly held the positions they had taken. In the end, after five days of furious fighting, the army command ordered the VIII Corps to bring its defensive front back to the positions of Mali Trebeshines-Chiaf Lusit-Spi and establish a strong connection to the XXV Corps near Arza di Mezzo and Muriçaj, and it was necessary to suspend the offensive and take a defensive stance. Despite the failure, the Italian action against Klisura mainly served to ease the Greek pressure on Berat and from the end of January, the Greek Command turned its efforts to the conquest of Tepeleni, a threatening salient that barred the Vojussa, Zagorias and Dhrinos valleys and that could be used by the Italian forces as a base for a massive counter-offensive.

Italian motorised column crosses a bridge in Berat, December 1940. (USSME)

Sergente Ugo Giavitto. (www.movm.it)

Tenente Colonnello Umberto Tinivella,
commander of the *Val Tagliamento* Battalion.
(www.movm.it)

Colonnello Gaetano Tavoni, commander of the
9th *Alpini*. (www.movm.it)

Blackshirt Aldo Spagnolo of the CLV Battaglione
CC.NN. *d'Assalto Matera*. (www.movm.it)

Alpine units marching in the high mountains, winter 1940–1941. (USSME)

Tenente Igino Urli of the 78th Infantry.
(www.movm.it)

Maggiore Lorenzo Savoré.

Maggiore Mario Ceccaroni (www.movm.it)

Maggiore Umberto Saracini (www.movm.it).

A defensive position of the Alpine troops with a heavy machine gun, in the high mountains, January 1941. (USSME)

Greek soldiers in the Klisura area near an M13/40 tank damaged in combat and abandoned by the Italians, January 1941.

Italian defensive position with a *Breda* machine gun, gug into the snow January 1941. (USSME)

Alpine ski patrol on Mount Cervino, on the Albanian front, January 1941. (USSME)

Alpini skiers engaged in combat on Mount Cervino, January 1941. (USSME)

A patrol of *Alpini* skiers during a transfer march, January 1941. (USSME)

7

The Battle of Tepeleni

On February 1, 1941, *Generale* Cavallero had a meeting with Mussolini in Bisceglie, Apulia, to take stock of the situation on the Albanian front: Cavallero complained, above all, about sending untrained units to the front line: '[This] is the cause of the low morale and, therefore, low performance of the units, of serious losses in troop numbers far greater than those that would be had with even medium-trained units…'[1] Cavallero was undoubtedly referring to the fact that on the front of the XXV Army Corps, the most active during the Battle of Klisura, the average weekly losses had risen from 800 to 1,200 men. Of course, the difficult conditions in which the Italians had to fight had to be taken into consideration, with temperatures around 15 degrees below zero, in the rain and snow, equipped with unsuitable clothing, which increased the cases of frostbite. The front had held, despite a myriad difficulties.

While waiting to prepare a new massive counter-offensive, the Italian Supreme Command began a reorganisation of the divisions: on 5 February, *Generale* Gastone Gambara replaced *Generale* Bancale in command of the VIII Army Corps. In the rear, along the coast, work was begun to increase the efficiency of the ports, while the reorganisation of the most tried divisions, such as the *Julia*, the *Lupi di Toscana*, the *Bari*, the *Siena*, the *Centauro and* part of the *Modena,* was being completed. On the front line, in addition to the reorganisation of the front, the most tried units were being rotated with those remaining in the second line, such as the *Pinerolo*, *Legnano*, *Brennero* and *Sforzesca*, as well as the arrival of new divisions: the *Cagliari* assigned to the VIII Corps and the *Cuneense Alpini* Division assigned instead to the XXVI Army Corps on the Macedonian front.

The Greek Attack

In the meantime, the Greek Command had planned a new offensive to take Tepeleni and this time, considering the failure of the previous offensive, the Greek generals discarded the idea of a frontal attack against the now well-established Italian positions, in favour of a pincer action, aimed at striking the flanks of the XXV Army Corps, led north along the Mali Trebeshines by the 5th Infantry Division and south by the 2nd Division. Once Tepeleni was reached, the road to Vlora would be open.

---

1   Mario Montanari, *L'Esercito Italiano Nella Campagna di Grecia*, Ufficio Storico Stato Maggiore dell'Esercito, page 521.

At 7.45 a.m. on 13 February, the *Ellinikí Vasilikí Aeroporía* (the Royal Hellenic Air Force) began to bombard the Mezgoranit Valley, Mali Shëndeli, Tepeleni and the Luzati Plain in successive waves, followed by artillery fire that began to hit the positions of the VIII and XXV Corps. The units of the Greek 5th Infantry Division moved from the northern section of the Trebeshines, from a height of 1308 to a height of 1925, overwhelming the few remaining Alpine elements defending the ridge. The garrison of Arza di Sopra, comprising two platoons, was also overwhelmed after furious hand-to-hand combat. After the fall of the garrison of Arza di Mezzo as well, the Greek units headed towards 1178 Shëndeli, which was occupied in the late afternoon. Towards evening, the Greek forces came within a few hundred metres of the right end of the Italian artillery groups' deployment: some pieces were moved from their positions to direct fire at the enemy. The fighting around height 1178 raged throughout the night, but in the end the Italian defences held. By the morning of 14 February, the entire Shëndeli ridge was still in the hands of the Italian troops. However, the losses had been heavy: the III/53rd had lost all company commanders in action and the XXIX Blackshirts Battalion had lost nine officers.

There have been numerous acts of heroism, such as that of *Caporale* Solideo D'Incau, born in Sovramonte, in the province of Belluno, in 1915, in the 7th *Alpini* Regiment. He died heroically on 13 February 1941, during a surprise attack by Greek troops, preceded by intense artillery fire that forced the Italians to take cover. When the Greek troops broke into the trenches manned by the 65th Company, *Caporale* D'Incau, after being isolated, was surrounded and captured by the enemy, but he had time to make his 8mm *Breda 37* machine gun useless. Invited by an enemy sergeant to remount the weapon, he refused several times, angering the Greek soldiers who bayoneted him to death. In the afternoon, an Italian counterattack recaptured the position and his body was found on the ground and underneath it, in the mud, was the *Breda* machine gun extractor that he had tried to hide. He was awarded the *Medaglia d'Oro al Valor Militare alla Memoria*, with the citation:

> Commanding a machine gun squad guarding an advanced position and attacked by overwhelming enemy forces and beaten by violent artillery and mortar fire, seeing his officer fall, he did not desist from mowing down the enemy with his weapon, encouraging his comrades to resist by word and example. After repeated assaults, valiantly thrown back, he was surrounded by the enemy and invited to surrender. Although wounded in the head, he refused to surrender and persisted in the fierce fight. Overcome, before falling into the hands of the enemy, in a supreme act of virile readiness, he dismantled his machine gun and rendered it useless to the enemy. Taken prisoner and the enemy trying to force him to reassemble the weapon, he preferred death to such ignominy, falling pierced by bayonet blows made at him with savage fury by the adversary. A shining example of a high sense of duty, of profound love of country, of sublime sacrifice. [Vendrescia (Greek front), 13 February 1941].

Sottotenente Luigi Rendina, from the *Feltre* Battalion of the 7th *Alpini* Regiment, born in L'Aquila in 1916, also fell in combat on 13 February, after being surrounded by enemy soldiers who ordered him to surrender. After grabbing his pistol, he pointed it at the Greek soldiers in a last attempt to return fire. He was awarded the *Medaglia d'Oro al Valor Militare alla Memoria*, with the citation:

> Commander of an advanced strongpoint, after strenuous resistance against repeated enemy attacks, with a garrison reduced to a handful of men, and with inefficient weapons, he was surrounded by overwhelming forces. Asked to surrender, he replied that 'the Feltre Alpine troops preferred death to surrender'. He then went out into the open and threw his pistol at the enemy, who was astonished by such heroism. Mortally wounded, he refused the help of the few surviving Alpine soldiers and encouraged them to resist. A shining example of patriotism and courage, he joined his father, who had fallen in the 1915–1918 war, in the supreme sacrifice. [Vendrescia (Greek front), 13 February 1941].

Lastly, *Tenente* Giorgio Maggi, of the 49th *Parma* Infantry, born in Alessandria on 12 November 1917: on 13 February 1941, while leading his platoon to take an important position, he was wounded. He refused all treatment and remained at the head of his men until victory was achieved. Late in the evening, when the position was taken, he was hit by an enemy grenade and killed. He was awarded the *Medaglia d'Oro al Valor Militare alla Memoria*, with the citation:

> Platoon commander, leading his men, with audacity and great valour, he rushed to the assault to recover an important position. Wounded, refusing all treatment, he continued his action and, having driven back the enemy, he bravely resisted the renewed attacks of overwhelming enemy forces. Late in the evening, having finally crushed the last and strongest enemy attack, while standing on the trench, praising the victory achieved and within sight of the fleeing enemy, he heartened his men, being hit by a grenade that ripped through his chest and legs, he fell as a hero. Shining example of heroic faith and indomitable courage. [Bregu Saliut (Greek front), 13 February 1941]'.

The Greek forces stood on the eastern slopes of Shëndeli, waiting to return to the attack. *Generale* De Cia decided to pre-empt the enemy, launching a counterattack to eliminate the Greek salient: for the action the I/67th of the *Legnano* and an Alpine company from Chiaf Mezgoranit moved towards Arza di Sopra, with the support of a battalion of the 53rd from Shëndeli, while a unit of Blackshirts of the VIII Corps was to descend beyond Arza di Mezzo. The counterattack was launched after a brief artillery barrage and was initially successful, forcing the Greek units to fall back beyond the Muriçaj stream, suffering heavy losses. Towards evening, the Italian units reached Arza di Sopra.

In an attempt to eliminate all enemy troops who had broken into the Italian positions, a concentric operation was planned to be launched in the early hours of 16 February, from Chiaf Mezgoranit to the north and from Shëndeli to the east by XXV Corps and with a couple of battalions from Arza di Mezzo to the south by VIII Corps. In support would be artillery fire from VIII Corps itself.

On 15 February, units of the 53rd Infantry (*Sforzesca* Division), while attempting to improve their positions, clashed with enemy units, unleashing fierce fighting that quickly extended to the entire attack front. Height 1178 was recaptured, then lost and then recaptured again by the Greeks. At the end of the day, the 53rd Infantry, which lamented the loss of 700 men among the fallen and wounded, found itself clinging to the western positions of Mali Shëndeli, while the part from height 1178 to Punta Nord was in Greek hands. The Greek units launched new attacks on the sides in an attempt to expand their breakthrough: new fighting occurred in the area between Muriçaj and Chiaf Mezgoranit.

On 16 February, the 54th *Sforzesca* Infantry, most of the 67th *Legnano* Infantry, the remnants of the Alpine battalions and the Blackshirts were thrown into combat. The Greek attacks were thus all repulsed and pushed back, from position to position, from height to height. At dawn on 17 February, the enemy attacks were completely exhausted: on the Shëndeli ridge, only height 1178 remained in Greek hands.

While the Greek 5th Division attempted to break through north of Klisura, the 2nd Division was busy launching attacks from 15 February onwards, in the Zagorias Valley and on Mount Golico, in order to undermine the XXV Corps' deployment. In the Zagorias Valley, the positions of the *Pizzi* group were attacked and on Golico those of the 48th *Ferrara* infantry. After three hours of furious fighting, the centre of the II/68th Infantry *Legnano* was overwhelmed and in the early afternoon the *Val Natisone* Battalion was forced to abandon the slopes of Brezhanit. Towards evening, new enemy breakthroughs also forced the *Belluno* and the I/68th to retreat. On the morning of 16 February, despite being subjected to a massive artillery and mortar bombardment, the Italian positions on the north-eastern slopes of the Golico continued to hold. On the right, however, the Italian soldiers had their backs to Vojussa.

On the rest of the front, as far as the sea, the Greek forces of the Army of Epirus continued to attack, particularly in the area of Mount Scutarà, on the Kurvelesh plateau against Lekdushaj, in the Dhrinos Valley and on the Golico chain. In the western sector, the divisions of the *Cuneo* and *Modena* nipped enemy attacks in the bud. On the right of Dhrinos, the Greek attacks were concentrated against the position of Mali Hormova, defended by a platoon of the 48th infantry from *Ferrara*, one from *Bolzano* and one from *Belluno*, in all about eighty men called to face two battalions of Greek infantry. After two hours of hard fighting, the Italian soldiers were forced to retreat towards Golico, where a company of the 48th Infantry arrived to reinforce them.

On 18 February, the Greeks resumed attacking along the entire front, but without achieving any significant results. In particular, they attacked in the direction of Shëndeli, Pesclani and Golico. The attacks against Shëndeli were stopped by counterattacks launched by the II/53rd and *Bolzano*, with considerable losses on both sides. Other attacks by elements of the 5th Greek Division from the Trebeshines were stopped by the defensive positions of the Italian strongholds, as well as breakthrough attempts that triggered furious hand-to-hand combat to no avail. On Golico, *Ferrara*'s counterattack against Mali Hormova met with a new attack from the Greek infantry: the 48th infantry company defending the position found itself surrounded. A desperate bayonet assault was then launched by that handful of brave men, which repulsed the enemy and broke the circle around the position.

In the course of the morning, the XXV Corps Command reported the losses of the last few days to the army: the *Sforzesca* sector had reported 91 officers and 2,074 troops, including fallen, wounded and missing. In particular, the 53rd Infantry had lost all senior officers. The *Legnano* sector had reported 43 officers and 1,696 troops. Among the officers were the commanders of the two infantry regiments.

Among the officers who distinguished themselves in these last battles, was *Maggiore* Cesare Campana, of the 53rd Infantry, born in Mondovì, province of Cuneo, in 1897, who fell on the Mali Scindeli on 17 January 1941 and was awarded the *Medaglia d'Oro al Valor Militare alla Memoria*, with the citation:

> Battalion commander, in four days of extremely hard fighting on wild and blizzard-beaten mountains, he led his battalion to attack against over-whelming enemy forces five times, crushing the offensive impetus of the best enemy assault troops. Exhausted and with the battalion reduced to a handful of men, attacked from the front and from the flank, in order to encourage his men, he placed himself at the head of the unit, and once again attacked with extreme vigour. Seriously wounded, he refused to be transported to the dressing station and continued to encourage his men who, animated by his example, fought with tenacious heroism. Wounded a second time, mortally, he ended his heroic existence at the contested position, while the enemy, admiring such valour, desisted from the enterprise and fell back to their original positions. [Quote 1540 and 1269 Mali Scindeli (Greek front), 14–17 February 1941].

Also among those decorated was Giovanni Lagna, born in Parella (Turin) on 9 May 1902, team leader (*Guida del Gruppo*) of the XII Blackshirts Mountain Battalion, who fell on 16 February 1941 on height 1046, struck full force by a bomb that blew off both of his legs. He was awarded the *Medaglia d'Oro al Valor Militare alla Memoria*, with the citation:

> Always first in every risky undertaking, during an intense bombing raid, struck full force by a bomb that took off both his legs, he refused all treatment so that the doctors would not be diverted from assisting his wounded comrades. Perfectly aware of his imminent end, he invited those present to sing the hymns of Fascist Italy and expired, exclaiming: 'Tell *Il Duce* for me that I have given all I can and I only regret that I cannot give more.' A sublime example of strength of mind and of the noble virtues of a soldier and a citizen. [Height 1046 – Greek front, 16 February 1941].

Reinforcements Arrive

Considering the heavy losses suffered, *Generale* Rossi requested the immediate dispatch of at least two *Alpini* battalions, one to be engaged on Shëndeli and the other on Golico. In the meantime, the II/3rd *Granatieri* were transferred to *Ferrara* to strengthen the defences on Golico and make the connection with the *Legnano* on the ridge at 1192 metres above sea level more stable. For its part, the Albanian High Command was preparing new reinforcements and an entire regiment of the *Puglie* Division was already in the rear of the VIII Corps, while the *Julia* was ready to return to the front line. *Generale* Cavallero placed great trust in the *Julia* and with it intended to eliminate the Greek breakthrough on Shëndeli and then launch a wider offensive. The plan envisaged a main attack in the direction of Arza di Sopra with the *Julia* and a secondary action along the Shëndeli ridge with the units already present in the sector. The entire VIII Corps was to be ready to exploit the success along the Trebeshines Ridge.

In the meantime, the fighting continued on the northern Shëndeli: the entire ridge was littered with dead, testifying to the harshness of the fighting. The attacks and counterattacks continued unabated, but the Italian defenders managed with great sacrifice to firmly hold onto their positions. The fighting also continued in the Zagorias Valley, between height 1192 and Pesclani: in this sector too, all the attacks were repulsed and serious losses were inflicted on the Greek divisions, whose soldiers began to show signs of weakening morale and there were numerous cases of desertion. The captured Greek prisoners revealed that even among their ranks there were numerous terrible cases of frostbite, despite the fact that their equipment was superior to that of the Italians.

The situation seemed to have stabilised: on the Golico was the II/48th of the *Ferrara* and in the second line, the II/3rd *Granatieri*, engaged in successfully repelling all enemy attacks. On Shëndeli, a formation battalion of the 41st Infantry and a Blackshirts battalion of the *Legnano* were engaged. The *Susa* Battalion was sent to Pesclani. Although the weather conditions continued to deteriorate, the fighting continued until 20 February, especially on Golico, at Pesclani and at height 1192. On Golico, the Greeks concentrated their efforts more on trying to take the summit: for three days and nights, the gallant II/48th Infantry, placed in defence of those positions, repelled all enemy attacks. In the end, reduced to only 96 men, it was forced to retreat to the stronghold at height 1615, the last northern elevation of the Golico. On the same day, the Pesclani position was also abandoned. On the rest of the front, the positions held and the enemy attempts to descend into the Vojussa Valley from Mount Groppa were all repulsed, with very heavy losses for the Greeks.

On the afternoon of 20 February, *Generale* Geloso met with Cavallero to discuss the situation in the XXV Corps sector: the critical point remained the Golico and as long as it held, there were no problems. In the meantime, while the *Susa* Battalion crossed the Devoli by cable car, the *Tolmezzo* Battalion of the *Julia* Division began the crossing of the Vojussa by boat. For the planned offensive, Geloso reported that the *Julia* alone would not be sufficient, so it was necessary to seek reinforcements. The *Puglie* Division was not yet available, the *Modena* had serious deficits in armament and the *Bari* was in much the same condition. At that point, it was decided to deploy the *Julia* in front of the Shëndeli in a defensive position, assigning the *Susa* Battalion to it.

The transfer of the units of the *Julia* took a couple of days and only on the 24th, *Generale* Rossi completed the orders for the Division to be in the line: the 8th Alpini on the Vojussa, with the *Tolmezzo* on the height 1615 Golico with the order to organise retaking the peak; the *Susa* and the *Cividale* in the Zagorias Valley; the *Gemona*, in the second line north of Dragoti. The 9th *Alpini* on the Shëndeli, with *L'Aquila* in the Mezgorani Valley with orders to resist to the bitter end and the *Vicenza* on Mount Beshishtit.

The Return of Julia

Between the end of February and the beginning of March, the Greeks returned to attack in the XXV Corps sector, reigniting the Battle for Tepeleni. This time, the Greek forces concentrated on a narrower front line, mainly engaging the units of the *Julia* and *Ferrara*. In particular, the *Julia*, reinforced by the *Pizzi Alpini* group, managed to defend the rear of the Dragoti narrows, but once again suffered heavy losses. The 48th *Ferrara* infantry, reduced to a few hundred men, reinforced by a grenadier battalion and then by two battalions of the 67th *Legnano* infantry, managed to repel enemy attacks in the Dhrinos Valley.

Between 24 and 27 February, the *Julia* began the movement of the front line units, to take over from the *Legnano* and the *Pizzi* group. Initially, the *Tolmezzo* Battalion, under the orders of *Tenente Colonnello* Ezio Leonarduzzi, was detached from the 8th *Alpini* and transferred to the *Ferrara*, to garrison stronghold 27 on height 1615 del Golico. And it was precisely on this height that, on 27 February, the commander of the 72nd company of the *Tolmezzo*, *Capitano* Mario Fregonara, born in Trecate (Novara) on 15 May 1899, was killed, alongside other Alpine soldiers. In the middle of a snowstorm, Fregonara led his men in the taking of an enemy position with hand grenades and daggers, capturing weapons and material. Overwhelmed by superior enemy forces, he counterattacked and regained the position until he was mortally wounded. For the courage he showed in the battle, he was awarded the *Medaglia d'Oro al Valor Militare*, with the citation

> At the head of an Alpine company, which he had forged into a solid instrument of war, he attacked, in near-impassable terrain and in prohibitive atmospheric conditions due to the frost and the raging storm, fortified enemy positions and with hand grenades and knives he succeeded in defeating the enemy who, forced to flee, abandoned weapons and materiel. Counterattacked for the first time and forced to retreat, he reorganised the survivors and, with extreme determination and indomitable courage, attacked again and repulsed the enemy, reoccupying the position. Overwhelmed again by overwhelming forces, he was always the first where the fight raged most, and desperately resisted until he was shot dead. A shining figure of a hero, a noble example of audacity, self-sacrifice and love of his country. [Height 1615 of Monte Golico (Greek front), 27 February 1941].

In the night of 27/28 February, the units of the *Julia*, together with the *Susa* Battalion of the 3rd *Alpini* assigned to the division, took over the positions of the *Legnano*, which was moved to the second line. On 28 February, *Generale* Girotti took control of the sector between Chiaf Mezgoranit and height 1065 del Golico. In the early hours of that same day, the Greeks detected the Italian units on the front line and attacked, planning to take advantage of the situation: the advanced positions on the left bank of the Vojussa, in particular those defended by the *Cividale* and *Suda* Battalions, were attacked. At the same time, the *Ellinikí Vasilikí Aeroporía* bombarded the area around the Dragoti Bridge and the area of the Kodra Monastery. Initially, the Greek infantry gained ground, but was immediately repulsed by a furious counterattack launched by the Italian units.

Giacomo Brunengo, *Sottotenente* of the 8th *Alpini* regiment, born in Pieve di Teco (Imperia) in 1911, died in combat on 28 February 1941 at height 739 del Golico and was awarded the *Medaglia d'Oro al Valor Militare alla Memoria*, with the citation:

> Commander of an Alpine platoon, during a violent attack by the enemy superior in numbers and means, he was struck by mortar shrapnel that broke his left arm, he continued to offer strong resistance to the enemy and forced him to retreat. Then, heedless of the intense fire, smiling and confident of victory, he launched himself at the head of the unit to counterattack with hand grenades. Wounded a second time, he did not give up the fight, but, having replenished himself with bombs, he threw himself back into the fight and with the example of his indomitable courage, made even more evident by his bleeding wounds, he increased the strength and fighting ardour of his Alpine men a hundredfold, forcing the enemy to flee and abandon their weapons. As he pursued the adversary, a machine gun burst hit him in the chest and ended his young, heroic existence. A shining example of military virtue and patriotism. [Zona Peschlani – Q. 739 di M. Golico (Greek front), 28 February 1941].

New Directives

On 1 March, *Generale* Cavallero issued new directives:

> Events are evolving towards a new decisive phase. While it is necessary to tighten the tempo of the offensive action, it is necessary to be ready to crush any adversary convoys especially towards Berat, Tepeleni and Valona.[2]

Due to the ever-looming threat to Vlora, the newly reorganised and trained *Lupi di Toscana* Division was transferred to the 11th Army, destined for the Sushiça Valley. This would allow the entire *Cuneo* Division to regroup on the Littoral, the 9th *Alpini* to regroup in the Smokthina Valley and the *Acqui* to be withdrawn to Mavrova for reorganisation.

At the beginning of March, the XXV Corps found itself deployed from Shëndeli to Kurvelesh:

---

2   DSCSFAA, f. 02749/op. date 1.3.1941.

Sforzesca Division on the Shëndeli with the 53rd and 54th Infantry, 41st *Modena* Infantry (minus one battalion), XXX Blackshirts Legion and *Signorini Alpini* Group (*Bolzano*, *Val Cismon* and *Cervino* Battalions);

Julia Division with 8th and 9th *Alpini*, *Susa* Battalion, *Alpini* Group *Pizzi*'(*Val Natisone*, *Val Fella* and *Val Tagliamento* Battalions), 2nd Bersaglieri and XXVI Blackshirts Legion;

Ferrara Division in the Dhrinos Valley with 47th and 48th infantry, LXXXII Blackshirts Legion and II/3rd *Granatieri*;

Modena Division on the Progonat Plateau with 232nd *Brenner* Infantry, 18th *Acqui* Infantry and XXXVI Blackshirts Legion;

Brenner Division at the head of the Salarije Valley with 231 Infantry and XLV Blackshirts Legion.

In reserve were the *Legnano*, the 5th Bersaglieri, the *Galbiati* Blackshirts Group and the 42nd *Modena* Infantry.[3]

During this period, there were some changes in the leadership of the large units engaged on the Albanian front: *Generale* Pirzio Biroli replaced *Generale* Vercellino in command of the 9th Army.

On the Greek side, after the latest setbacks, there were also some changes: the command of the Western Macedonia Army passed to *Genikós* Tsolakoglou, while *Genikós* Pitskias took over the command of the Epirus Army from *Genikós* Drakos. The Greek High Command was apprehensive, as on 1 March 1941 Bulgaria had joined the Tripartite Pact, with Germany's promise of Thrace giving access to the Aegean Sea. The next day, 2 March, German troops of Marshal von List's 12th Army, destined for the imminent invasion of Greece, began to deploy on Bulgarian territory. In practice, the Greeks expected an imminent attack by German and Bulgarian forces in Thrace, which would result in the necessary transfer of troops from the Albanian front.

Resumption of Greek Attacks

For a few days, the Greek units limited themselves to carrying out local attacks, day and night, while the XXV Corps completed its defensive set-up. Then, at dawn on 7 March, the Greek artillery began to hit height 1615 of Golico, where the *Gemona Alpini* troops were and the right flank of Dhrinos. *Ferrara*'s artillery batteries immediately returned fire, hitting the Golico Ridge while the Greek 11th Infantry Regiment launched themselves against height 1615 and the 34th against the north-eastern ridge of the peak. At the same time, the *Ellinikí Vasilikí Aeroporía* bombarded the

---

3   Mario Montanari, *L'Esercito Italiano Nella Campagna di Grecia*, Ufficio Storico Stato Maggiore dell'Esercito, pp.559–560.

Beshishtit and Dragoti areas. At around 8:00 a.m., connections between the divisions began to break down due to enemy fire. At 9 a.m., there was a new attack by the Greek 17th Infantry Division against the positions in the Mezgorani Valley. Initially, it was a company of *L'Aquila* Battalion that was engaged in combat, then it was the turn of the XXVI Blackshirts Legion that was hit by the Greek units coming down from the Trebeshines: the Blackshirts supported by mortar fire managed to hold for about an hour, then began to fall back, allowing the enemy to outflank the Mezgorani stronghold from below. In the meantime, news arrived that the Greeks had reached height 1615: at 11:15, the 8th *Alpini* reported having received a message from the commander of the *Gemona*, *Maggiore* Giuseppe Perrot:

> 10 o'clock. The troops of the *Gemona* Brigade have been overrun on height 1615. I launched a counterattack with the 70th, but it was broken at height 1500 west of 1615. The 70th resisted there but the commander died and many officers were wounded. The 69th destroyed. The 71st almost entirely destroyed. Urgent provision must be made in the general interest for fresh troops to prevent the Greeks from coming down. The action of our artillery was not very effective. The shells did not explode. I came down last from the height and was slightly wounded. The losses are very heavy. Everyone did their duty, especially the officers…

As reported in the previous message, among the fallen of the *Gemona* was the commander of the 70th Company, *Tenente* Benvenuto Ratto; born in Ceva (Cuneo) in 1915. He was killed on 7 March 1941, on Monte Golico, at height 1615: after the position had been abandoned under pressure from superior enemy forces, he regained it with momentum and although wounded, Ratto, clinging to the rocks with his Alpine troops, resisted the repeated attacks until he was mortally wounded. He reached the valley, carried on the shoulders of his Alpine soldiers. He was awarded the *Medaglia d'Oro al Valor Militare alla Memoria*, with the citation:

> Commander of an Alpine company, of legendary valour, distinguished several times for heroic conduct and decorated several times during the Albanian campaign, during a fierce battle for the possession of a contested position, he rushed with irresistible impetus at the head of his men. Wounded, he continued his action, arriving first at the enemy positions. Clinging to the rocks with his Alpine men, he tenaciously resisted the enemy's repeated attacks, preventing him from advancing even one metre, until he was struck again and found a glorious death. A magnificent figure of an intrepid and reckless young commander, a shining example of courage, abnegation and spirit of sacrifice pushed to the point of holocaust. [Monte Golico – height 1615 (Greek front), 7 March 1941].

On the right bank of the Dhrinos, the Greeks had attacked the positions of the 48th Infantry *Ferrara*, which had in the front line on the western slopes of Golico, the 3rd Battalion, reduced to less than 500 men, and the 1st Battalion, reduced to about 200 men. In reserve was the 2nd battalion, comprising 140 men at Kodra and the II/3rd

Granatieri at height 1615. After holding out against the first attacks, the Italian regiment found itself completely exposed to enemy fire after the heights fell, so it was necessary to move the units. In the course of the night, two battalions of the 67th Infantry and the LXVIII Blackshirts Battalion arrived to reinforce them. In order to face the new enemy attacks, *Generale* Girotti requested the dispatch of the *Val Fella* Battalion, which had already been put on alert in Kodra and was immediately transferred partly to Golico and partly to the rocky spurs south-east of Beshishtit.

In the afternoon, the entire front of the *Julia* was affected by the fighting. To the north, the Greeks had reached the high eastern slopes of the Shëndeli, where one company of the Battalion *L'Aquila*, completely isolated, and the Battalion *Vicenza* continued to tenaciously resist. To the south, the *Cividale* and *Susa* Battalions had managed to repel the attacks of the Greek 34th Regiment. The Val Tagliamento, which moved from Turan, was also ordered to help.

Towards evening, despite the darkness, the Greek units continued to attack and after taking height 1615, below which the remnants of the *Gemona* continued to resist, they were about to take the Beshishtit. At 10 p.m., the Greeks also seized height 1437, the eastern spur of the Shëndeli. In the course of the night, while the Italian units were preparing to launch counterattacks, the Greeks occupied height 739 in the Vojussa Valley. In the early hours of 8 March, the Italian counterattacks began: elements of the *Vicenza* recaptured height 1437 of the Shëndeli. At dawn, *the Cividale* recaptured height 739 and around 6:00 a.m., the *Val Fella* began to advance towards the northern tip of Golico. In the late morning, after a hard fight, height 1615 was also recaptured.

Sottotenente Egidio Aldo Fantina, born in Fietta di Paderno del Grappa, province of Treviso, on 1 January 1915, serving with the *Val Fella* Battalion, died on 8 March 1941 during an attack on Monte Golico. After finding himself alone in an enemy position, he was hit in one arm and one leg by shrapnel; when he was reached by the other Alpine soldiers, he continued to encourage them and went on the attack when a hand grenade hit him in the face. He managed to get up immediately, threw a hand grenade and gave a last cry of encouragement that was immediately cut short by the rifle shot that killed him. For the courage he showed in combat, he was awarded the *Medaglia d'Oro al Valor Militare alla Memoria*, with the citation:

> Worthy son of a line of heroes, he participated enthusiastically in all the actions of his unit and his every act was one of valour. In the retaking of a strongly fortified position, at the head of his daring men, he launched himself against the enemy, jumping first into the enemy trench. Wounded in several places on his body by numerous pieces of shrapnel, he did not bother to seek medical attention, but stood his ground in the position he had taken. Hit a second time and severely in the head and chest, he continued to encourage his Alpine soldiers, until a rifle shot at point-blank range caused him to fall mortally wounded. But the lacerations of the flesh did not weaken his heroic spirit, and to the Alpine soldiers who carried him to the dressing station he kept repeating: 'Don't mind me, go on, go on always for the greatness and glory of Italy.' A shining example of the purest heroism. [Monte Golico, 8 March 1941].

During the fighting on the Shëndeli, *Tenente* Giuseppe De Martini, born in Thiesi, Sassari province, in 1912, commander of the 61st Company of the *Vicenza* Battalion, who fell on 8 March 1941, distinguished himself and was awarded the *Medaglia d'Oro al Valor Militare alla Memoria*, with the following citation:

> Commander of an Alpine company forged by him and tempered to every test; in long months of a hard military campaign he gave an admirable example of conscious daring and uncommon command ability. In an action to recapture an important height, when an infantry unit found it difficult to overcome the enemy's resistance, he attacked with the few survivors of his heroic company and occupied the position, capturing numerous weapons. He then remained undaunted under violent enemy mortar fire, crushing an attempted counterattack. Wounded, after a few days of treatment, he escaped from the hospital to return, still not fully recovered, to the unit. Subsequently, in the most delicate and difficult phase of a tough battle, he once again, on his own initiative, took the lead of the unit, impetuously dragging it into a furious counterattack on a nearly inaccessible enemy position, and during this action he died during a bloody night melee. [Mali Scindeli (Greek front), 28 October 1940 – 8 March 1941]

In the afternoon of 8 March, the Greek attacks resumed south of Vojussa, in the XXV Corps sector. The *Susa* Battalion, reduced to about a hundred men, after suffering heavy losses, was forced to retreat after repelling numerous enemy attacks, leaving the *Cividale*'s flank uncovered, which remained with about 250 men. On 9 March, while the IV and VIII Corps launched their offensive, the defensive fighting continued, becoming more and more bloody for the *Alpini* battalions: most of the company commanders had fallen in combat and the companies were left with only a few dozen men each. The positions were held only by great sacrifices and the only support came from the artillery fire of the *Julia* and *Ferrara*. When night fell, the Greeks had reached the eastern positions of Beshishtit and the north-eastern spur of Golico.

Tenente Antonio Cavarzerani of the 8th *Alpini* Regiment, born in Udine in 1914, distinguished himself in these battles. After being seriously wounded in the abdomen by machine gun fire on 9 March 1941 at height 1143 Monte Golico, he died at Field Hospital 628 six days later. He was awarded the *Medaglia d'Oro al Valor Militare alla Memoria*, with the following citation:

> A war volunteer, always first in every difficult and risky undertaking, already distinguished in bitter battles for bravery and valour, in the course of a very hard action, he voluntarily carried out delicate and dangerous missions, crossing areas intensely beaten by enemy artillery and automatic weapons. During bitter combat, when a dangerous enemy infiltration occurred, he voluntarily took command of a unit and threw himself to face the adversary. Repeatedly attacked by overwhelming forces, he resisted with unwavering tenacity and counterattacked the enemy at the head of his men and was mortally wounded. Aware of his imminent end, with sublime words of

faith and patriotism, he continued to encourage his Alpine soldiers to the fight and said he was happy to have been able to fulfil his duty as a soldier to the ultimate sacrifice. A shining example of a high sense of duty and eloquent military virtues. [Height 1615 – height 1143 of M. Golico (Greek front), 27 February –9 March 1941].

Throughout the next day, 10 March, the Italian troops were engaged in recapturing those heights, while on the Greek side, attacks continued to reach height 1615. But neither effort succeeded, the units on both sides were exhausted. A few hours of relative calm followed, allowing both sides to catch their breath and reorganise their divisions. At 14:00 on 11 March, the Greeks returned to the attack, concentrating their efforts on the two pillars of the Dragoti hold. Attacks against the Beshishtit were still repulsed, as were those against height 1615. More attacks against the two positions followed, but in vain.

After five days of futile efforts, on 12 March the Greeks moved their attacks along the right flank of the Vojussa Valley alone, in an attempt to isolate the defences on the heights and then force the defenders to surrender. In the morning, the units of the Greek 17th Infantry Division attacked the rocky ridge south-east of Beshishtit, defended by the remnants of the XXVI Blackshirts Legion, which failed to hold the position, allowing the enemy to hit the neighbouring units on the flank. In a short time, the entire left wing of the defence position at the bottom of the valley was overwhelmed and only the intervention of all available artillery, the 2nd Bersaglieri and the *Val Tagliamento* Battalion, succeeded in stopping the enemy advance. The Greeks for their part had suffered heavy losses and were unable to continue their offensive thrust. With the arrival of new reinforcements, a supplementary battalion of the 8th *Alpini* and one of the 68th *Legnano* Infantry, the situation was completely restored. The Italian losses between 7 and 12 March were heavy: 446 officers and 8,000 non-commissioned officers and soldiers killed and wounded.

At the close of the Battle of Tepeleni the *Lupi di Toscana* Division entered the Vojussa sector: on the evening of 12 March, *Generale* Geloso had decided to transfer the division to the XXV Corps to defend the barrage at the bottom of the Vojussa Valley and to protect the Dragoti Bridge. The long defensive battle begun in early December to defend the key positions of Vlora, Tepeleni and Berat could be considered won. It was necessary at this point to regain the initiative of the operations with an offensive.

Generale Gastone Gambara.

Caporale Solideo D'Incau, serving with the 7th *Alpini* Regiment. (www.movm.it)

Sottotenente Luigi Rendina, from the Feltre Battalion of the 7th *Alpini* Regiment. (www.movm.it)

Tenente Giorgio Maggi, of the 49th *Parma* Infantry. (www.movm.it)

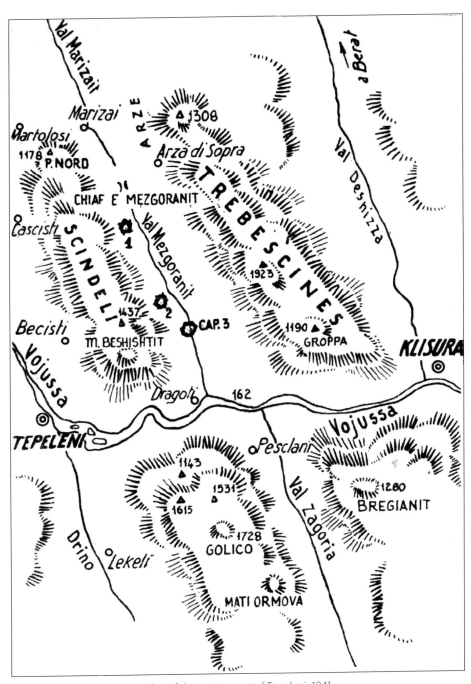

Map of the sector west of Tepeleni, 1941.

Alpini skiers in a defensive position, engaged in high mountain fighting to repel an enemy attack, January 1941. (USSME)

Alpini skiers on a high mountain march, February 1941. (USSME)

Mount Golico seen from the Vojussa Valley. (USSME)

CESARE CAMPANA

Maggiore 53° Reggimento fanteria, da Mondovì (Cuneo), alla memoria.

« Comandante di battaglione, in quattro giorni di durissima lotta su montagne selvagge e battute dalla tormenta, conduceva per ben cinque volte il suo battaglione all'attacco contro forze nemiche sover-chianti, stroncando l'impeto offensivo delle migliori truppe d'assalto nemiche. Stremato di forze e ridotto il battaglione ad un pugno di uomini, assalito di fronte e di fianco, per incuorare i suoi, si poneva alla testa del reparto, e contrassaltava ancora una volta con estremo vigore. Gravemente ferito, rifiutava di essere trasportato al posto di medicazione e continuava ad incitare i suoi uomini che, animati dal suo esempio, si battevano con tenace eroismo. Colpito una seconda volta, mortalmente, chiudeva la sua eroica esistenza sulla posizione contrastata, mentre il nemico, ammirato da tanto valore, desisteva dall'impresa e ripiegava sulle posizioni di partenza. »

(Quote 1540 e 1269 del Mali Scindeli, fronte greco, 14-17 febbraio 1941-XIX)

Contemporary postcard commemorating the award of the *Medaglia d'Oro al Valor Militare* to *Maggiore* Cesare Campana.

Maggiore Cesare Campana of the 53rd Infantry Regiment. (www.movm.it)

Giovanni Lagna, *Guida del Gruppo* of the XII Blackshirts Mountain Battalion. (www.movm.it)

The commander of the 72nd Company of the *Tolmezzo* Alpine Battalion, *Capitano* Mario Fregonara. (www.movm.it)

Sottotenente Giacomo Brunengo, 8th *Alpini* Regiment. (www.movm.it).

GIOVANNI
LAGNA

*Capo squadra XII Battaglione
CC. NN. da montagna,
da Parella (Aosta), alla memoria.*

«Sempre primo in ogni impresa rischiosa, durante un intenso bombardamento, colpito in pieno da una bomba che gli stroncava ambedue le gambe, rifiutava ogni cura, perchè i medici **non** fossero distolti dall'assistenza ai camerati feriti. Perfettamente conscio della imminente fine, invitava i presenti ad intonare gli inni dell'Italia fascista e spirava esclamando : «Direte per me al Duce che ho dato tutto quello che potevo e mi dolgo solo di non poter dare di più». Sublime esempio di forza d'animo e di elette virtù di soldato e di cittadino.»

*(Quota 1046, fronte greco,
16 febbraio 1941-XIX)*

Contemporary postcard commemorating the award of the *Medaglia d'Oro al Valor Militare* to *Guida del Gruppo* Giovanni Lagna.

New troops from Italy just disembarked from planes at the Shkodra airfield in Albania, January 1941. (USSME)

Italian artillerymen engaged in positioning a piece, March 1941. (USSME)

Greek officers, observing their units' attack on Italian positions, March 1941.

Generale Pirzio Biroli, the new commander of the 9th Italian Army.

Tenente Benvenuto Ratto, commander of the 70th Company of the *Gemona* Battalion. (www.movm.it)

Generale Mario Girotti, March 1941. (USSME)

Sottotenente Egidio Aldo Fantina, in the *Val Fella* Battalion. (www.movm.it)

Tenente Giuseppe De Martini, commander of the 61st company of the *Vicenza* Battalion. (www.movm.it)

Sottotenente Antonio Cavarzerani of the 8th *Alpini* Regiment. (www.movm.it)

ANTONIO CAVARZERANI

Sottotenente 8° Reggimento alpini, da Udine, alla memoria.

« Volontario di guerra, sempre primo in ogni impresa difficile e rischiosa, già distintosi in aspri combattimenti per ardimento e valore, nel corso di una durissima azione, assolveva volontariamente delicate e pericolose missioni, attraversando zone intensamente battute dall'artiglieria e dalle armi automatiche nemiche. Durante aspro combattimento, verificatasi una pericolosa infiltrazione nemica, assumeva volontariamente il comando di un reparto di formazione e si lanciava a fronteggiare l'avversario. Ripetutamente attaccato da forze preponderanti, resisteva con incrollabile tenacia e contrassaltava il nemico alla testa dei propri uomini, rimanendo mortalmente ferito. Conscio della prossima fine, con sublimi parole di fede e di amor patrio, continuava ad incitare i suoi alpini alla lotta e si diceva lieto di aver potuto compiere fino all'estremo sacrificio il proprio dovere di soldato. Fulgido esempio di elevato sentimento del dovere e di elette virtù militari. »

(*Quota 1615 - quota 1143 di M. Golico, fronte greco, 27 febbraio - 9 marzo 1941-XIX*)

Contemporary postcard commemorating the award of the *Medaglia d'Oro al Valor Militare* to *Sottotenente* Antonio Cavarzerani.

8

The March Offensive

The entry of German troops into Bulgaria had not only alarmed the Greek Command, but also Mussolini himself, who feared a blitzkrieg action in Macedonia by his allies. Driven by the desire to get ahead of Hitler in the conquest of Greece, he hurriedly ordered a new offensive. And thus, on 2 March 1941, *Il Duce* personally went to Tirana. He visited all the corps commands, and held discussions with all the generals. In Rehova, where the VIII Corps command was located, during his speech to the generals, he also set the date for the new offensive:

> First of all, I thank you for having exposed the situation in an ideal manner, that is, without hiding the difficulties and deficits. These deficits require that the action be delayed. This morning with Cavallero we were already talking about making it to 9 [March]. This action is of great importance. It must not be started unless everything is in place. Men, means and services must be arranged so that the action, once begun, has no uncertainties and proceeds with an energetic and decisive rhythm…

The preparation of the new offensive was entrusted to *Generale* Gastone Gambara, a veteran of the war in Spain, held in high esteem by *Il Duce*, who had been in command of the VIII Army Corps since February 1941. Gambara's plan of attack had convinced Mussolini, despite the doubts expressed by Cavallero, who had recommended an action further north, on the left side of the front, where the Greek forces were weaker. Instead, Gambara decided to attack the strongest core of the Greek Army, the one facing Valona. If successful, the Greek forces would have suffered a heavy defeat and the Italian forces would have permanently averted the risk of being thrown back into the sea. The offensive had as its main objective the reconquest of Klisura and as a direct consequence the easing of Greek pressure on Tepeleni and Vlora. Gambara's plan envisaged the use of *Generale* Carlo Spatocco's IV Army Corps (north-east) and *Generale* Gambara's VIII Army Corps (centre), also with the possibility of later intervention by *Generale* Mario Vercellino's XXV Army Corps (south-west). In all, 6 to 7 divisions were adequately supported by over 300 pieces of artillery and a hundred or so medium-calibre pieces plus the *Regia Aeronautica*, which was to pave the way for the ground units with a massive bombing effort.

At the time, the IV Army Corps included the *Cacciatori delle Alpi* Division. The VIII Army Corps, the *Pinerolo, Cagliari, Puglie, Bari* and *Siena* Divisions. The XXV Army Corps, the *Sforzesca* Division, the *Signorini Alpini* Group and the *Galbiati* Blackshirts Regiment.

The Attack Begins

On 8 March 1941, orders were issued for the attack christened 'The Spring Offensive', although in reality it was still winter. The start time for all units was set at 8.30 a.m. the next day. In the Deshnicës Valley sector, the IV Corps had 11 battalions, while on the other side the Greeks fielded the 11th Infantry Division of 8 battalions. In the central sector, the VIII Corps fielded as many as 38 battalions from the *Pinerolo, Cagliari, Puglie, Bari* and *Siena* Divisions, against the Greek II Corps, which fielded some 19 battalions. In the southern sector, the XXV Corps fielded the *Sforzesca*, the *Signorini Alpini* Group and the CC.NN *Galbiati* Group with a total of 12 battalions against the Greek 5th Infantry Division with 10 battalions.

Between 7 a.m. and 7.30 a.m. on 9 March, artillery preparation fire began on the entire front of the 11th Army along the Deshnicës Valley. This was followed by the intervention of the *Regia Aeronautica*, with massive bombardments from high altitude; this did not, however, inflict many losses on the enemy. In the northern sector, the divisions of the IV Corps initially advanced deep on the left of the Osum. Around noon, *Generale* Mercalli reported that his forces were near the heights of Bregu Gliulei and Spadarit. Towards evening, the *Cacciatori* were blocked by the massive barrage unleashed by the Greeks and some counterattacks. Further north, the *Pusteria* units had halted in the village of Selanij, where the fighting continued. In the meantime, the commander of the IV Corps reported a problem with supplies and asked the Army Command to send trucks to solve it.

Further south, the XXV Corps also encountered considerable difficulties, having to face from Beshishtit to Golico continuous Greek attacks that did not allow the *Sforzesca* to take part in the offensive action. At 9.30 a.m., *Generale* Geloso ordered *Generale* Rossi to continue the attack, particularly with the *Sforzesca*'s left column. At the end of the day, the column led by *Colonnello* De Renzi attacked and captured the position of Arza di Sopra, while the *Signorini* Group advanced slowly to Chiaf Mezgoranit.

In the centre, in the VIII Corps sector, artillery preparation fire began at 7.00 a.m. and also lasted about an hour and a half. Immediately afterwards, the three front line divisions moved from their starting positions: the 63rd Infantry from *Cagliari* was almost immediately stopped without being able to reach Bregu Rapit. After a new artillery intervention of about a quarter of an hour, the attack was renewed, also engaging the 64th Infantry on the right. However, this attack was similarly unsuccessful and towards evening, the division had only advanced a few hundred metres.

In the Monastero area, the units of the *Puglie* Division, after a promising start, were driven back almost to their initial positions by a strong enemy counterattack. Further south, the *Pinerolo* Division was engaged, whose units, after having moved towards Chiaf and Lusit and having overcome the advanced enemy positions, began to encounter strong resistance and above all ended up under massive enemy fire coming from the Trebeshines and in particular from height 1308. The fire of all available artillery was then concentrated on this height, on which repeated aerial bombardments were also carried out. But no results were achieved, both because no heavy artillery was available and because the aerial bombardment from very high altitudes proved to be inaccurate.

The battle had taken on a caustic character, i.e. it was hard on attackers and defenders alike, causing considerable casualties, but only allowing the tangible result of gaining little ground. It must also be said that automatic weapons, quickly emplaced by the defenders, were able to stop any frontal effort: nor was divisional artillery sufficient to silence them, because their detection was very difficult. The only truly appreciable advantage obtained by the Italian side was that of forcing the enemy to desist from fuelling the effort against the Shëndeli.[1]

At 19:00, considering the strong enemy resistance, *Generale* Geloso ordered all divisions to remain in close contact with the enemy by engaging strong patrols and to strongly hold the positions they had reached.

Counter-offensive Resumes

At dawn on 10 March, the Italian counter-offensive resumed. In the IV Corps sector, the *Alpini* troops of the 11th attacked in dense fog and in the rain: the *Feltre* Battalion decisively attacked the Greek positions and around midday managed to reach the summit of Spadarit. However, it had to be supported in its action by the CIV Blackshirts battalion, which was left without officers and was unable to contribute much, giving the Greeks the chance to counterattack. The other two *Alpini* battalions, which were left behind due to fog, also failed to lend their support. At the same time, the *Cacciatori*'s attack also had no effect.

In the VIII Corps sector, the *Puglie* Division, which had initially managed to reach the southern slopes of Bregu Rapit, was repulsed in the afternoon by a strong Greek counterattack and *Generale* Gambara was forced to send the Blackshirts group as reinforcement. The *Pinerolo* Division, on the other hand, was able to continue its offensive towards Chiaf and Lusit, but failed to break through. The *Cagliari* Division for its part made no progress and in the meantime its commander had fallen ill and was temporarily replaced by the commander of the 63rd Infantry.

In the XXV Corps sector, the Italian units were still repelling the Greek attacks, mainly on Golico, without the possibility of providing support to the VIII Corps. The Greeks had concentrated their attacks mainly on the Golico, attempting to bypass it north of the Vojussa. The Italian positions, also reinforced by the arrival of the *Legnano*, held. *Generale* Rossi was mainly focused on the position of Tepeleni, which he knew he had to defend at any cost. The resistance around the Golico attracted the attention of the high commands and Mussolini himself. Artillery fire was also used more in support of the positions on the Golico than in support of the attacks towards Chiaf Mezgoranit and on the Arze.

From the beginning of the counter-offensive, Mussolini had moved to the observatory on Mount Komarit to monitor the operation. He was very confident and had informed Cavallero about Yugoslavia's forthcoming accession to the Tripartite Pact.

1   Mario Montanari, *L'Esercito Italiano Nella Campagna di Grecia*, Ufficio Storico Stato Maggiore dell'Esercito, pp.613–615.

Also considering the Bulgarian and German threat on the Greek borders, he hoped for an imminent retreat of the Greek forces to the Albanian front. However, this did not happen; on the contrary, the Greek units continued to hold their positions firmly and even launched counterattacks. *Generale* Geloso then ordered the *Siena* to move to the Zehanj area, behind the artillery positions of the corps and the *Centauro* to transfer some of its elements to Gllava, two tank battalions and two bersaglieri battalions. Seeing the poor results, Mussolini decided to immediately bring in two divisions from Italy, the *Casale* and the *Firenze*.

On 11 March, the *Puglie* units attacked again, in an attempt to outflank Bregu Rapit. But as early as 10am, they were stopped. At the same time, the *Bari* divisions were ordered to insert themselves between those of the *Puglie* and *Cagliari* divisions, in order to aim towards the Deshnicës Valley. At 18:00, all divisions on the front line moved to attack, but without achieving any significant results. The night attack by the *Bari* battalions along the northern slopes of the ridge leading from Monastero to a height of 731 was also unsuccessful. The Greeks continued to resist tenaciously and the situation appeared without any possible tactical or strategic outlets. In the high commands, some began to think about suspending the offensive, since at least the objective of easing the enemy pressure on Tepeleni had been achieved. However, on the evening of 11 March, *Generale* Geloso communicated to the army corps commanders the directives to resume the offensive. The *Siena* Division was to move to the front line. The VIII Corps was to continue its attacks to open a gap to penetrate the Deshnicës Valley, while the *Siena* was to attack the Trebeshines from the northern slopes aiming at the 1308 height. The XXV Corps, with the *Lupi di Toscana* defending the Vojussa Valley, was to resume the attack with the *Sforzesca* and an Alpine grouping together with the *Siena* on the Arze and at Chiaf Mezgoranit, aiming at the Trebeshines. In the end, nothing happened, as *Generale* Cavallero preferred to suspend all offensive action on the Trebeshines, primarily to avoid further unnecessary losses.

At dawn on 12 March, the *Bari* divisions attacked instead, but were held by the massive barrage of Greek fire. During the previous night, the *Cagliari* had been attacked on the right, but the Greek divisions had been repulsed. In the morning, however, the Division's units were unable to attack. The *Puglie* Division, exhausted from the previous fighting, was withdrawn from the front line.

Towards evening, Mussolini met with *Generale* Geloso to take stock of the situation:

> The infantry of the three attacking divisions made little progress: the *Pinerolo*, the most dynamic, did little; the *Puglie* did even less; the *Cagliari* practically did not move. I almost immediately had the feeling that the action was not proceeding well. Yesterday, *Bari* got on the line, but so far it has done nothing. Conclusion: we have four stationary divisions. We must disengage them, bearing in mind that we have two more divisions available, two must come from Italy and, if necessary, I will bring two more. We must continue this attack…. We cannot think of other operations because we lack time. Germany will attack at the beginning of April and will give us six days' notice. I cannot ask Hitler to delay his action because this could

have fatal consequences; in fact, any delay would allow the British troops in Greece to increase (one division is already landing in Attica). Before Germany intervened, it was essential to achieve military success because otherwise the Germans would have every reason to say that the Greeks had succumbed because of them. So the action must continue: if still possible with the breakthrough, otherwise with wear and tear, which must, however, be swift enough so that decisive results can be achieved by the end of the month: we have 19 days to go.... We must attack tomorrow, for otherwise the troops will begin to take root on the ground and believe that the action is over. The Greeks must be held all day under our fire. The antidote to the mortar is celerity of movement...[2]

Immediately afterwards, Mussolini called *Generale* Pricolo on the telephone and ordered him to make all serviceable aircraft available for the next day: 'The aircraft must drop at least 1,500 bombs on height 1308 and all planes must intervene...' Pricolo ensured the bombing of Chiaf Sofiut and height 1308, from 9 to 11 am and from 2 to 6 pm.

New Offensives

On the afternoon of 13 March, the VIII Corps returned to the attack with the *Cagliari*, *Bari* and *Pinerolo* Divisions in the front line between Bregu Rapit and Proj Math: the *Bari* Divisions were to penetrate as far as Hanj Vinocasit, while the *Cagliari* and *Pinerolo* divisions were to launch diversionary attacks on the flanks to deceive the enemy. The *Siena* Division was to remain in the second line. The new attack was supported by the *Regia Aeronautica*, which from 14:00 to 17:30 heavily bombarded the Trebeshines, and by the entire artillery of the VIII and XXV Corps. In the Mali sector and in the Arze sector, the units of the IV Corps and the *Sforzesca* engaged the enemy to prevent them from transferring forces to the most threatened points. The bloodiest fighting always took place in the Desnizza Valley (Deshnicës) where the Italians were particularly heavily engaged in taking a hill, a Karst peak, a key position for the defence of Berati, around which the Greeks had created a defensive structure on five levels: Height 731 di Monastero. This peak (also known as Height Monastir) was an important strategic site 20km north of Klisura at the foot of Mount Trebeshines, in the heart of the Greek defensive line.

> While the ground was seething with outbreaks, a rough hump in the terrain was also pointed out to Mussolini, a barren hill whose reconquest was considered very important for the protection of Berat. That hill was referred to as the Monastero locality because of the low buildings of a convent, reduced to rubble, that stood there with other hovels.[3]

---

2   Cavallero diary, dated 12.3.1941.
3   Mario Cervi, *Storia Della Guerra di Grecia* (Milan: Gruppo Mondadori, 1965), p.265.

But once again, the VIII Corps' attack was unsuccessful, despite repeated infantry attacks and heavy bombardment, with the Greek defenders managing to hold their positions by cleverly exploiting the geography of the terrain. The *Bari* units repeatedly attacked the Monastero area but were unable to break through the Greek defences: the 140th Infantry left its regimental commander and a battalion commander on the field.

Colonnello Luigi Biasucci, born in Rome on 13 April 1890, had taken command of the 140th Infantry Regiment of the *Bari* in January 1941. He fell in combat at height 731 di Monastero on 14 March 1941 and was awarded the *Medaglia d'Oro al Valor Militare alla Memoria*, with the following citation:

> Commander of a regiment, courageous and shrewd, with passionate and constant action as animator and leader, he made his battalions a superb fighting tool. Having received the order to attack a fortified enemy position, he calmly and skilfully gave the necessary orders to carry out the task entrusted to him. In the course of the action, at the head of his battalions, an infantryman among infantrymen, valiant among the valiant, he rushed the enemy and, mortally wounded, he fell, singing the praises of victory. [Height 731 Monastero area (Greek front), 13–14 March 1941]

Maggiore Gino Valentini, commander of the 3rd battalion of the 140th Infantry Regiment, born in Muggia (Trieste) on 20 June 1909, also fell during the fighting for height 731 and was awarded the *Medaglia d'Oro al Valor Militare alla Memoria*, with the following citation:

> War volunteer. Superbly decorated, animator, organiser, with an exceptional fighting spirit, he launched himself and his battalion into the attack of a heavily fortified position that was a bulwark of enemy resistance and, despite extremely heavy losses, he kept the unit he had forged strong. He also took command of the remains of another unit, which had been left without officers, and at the head of the troops he renewed the attack, heedless of the violent enemy reaction. With reckless disregard for danger and indomitable valour, he conquered the terrain inch by inch and succeeded in bringing his decimated units within assault distance. In the final bayonet attack, to the cry of '*Savoia*', he was the first to reach the contested height, where, mortally wounded, he fell valiantly. [Monastero – Q. 731 (Greek front), 13 – 14 March 1941].

The soldiers of the *Cagliari* Division managed to twice occupy the position of Bregu Rapit and were twice driven back by strong enemy counterattacks.

The *Pinerolo* units, engaged in supporting the *Bari* advance, also suffered heavy losses, including that of the commander of the 13th Infantry, *Colonnello* Francesco Franceschetti.

Generale Cavallero went to the front line to see the situation for himself: the *Cagliari* had lost around 500 men from each regiment and the soldiers were totally disheartened at not being able to approach the Greek positions. The divisional artillery commander also reported that with the calibre at his disposal, he would never be able to open the way for the infantry units.[4]

The losses of the VIII Corps in the last six days of battle were 300 officers and 7,600 non-commissioned officers and soldiers, killed, wounded and missing.

Further north, the divisions of the IV Corps were being reorganised: *Generale* Mercalli had transferred the 11th Alpini and the CV Blackshirts Legion to the *Pusteria*, for the recapture of Spadarit: the position was taken by the Italian divisions but was lost again soon after.

On 15 March, Mussolini, embittered by the failure of the offensive, during a meeting near Posto 34 in Devoli with *Generali* Cavallero, Geloso and Gambara, suggested that the attacks should be moved further south (starting on 28 March) with Klisura as the target:

> We have an effort underway that engages C.A. IV, VIII and XXV. This effort responds to the concept of waging war of attrition, in that we are acting here in correspondence with the adversary's strongpoint, and to offer us chances for tactical success. On the other hand, the only area on the 11th Army front where our success can have a name is Klisura. If we achieve this, it will result in the collapse of Greek morale. The objectives are, therefore: to hold Tepeleni at any cost; to reach Klisura at any cost…

The Last Assault

The Italian offensive came to a halt between 16 and 18 March, allowing the Greeks to bring forward their reserves and begin a gradual reinforcement of their line. On 19 March, the Italian commanders decided to launch a new attack against height 731, this time also supported by tanks (four M13/40 tanks) led by *Tenente* Luigi Camera and by specialist volunteers in assault units, which were to penetrate the enemy defences, disrupt them and create confusion, while waiting for the arrival of the bulk of the infantry launched on the assault. *Capitano* Giorgio di Borbone Parma, born in Milan on 20 May 1900, serving in the 31st *Siena* Infantry Regiment, was placed in command of these 150-odd men. Aiming directly at height 731, the armoured vehicles managed to open a few gaps in the defences, through which the assault troops threw hand grenades. *Capitano* di Borbone Parma was among the first to reach between the Greek defences, and then succeeded with his men in permanently occupying a position between the enemy lines, a part of height 731. It remained in place to wait for reinforcements to arrive, but the wait was in vain as the infantry of the *Bari* Division were stopped further down the valley by Greek artillery fire. Unable to move forward, they were eventually forced to return to their original positions. Left completely isolated, *Capitano* di Borbone Parma continued

---

4 In fact, in general, there was no coordination between the artillery groups and the battalions launched to the attack: after the first 50 or 60 metres of movement, the batteries, by not extending their fire and remaining stationary on the initial coordinates, allowed the Greeks a limited retreat and then to launch rapid counterattacks.

to fight, repelling the attacks of the Greek infantry. After exhausting all ammunition and hand grenades, a rifle shot hit him in the head, killing him instantly. Along with him, 66 of his volunteers also fell, while 23 others were seriously wounded.

Di Borbone Parma was awarded the *Medaglia d'Oro al Valor Militare alla Memoria*, with the citation:

> Commander of an Arditi company, three times war volunteer, already wounded in previous actions in which he had valiantly distinguished himself, he obtained, after strong pleading, the return to his unit. In bitter combat, with unparalleled audacity and reckless disregard for danger, he threw himself, at the head of his troops, against a fortified enemy position. Hit the first time, he continued to advance and reached the enemy line, taking it and dispersing the defenders with fierce throwing of hand grenades. Surrounded by an overwhelming force, he persevered undaunted in the unequal fight until, having exhausted the bombs and the ammunition from his gun against his nearest adversaries, he was overwhelmed and fell a hero. [Q. 731 Monastero (Greek-Albanian Front)]

The attacks against the Greek positions continued with less intensity until 24 March, but without achieving any significant results. A sad balance of Italian losses suffered in this last offensive remained to be recorded: around 12,000 men, dead and wounded.

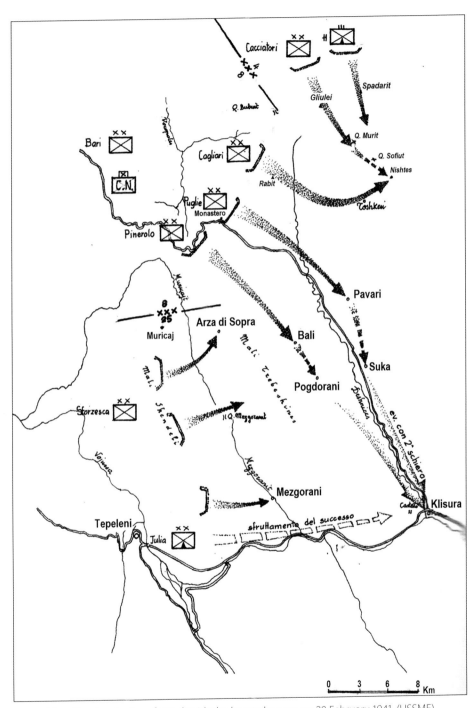

Map: Gambara's plan of attack with the latest changes on 28 February 1941. (USSME)

An Italian machine gun squad on the attack, March 1941. (USSME)

Italian soldiers advance along a slope, March 1941. (USSME)

A heavy machine gun provides supporting fire to attacking infantry units, March 1941. (USSME)

Mussolini at the observatory of the 9th Army, March 1941. (USSME)

Italian infantry units attacking a hill, completely destroyed by artillery fire, March 1941. (USSME)

The half-destroyed buildings on Monastero at elevation 731, the scene of bloody battles between Italian and Greek troops in March 1941.

LUIGI BIASUCCI

Colonnello 140° Reggimento fanteria,
da Roma, alla memoria.

« Comandante di reggimento, coraggioso e sagace, con azione appassionata e costante di animatore e di capo, faceva dei suoi battaglioni un superbo strumento di lotta. Ricevuto l'ordine di attaccare una munita posizione avversaria, dava con calma e sicura competenza le necessarie disposizioni per la realizzazione dell'impresa affidatagli. Nello svolgimento dell'azione, alla testa dei suoi battaglioni, fante fra i fanti, valoroso fra i valorosi, faceva impeto sul nemico e ferito mortalmente, cadeva inneggiando alla vittoria. »

(Quota 731 zona Monastero, fronte greco, 13-14 marzo 1941-XIX)

Contemporary postcard commemorating the award of the *Medaglia d'Oro al Valor Militare* to *Colonnello* Luigi Biasucci.

Italian infantry during an attack on enemy positions, March 1941. (USSME)

Colonnello Luigi Biasucci, commanding the
140th Infantry Regiment of *Bari*. (www.movm.it)

Maggiore Gino Valentini, commander of the
3rd Battalion of the 140th Infantry Regiment.
(www.movm.it)

Capitano Giorgio di Borbone Parma,
serving with the 31st Infantry
Regiment *Siena*. (www.movm.it)

GIORGIO DI BORBONE

Capitano del 31° Reggimento fanteria, da Milano, alla memoria.

«Comandante di una compagnia arditi, tre volte volontario di guerra, già ferito in precedenti fatti d'arme in cui si era valorosamente distinto, otteneva, dopo varie insistenze, di rientrare al proprio reparto. In aspro combattimento si lanciava con impareggiabile audacia e sprezzo del pericolo, alla testa dei suoi arditi, contro munita posizione avversaria. Colpito una prima volta, seguitava ad avanzare e giungeva sulla linea nemica conquistandola e disperdendone i difensori con accanito lancio di bombe a mano. Accerchiato da forze soverchianti, persisteva imperterrito nell'impari lotta, finchè, esaurite le bombe ed i colpi della propria pistola contro i più vicini avversari, veniva sopraffatto e cadeva da eroe.»

(Quota 731 di Monastero, fronte greco, 19 marzo 1941-XIX)

Contemporary postcard commemorating the granting of the *Medaglia d'Oro al Valor Militare* to *Capitano* Giorgio di Borbone Parma.

Mussolini during his inspection tour on the Albanian front, surrounded by his top department commanders, March 1941. (USSME)

9

The Invasion of Yugoslavia

As early as November 1940, immediately after the Italian attack on Greece, Hitler had ordered his General Staff to plan an action to attack the country, which was code-named Operation MARITA. Hitler was not directly interested in Greece, but feared a British intervention in the Balkan peninsula and especially feared the threat to the Romanian oil wells in Ploiesti. The British had already started sending aid to Greece in early November 1940: an infantry brigade was sent to garrison the island of Crete and the Royal Air Force sent a squadron of Bristol Blenheim light bombers, followed in later weeks by other squadrons of Blenheim and Vickers Wellington bombers and Gloster Gladiator fighters. The latter aircraft were passed over to the Greeks and replaced by the more modern Hawker Hurricane fighters.

On 16 November 1940, 2,200 British soldiers and 310 vehicles of the RAF ground support units arrived at the port of Piraeus, followed by anti-aircraft artillery units with another 2,000 men and 400 vehicles. Command of the British divisions in Greece was then taken over by Air Vice Marshal John D'Albiac. When German forces entered Bulgaria in March 1941, the British decided to send an expeditionary force to Greece to face a possible German invasion. On 2 March, the Operation LUSTRE was launched; the transport of troops and materiel to Greece, which was completed on the 26th with the arrival in the ports of Piraeus and Thessaloniki. The British expeditionary corps, also known as 'Force W', comprised around 54,000 men, formed as a British armoured brigade, two Australian divisions, a New Zealand division and a Polish brigade; all units from the North African front. The troops were placed under the orders of General Henry Wilson.

Yugoslav Betrayal

The presence of the British Expeditionary Force in Greece accelerated the German plans. In order to invade Greece, there were two possibilities: go through Yugoslavia or pass through Hungary, Romania and Bulgaria. The first solution was of course more advantageous as it would have saved a lot of time. So after having succeeded in getting Romania, Bulgaria and Hungary to join the Tripartite Pact, Hitler also started diplomatic talks with Yugoslavia, with the regent Prince Paul. And so, on 25 March 1941, after heavy pressure and the promise of the port of Thessaloniki in Greece, the Yugoslav government joined the Tripartite Pact. On the same day, the decision was also taken to delay Operation BARBAROSSA by four weeks for the invasion of Greece. But on the night of 26/27 March, a group of Serbian officers opposed to the Axis agreement, led by *General* Dusan Simovic, overthrew the government of the regent Paul in a coup d'état. The young Peter II ascended the throne and entrusted the task of forming a new government to *General* Simovic himself. In the streets of Belgrade, the Serbian population greeted the event warmly and British and French flags were displayed from the windows of houses. For Italy and Germany, the Serbian coup was an unacceptable provocation. Hitler immediately issued orders to 'crush Yugoslavia militarily and politically', which were summarised in instruction sheet number 25:

> It is my intention to invade Yugoslavia with powerful forces in the direction of Belgrade and the southernmost territory, in order both to inflict a decisive defeat on the Yugoslav Army and to separate the southern part of the country from the rest of it in order to turn it into a base for further land operations. In particular, I order the following: as soon as the concentration of sufficient forces is completed and weather conditions permit, all ground installations and the city of Belgrade are to be destroyed by continuous air attacks by day and night.

As early as 27 March, after Hitler had ordered his generals to prepare for the attack on Yugoslavia and Greece, set for 6 April 1941, Hitler himself sent Mussolini a telegram to coordinate military operations against Yugoslavia:

> And now I cordially request you, *Duce*, not to begin any further operations in Albania during the next few days. I consider it necessary that you cover and protect with all available forces the most important passes between Yugoslavia and Albania …. I also consider it necessary, *Duce*, that you reinforce your units on the Yugoslav-Italian frontier with all available means and with the utmost speed.

In practice, Hitler was asking the Italian armed forces for an offensive action along the 'Julian' border[1] to protect the flank of the attack of the German forces coming from Austria. Along the Greek-Albanian front it was necessary to take a defensive stance while awaiting the junction with the German troops coming from Bulgaria in the direction of Skoplje and then continue south against the Greek and British forces.

Il Duce replied to Hitler:

> Orders have already been given by me personally to *Generale* Cavallero to suspend the offensive [in Albania ed.], the start of which was imminent. Infantry divisions are flowing towards the northern frontier and are taking up positions in the three directions of a possible Yugoslav attack. Orders have been given for seven divisions to flow towards the eastern Alpine

---

1   The Julian Border is actually the border between Italy and Slovenia that was established after World War II although the term 'The Julian Marc' for the area dates to 1863 (ed.).

frontier, which will join the existing ones, plus fifteen thousand men to guard the frontier. In the same area, the 2a air squadron is ready to operate.

Italian Forces in the Field

The Italian attack against Yugoslavia took place in three different areas: along the 'Julian' border, from the stronghold of Zadar and from the Albanian border. In the north was the 2nd Army (comprising 5 army corps) of *Generale* Vittorio Ambrosio. In Zadar, there were approximately 9,000 men who were raised to the rank of a division. On the Albanian border was the 9th Army of *Generale* Pirzio Biroli and the 11th Army of *Generale* Geloso.

At the beginning of March, the 2nd Army comprised:

> XI Army Corps (*Reale, Isonzo* and 3rd *Alpini* Infantry Divisions)
> V Army Corps (*Sassari, Bergamo* and *Lombardy* Infantry Divisions)
> The 1st *Esprimere* Division
> Some units of *Guardia di Frontiera*, reinforced with battalions of Blackshirts

Before the start of operations, the army received reinforcements in the form of three additional corps, three infantry divisions (*Assietta, Ravenna* and *Piave*) and other units.

> VI Army Corps (*Friuli* Infantry Division)
> The motorised Army Corps (*Littorio* Armoured Division, *Pasubio* and *Torino* Infantry Divisions)
> The *Celere* Army Corps (*Eugenio di Savoia, Emanuele Filiberto* and *Principe Amedeo Duca d'Aosta* Divisions).

German Forces

The Germans invaded Yugoslavia from the north with the 2nd Army under *Generalmajor* Maximilian von Weichs:

> XLIX Corps and LI Corps from Austria;
> XLVI Armoured Corps from Hungary.

From the north-east with Field Marshal List's 12th Army: the 1st Armoured Group under *General* Ewald von Kleist comprised three Army Corps: XLI Motorised Corps, was to move from Romania with the objective of aiming for Belgrade. XI and XIV Corps from Bulgaria with the objective of targeting Nis and then also converging on Belgrade. Further south and still from Bulgaria XL, XVIII and XXX Corps were to move from Bulgaria with the objective of carrying out Operation MARITA.

Satellite Forces

Hungary took part in the operations from 11 to 13 April, with the 3rd Army (three Army Corps) comprising a total of eight infantry divisions and two motor brigades. Romania and Bulgaria did not participate directly in the conflict, only allowing the transit of German troops.

Yugoslav Forces

On the eve of the German-Italian invasion, the Yugoslav Army had a total of about 30 infantry and 3 cavalry divisions, plus a few armoured regiments. The forces included:

> 1st Army Group (7th Army and 4th Army), under the orders of *General* Petrovic, stationed along the borders with Italy and Austria;
> 2nd Army Group (1st Army and 2nd Army), under the orders of *General* Milutin Nedic along the Hungarian and Romanian borders;
> 3rd Army Group (3rd Army, 5th Army, 6th Army and 3rd Territorial Army), under the orders of *General* Milan Nedic along the southern Romanian, Bulgarian, Greek and Albanian borders.

The armament of the Belgrade Army was poor and antiquated, especially when compared to that of the German Army, but not so poor when compared to that of the Italian Army. The heavy armament dated to the First World War and the few trucks available were outdated (mostly French FT trucks) and allocated in a disorganised manner to the various infantry units. The situation of the *Vazduhoplovstvo Vojske Kraljevine Jugoslavije* (Yugoslav Air Force) was no better, which could count on some 500 efficient aircraft, but most of which were destroyed on the ground at the beginning of hostilities by the *Luftwaffe*, thus making their eventual operational contribution negligible.

Fire on Belgrade

At dawn on 6 April 1941, the German *Luftwaffe* began Operation CHASTISEMENT, the code name given to the bombing of the Yugoslavian capital: waves of Stuka dive-bombers unleashed their lethal load of death on Belgrade, striking it repeatedly over three days and three nights, reducing entire neighbourhoods to a heap of rubble. The German planes were able to act undisturbed as the capital had been declared an open city and therefore had no anti-aircraft defence. Moreover, the *Vazduhoplovstvo Vojske Kraljevine Jugoslavije* no longer existed, since, as mentioned, most of the aircraft had been systematically destroyed on the ground by the *Luftwaffe*. The massive bombing of Belgrade had been ordered by Hitler as 'punishment' for the Yugoslav government's turncoat and to force it to surrender in order to avoid the use of ground troops. Instead, the Yugoslav government wanted to continue resisting, perhaps hoping for some help from the Western Powers, but which could not have come at that time. Therefore, directives for the invasion were issued to the German-Italian ground troops.

The Invasion

The invasion plan envisaged a convergent action on Belgrade, conducted simultaneously from the north and northeast by von Weichs' 2nd Army and from the south by von Kleist's Armoured Corps. To the west, *Generale* Ambrosio's 2nd Italian Army would act. The other forces of List's 12th Army were to target Skoplje in Macedonia and join the Italian forces from Albania. On 9 April, German divisions stationed in Austria, Hungary and Romania invaded Yugoslav territory. By 10 April, Zagreb was already in German hands: in the Croatian capital, the Germans were welcomed as liberators, and the next day Slavko Kvaternik proclaimed the independence of Croatia. As early as 7 April, Italian troops operated offensive operations across the border, hindered only by massive enemy artillery fire, which, however, failed to slow down the eastward movement.

On 11 April, two motorcycle platoons of the 11th Bersaglieri Regiment preceded the entrance of the German columns into Ljubljana: the operation conceived by *Generale* Roatta was above all a political and propaganda success. The capital of Slovenia was within the Italian operational area, but some Italian agents had reported the advance of a German motorised column towards the city. *Generale* Roatta, using all available means, formed a motorised column and launched it at full speed towards Ljubljana. The Slovenians were greatly surprised when shortly before 6 p.m., instead of the German troops, they saw Italian soldiers enter the city. Shortly afterwards, the other divisions of the 11th Bersaglieri Regiment and the L tanks of the *San Giusto* Armoured Group arrived in Ljubljana, completing the occupation of the city. On 12 April, in the early hours of dawn, the 12th Bersaglieri Regiment, reinforced by a Blackshirts battalion, occupied Karlovac, joining the German forces that had also arrived in the Croatian city.

After reaching the objectives to the east of the offensive line established with the Germanic command, the troops of the 2nd Italian Army began to push along the Dalmatian coastline, to continue covering the right flank of the German offensive. It was also necessary to prevent the routed Yugoslav forces from reaching the so-called 'Bosnian Redoubt', an ideal area to organise an all-out resistance, due to its morphological conformation. In addition, it was necessary to join the forces from the Zadar garrison and take the Yugoslav forces stationed along the northern border of Albania from behind.

The Taking of Belgrade

The units of the German XLI Armoured Corps from Romania, having reached Pancevo on 10 April, continued on their way to the Yugoslav capital. On 12 April, *SS-Hauptsturmführer* Fritz Klingenberg of the 2nd company of the motorcycle battalion of the SS *Das Reich* Division crossed the Danube and with only nine men achieved the surrender of Belgrade. For this valiant and daring action, Klingenberg was decorated with the Knight's Cross. On the same day, Hungarian troops recaptured their former territories south of the Drava and the Danube lost after the First World War, almost without a fight.

From Bulgaria, the other two corps (XIV and XI) of von Kleist's Armoured Corps reached Nis on 9 April and Krusevac on the 10th. From there they also began to push towards Belgrade along the course of the Morava; on 12 April, in the sector of Mount Avala they clashed with some Yugoslav divisions that put up strong resistance. For almost two days, Kleist's panzers were pinned down by enemy fire, until the *Luftwaffe*, by now masters of the Balkan skies, intervened to crush the enemy resistance. On the 13th, von Kleist's armoured columns reached Belgrade.

Further south, from Bulgaria, the other German forces of List's 12th Army, after a few clashes with enemy units, reached Skoplje on 7 April, then pushed on towards Monastir along the Greek border and joined the Italian forces from Albania there as well.

The Zadar Front

The Italian garrison in Zadar immediately found itself on the front line after the Belgrade coup. There were about 9,000 men in the stronghold under the orders of *Generale di Brigata* Emilio Giglioli. Since 28 March, Italian intelligence services had reported the presence of considerable enemy forces and located several artillery positions around the city. On 2 April, the evacuation of the civilian population was arranged and the defence works were reinforced. Against the Italian garrison, the *Jadranska* Division was deployed in the front line and the *Mostar* and *Šibenik* Divisions were ready to intervene. From the Supreme Command came the order to resist to the bitter end.

In an attempt to loosen the enemy's grip around the town, an air raid by the *Regia Aeronautica* on enemy positions was ordered on 8 April. In retaliation, the *Ellinikí Vasilikí Aeroporía* in turn carried out raids on the city, which caused damage mainly to civilian dwellings. From that moment on, *Generale* Giglioli requested the continuous presence of fighters over the city's skies to prevent further enemy air raids. The situation changed radically after 11 April: with the Italian-German forces already in Croatia, the enemy units around Zadar began to retreat inland. Thus an offensive was ordered by the Supreme Command towards Knin in order to put the entire enemy front in crisis. *Generale* Giglioli formed an attack column, under the orders of *Colonnello* Eugenio Morra, comprising the *Zara* Bersaglieri Battalion, a motorised infantry battalion, a motorised artillery group, a tank company and other minor units.

The column, supported by intense artillery fire, moved at dawn on 12 April and immediately reached Zemonico Inferiore. The next day, the column came under heavy enemy artillery fire. *Generale* Giglioli, who had joined his men in the meantime, ordered *Colonnello* Morra to send the tanks forward. There followed furious fighting that saw the bersaglieri of the *Zara* battalion engaged against superior enemy forces supported by the *Vazduhoplovstvo Vojske Kraljevine Jugoslavije*. There were many dead and seriously wounded, including *Colonnello* Morra himself; the command of the column was taken over by Bersaglieri *Maggiore* Pietro Testa. Throughout the night of 13 and the morning of 14 April, the Italian units had to defend themselves against repeated attacks by the *Jadranska* Division.

The Yugoslav Collapse

On 14 April, the units of the *Turin* Division, having obtained the surrender of the Gracac garrison, quickly pushed towards the positions held by Giglioli's column, forcing them to flee. The combined forces thus continued their advance towards Knin. After losing control of all the advanced outposts, the Knin garrison surrendered to the Italian forces. On 15 April, facing the imminent catastrophe, the young King Peter fled to Greece to put himself under British protection; on the same day, a regiment of the *Turin* Division reached Šibenik while other regiments of the Division took Split. On 16 April, German forces entered Sarajevo, completing the annihilation of the Yugoslav Army. On 17 April, the motorised Army Corps entered Ragusa, meeting the Italian divisions of the XVIII Army Corps from Albania. Also on the 17th, Mostar, the former capital of Herzegovina, was taken.

Operations on the Albanian Front

As Hitler had expressed to Mussolini, the favourable outcome of Operation MARITA depended, above all, on the tightness of the Italian troops along the Albanian-Yugoslav border. In fact, immediately after the worsening of the political situation in Yugoslavia, Italian military command had ordered the reinforcement of the defensive line along the border between Albania and Yugoslavia, where an enemy offensive action was expected. The Italian defensive deployment along the Albanian-Yugoslav front had weakened during the military operations against Greece, turning into only a thin security line, defended by the Frontier Guard and some units of the *Carabinieri* and *Guardia di Finanza*. Starting in March 1941, the commander of the Italian Armed Forces in Albania, *Generale* Ugo Cavallero, therefore had numerous divisional and regimental units stationed in northern Albania in preparation for a possible offensive action against Yugoslavia, considering that the enemy on the other side deployed a force of approximately 130,000 soldiers.

On the eve of the start of operations against Yugoslavia, Italian forces were regrouped:

> XVII Army Corps under *Generale* Giuseppe Pafundi, committed to controlling the entire northern and north-eastern sector, composed of the *Centauro* Armoured Division, the *Messina* Infantry Division, the *Marche* Infantry Division, the *Diamanti* Blackshirts Regiment, the 19th *Guide* Cavalry Regiment and other smaller units.

XIV Army Corps (*Generale* Giovanni Vecchi), engaged in defending the eastern sector protecting Tirana, composed of the *Cuneense Alpini* Division, the *Puglie* Infantry Division, the 6th *Lancieri Aosta* Regiment and other smaller units.

the so-called 'Librazhd Sector' (*Generale* Nasci), committed to defending possible attacks from Dibrano and Struga,[2] comprising the *Arezzo*, *Florence* and *Pinerolo* infantry divisions, the 7th *Milan Lancieri* Regiment, the 4th Bersaglieri Regiment, the *Biscaccianti* Blackshirts Regiment and other smaller units.

The first to attack were the Yugoslavs, *General* Brusić's 3rd Army, relying on their numerical superiority and also taking advantage of the fact that the Italian units were still completing their deployment. On 6 April, enemy units had attacked in the Shkodra sector, defended by the XVII Army Corps, supported by heavy artillery fire and also by aerial bombardment over Shkodra itself. In the Puka sector, the Morina border post was overrun, despite the strenuous resistance of the Italian troops; in order to prevent the enemy from penetrating deeper, the bridge over the Lumes River was blown up. The next day, the enemy assaults became more intense, but the Italian soldiers held their positions remarkably well, counterattacking when they could. In the Kukës sector, however, the Italians had to retreat due to strong enemy pressure: Kukës was abandoned and the bridge over the Drin river was blown up. The *Regia Aeronautica* intervened and carried out several low-level attacks, forcing the Yugoslav forces to retreat.

Over the following days, in the Puka and Kukës sectors, Yugoslav assaults were repeated almost uninterrupted; they were, however, all repulsed thanks in part to counterattacks carried out by the tanks of the *Centauro* Armoured Division but also by the stubborn resistance of the Italian troops. On 13 April, the Yugoslavs unleashed a massive new offensive in the Shkodra sector, by four infantry regiments supported by tanks. First the *Centauro* tanks counterattacked and then a counterattack was launched by the 19th *Guide* Cavalry Regiment and the XXIII Militia Legion: they fought furiously until sunset, when the Yugoslav forces were forced to retreat and the situation was restored. Another attack in the Tarabosh sector was stopped by the soldiers of the *Messina* Division thanks to some counterattacks with hand-to-hand weapons.

In the XIV Army Corps sector, no major clashes occurred, with the Italian units mainly engaged in countering the enemy's attempts to penetrate the line.

On 15 April, the initiative passed into the hands of the Italians: units of the 31st tank regiment of the *Centauro*, despite intense enemy artillery fire, successfully carried out raids across the Yugoslav border. The enemy's forces were now nearing exhaustion, and on the 15th, a proposal for an armistice was presented by *Genikós* Petrovic, commander of the *Zetska* Division. The commander of the *Centauro*, *Generale* Pizzolato reserved the right to reply, and after a meeting with *Generale* Cavallero, it was decided not to accept any armistice but only unconditional

---

2   The Librazhd region was of crucial importance, as it covered the rear of the 9th Army, and also barred access to Tirana and formed the hinge of the entire defence towards Yugoslavia.

surrender. The offensive was thus resumed: with the Italian forces deployed in the Scutari sector, two columns were formed, one called 'North' comprising the *Centauro Division* and the *Marche* Division with the objective of targeting Ragusa and one 'South' comprising the *Messina* Division with the objective of targeting Kotor. The northern column, after occupying Niksic, reached Ragusa at 13:30 on the 17th. The South, after occupying Cettigne, the former capital of Montenegro, reached Kotor on 18 April.

Also in the sector held by the XIV Army Corps (*Puglie* Division, *Cuneense*, *Firenze* and other units), further south, north-west of Lake Ohrid, the Italian forces went on the offensive from 9 April. On 11 April, the motorcycle company of the 4th Bersaglieri entered Ohrid, joining the German units from Bulgaria. With the army now in disarray, the Yugoslav plenipotentiaries signed the act of surrender in Belgrade, which came into effect at 12 o'clock on 18 April. *General* Kalafatovik signed for Yugoslavia, for Italy *Colonnello* Bonfatti, the military attaché in Belgrade, and for Germany *General* von Weichs.

The Partition of Yugoslavia

After the armistice, the Yugoslav territory was divided among the various occupiers. To Germany went Northern Slovenia, Styria and Carinthia, the administration of Eastern Banat (inhabited by Romanian minorities) and the establishment of a military regime in Serbia, which was returned to the borders of 1914. Italy obtained part of Dalmatia and the Province of Kotor. Southern Slovenia with Ljubljana was directly annexed into the Italian national territory. Some territories in Macedonia and Kosovo were incorporated into Italian Albania. The territory of Montenegro was declared independent, as an Italian Protectorate. Croatia, with Slavonia, Bosnia-Herzegovina and part of Dalmatia formed the Independent State of Croatia, placed under dual Italian (in the west) and German (in the east) influence. On 15 May 1941, Croatia was established as a Kingdom, and Premier Ante Pavelic offered the crown to *Duca* Aimon of Spoleto of the House of Savoy. Other 'strips' of Yugoslav territory went to Bulgaria (much of Slav Macedonia) and Hungary (half of Vojvodina and other areas).

Generale Vittorio Ambrosio. (USSME)

Motorised column of the *Grossdeutschland* regiment marching on a Hungarian road, April 1941.

April 1941, bersaglieri on the march in Yugoslav territory. (USSME)

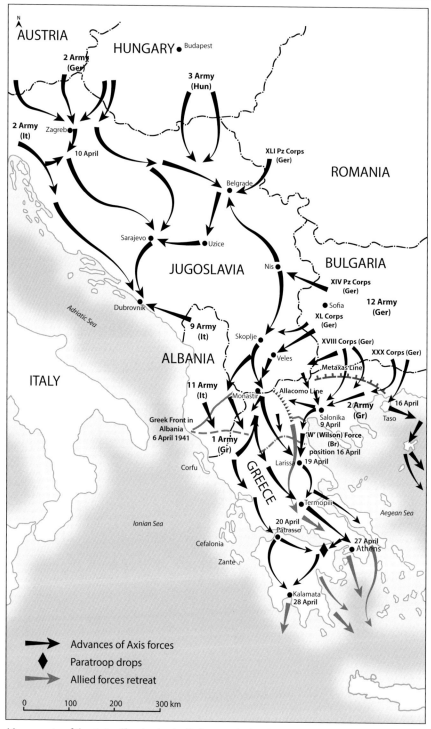

Movements of the Axis offensive in the Balkans with the deployment of the forces engaged throughout the campaign.

An Italian motorised column prepares to cross a watercourse on a bridge built by engineers near the border with Yugoslavia, April 1941. (USSME)

Julian Front, April 1941: Italian troops, after crossing the border into Yugoslavia, penetrated into Sussak, a suburb of the city of Rijeka. (USSME)

Italian troops parade through the streets of Ljubljana, April 1941. (USSME)

Italian soldiers attacking on the Yugoslav front, April 1941. (USSME)

Italian soldiers attacking on the Yugoslav front, April 1941. (USSME)

The 12th Bersaglieri Regiment enters Karlovac, April 1941. (USSME)

Yugoslav soldiers surrender to the Germans, April 1941.

Zadar Front: Italian Bersaglieri engaged in combat in the hinterland of the Dalmatian city, April 1941. (USSME)

Bersaglieri in the streets of Ragusa (Dubrovnik), April 1941 (USSME)

April 1941, Italian L tanks moving into Yugoslav territory. (USSME)

Italian motorcyclists and trucks enter Mostar, April 1941. (USSME)

Albanian Front, Spring 1941: the 131st Artillery Regiment of the *Centauro* Armoured Division,
deployed on the eve of operations against Yugoslavia. (USSME)

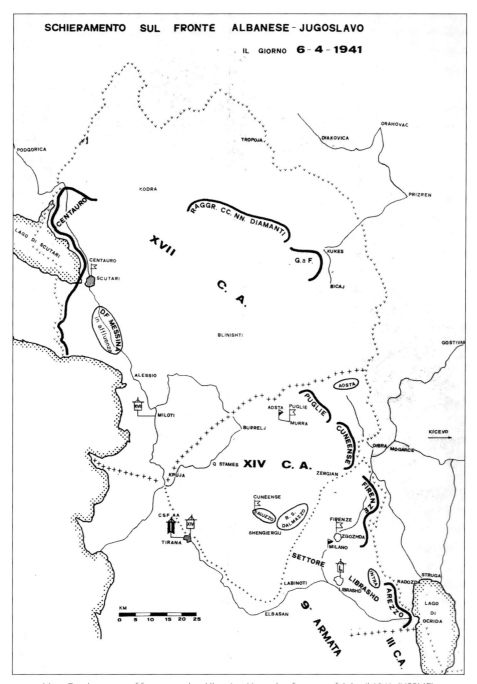

Map: Deployment of forces on the Albanian-Yugoslav front as of 6 April 1941. (USSME)

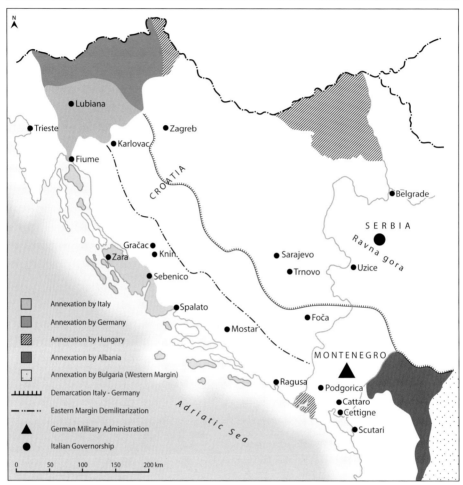

Map: Partition of Yugoslav territory after the capitulation, 1941–1943. (USSME)

Tanks of the *2.Panzer-Division* parade through Sofia, Bulgaria, on the eve of the attack on Greece and Yugoslavia, April 1941.

10

The Invasion of Greece

The invasion of Yugoslavia had changed the plans for the invasion of Greece: the original German plan envisaged an offensive action from Bulgaria aimed against the *Metaxas* line (an impressive complex of bunkers and trenches stretching from the Vardar Valley along the border between Macedonia and Bulgaria) and towards Thessaloniki. The possibility of entering Yugoslav territory gave the German forces the advantage of bypassing the *Metaxas* line via Skoplje and cutting their enemy's line in two. The bulk of the Greek forces (1st Army) was deployed along the Albanian border with the intention of confronting the Italian forces. Along the border with Yugoslavia, there were 4 Greek divisions and General Henry Maitland Wilson's British Expeditionary Corps, comprising 4 British divisions (including one from New Zealand and one from Australia) and a Polish brigade. Defending the *Metaxas* line were the three and a half divisions of the 2nd Greek Army.

The invasion of Greece began on 6 April by *General* List's German 12th Army. The mountain divisions of *General* Boehme's XVIII Corps attacked the *Metaxas* line near the Rupel Pass frontally, while the 2nd Panzer Division outflanked the same fortified line aiming at Strumica. On 9 April, the Germans reached Thessaloniki. Despite strong resistance, the Greek forces were overwhelmed by the momentum of the German armies, bowing to the firepower of the panzers and Stukas. Wilson's British barricaded themselves on Mount Olympus in an attempt to stop the German attack; the *Leibstandarte SS Adolf Hitler* attacked and after furious fighting forced the British to flee towards Thermopylae. Here Wilson with only the New Zealand division temporarily halted the German advance to give the remaining troops of the British Expeditionary Corps time to embark and escape capture. As at Dunkirk a year earlier, the British sought escape by sea. On the 24th, after a massive attack, the Allies fell back on Thebes, establishing a new defensive line, which was overrun on 26 April, forcing the British troops to retreat to the southern ports of Greece. On the same day, German paratroopers occupied the Corinth Bridge, allowing ground troops to enter the Peloponnese. Thanks to the resistance of General Wilson, Admiral Cunningham managed to evacuate some 43,000 soldiers out of 60,000 before the Germans occupied all the ports of Attica and the Peloponnese. In addition to a large amount of equipment and heavy armament, 11,000 prisoners also remained in German hands.

The Resumption of the Italian Offensive

The start of military operations against Yugoslavia had changed the Italian plans on the Albanian front, where a new offensive towards Klisura was planned for 28 March. The Italian generals breathed a sigh of relief, mainly because new and unnecessary losses were avoided. On the other hand, even Hitler himself, as noted above, had advised Mussolini not to undertake any offensive on the Albanian front at least until the German intervention in Greece began. For their part, the Greeks stubbornly continued to face the Italian forces in Albania, leaving very few units in the eastern sector against the German armies. On the Albanian border as many as 15 Greek divisions were deployed, while on the Bulgarian border there were only 4 divisions and 2 brigades.

At the beginning of April, the Greek forces attempted one last offensive against the Italian forces, on 4 April on the front of the 9th Army and on 5 April on that of the 11th army: all attacks were easily repulsed by the Italian units, which were not surprised in their positions. With the arrival of German troops in Greece and Yugoslavia, the situation changed radically and after the fall of the Slavic cities of Skopje (8 April) and Monastir (9 April), the Greek Command ordered the retreat of its forces to the Albanian front to avoid encirclement by German motorised formations. At the same time, the Italian forces in Albania immediately moved in pursuit of the enemy, who, although retreating, continued to stubbornly contest every inch of ground, engaging numerous forces with the rearguard. On 14 April, Coriza was recaptured and the infamous height 731 in Monastir, where Greek and Italian soldiers had clashed several times in furious and bloody fighting, was finally taken. The Italian troops then broke into the Deisnizza Valley.

On 17 April, after furious fighting in which the *Legnano* and the *Sforzesca* divisions and the 3rd *Granatieri* were engaged, Klisura was recaptured. On the same day, troops of the *Casale* Division (*Generale* Enea Navarini), together with those of the *Ferrara* Division, entered Gjirokastra.

Sergente Maggiore Antonio Mendolicchio, born in Foggia on 22 May 1915, of the 47th *Ferrara* Infantry Regiment, was killed in combat on the Argirocastro road on 14 April 1941. He was decorated with the *Medaglia d'Oro al Valor Militare alla Memoria*, with the citation:

> Volunteering on a daring military mission, he carried out his task with unparalleled enthusiasm, faith and valour. Leading his own squad, he penetrated between the enemy lines, firmly occupied an important position and held it for two days. Severely wounded in his left arm from the beginning of the fight, he bandaged himself, refusing all help. When his officer fell, he replaced him in command and, although surrounded and wounded again in various parts of his body, remained at his fighting post. At dawn, as reinforcements arrived to free him from the enemy's grip, a bomb severed his leg. Not at all shaken in his soldierly faith, he encouraged his fellow soldiers in defence and, standing on his one leg, gave orders, as before, with unparalleled energy and contempt for the now certain death. Having had his chest ripped open by a machine gun burst, he fell to the ground, sending his final farewell to his distant Homeland, content to give it his life. [Q. 350 of Km. 21 Argirocastro (Greek front), 13–14 April 1941]

In the meantime, the units of the *Venezia* Division took Ersekë and units of the *Bari* Division took Premeti. The first unit to enter Premeti on 17 April was the 1st Battalion of the 139th Infantry Regiment *Bari*, under the orders of *Tenente Colonnello* Achille Lauro, born in Naples on 5 December 1892. During the subsequent clashes with the Greek forces in the Ponte Perati area, he was killed in combat during an assault on enemy positions and was decorated with the *Medaglia d'Oro al Valor Militare alla Memoria*, with the citation:

> Senior officer of distinguished military virtue, his *colonnello* having been wounded, he took command of the regiment during a bitter fight. Twice wounded, he refused to leave his position in order to get aid, in a particularly delicate moment, his contribution to the achievement of success. While the last enemy resistance was being crushed, he was hit again and fell as a hero at the head of his men launched towards victory. [Premeti – Perati Bridge Zone (Greek front), 18–22 April 1941]

The Greeks Surrender

The rapid advance of the Italian forces stopped on 22 April at Ponte Perati, which was found to be occupied by a German formation. Starting at dawn, the motorcycle company of the 4th Bersaglieri, the *Lancieri di Milano*, the 63rd Infantry from *Cagliari* and the 140th from *Bari* arrived at Perati. In the words of the account of *Colonnello* Giorgio Morigi, commander of the *Lancieri di Milano* regiment:

> The *Lancieri di Milano* arrived at 7.15 a.m., still in time to cut the retreating enemy column in two. The orders from the commander of the army corps to advance into Greek territory were strict, but the Germans categorically forbade me to pass and I angrily saw the Greek column parading in front of me without being able to attack it.

The Italian troops were therefore not allowed to attack a retreating Greek column. The Germans had been ordered to avoid any further contact between Italian and Greek troops, as surrender negotiations were in progress. In the meantime, on the left wing, the *Pusteria* Division had reached the Grammos Ridge and then descended over Sarandaporos towards Konitsa. The operations lasted until the 23rd when the war officially ended.

Despite the successes achieved, Italian losses were considerable. Between 14 and 22 April, the 9th Italian Army suffered losses of 14 officers killed and 46 wounded, 131 non-commissioned officers and men killed and a further 736 wounded. The 11th Army suffered 65 dead, 250 wounded and 5 missing officers, with 900 dead, 3,500 wounded and 100 missing NCOs and rank and file.

On 23 April, after a series of contacts and discussions between the Italian and German military high commands, the act of surrender of the Greek Army was signed in Thessaloniki. For Italy *Generale* Ferrero signed, for Greece *Genikós* Tsolakoglou and for Germany *General* Jodl. On the same day, King George of Greece fled to Crete eager to continue the fight against the Axis forces.

The Italian Armed Forces Headquarters issued the following extraordinary communiqué number 321 on 23 April:

> The enemy army of Epirus and Macedonia has laid down its arms. The surrender was presented at 9.04 p.m. last night by a military delegation to the Commander of the 11th Italian Army on the Epirus front. The details of the surrender are being worked out in complete agreement with the German Allied Command.

On 28 April, the German and Italian troops made their triumphal entry into Athens. To the soldiers engaged on the Greek front, Il Duce sent the message:

> Victory consecrates your bloody sacrifices, especially grave for the land forces, and illuminates your flags with new glory. The Fatherland is proud of you as never before. At this moment, the Italian people remembers and salutes with emotion its heroic sons who fell in the Battle of Albania and expresses to you, who avenged them, its imperishable glory.

On 3 May 1941, during the victory parade through the streets of Athens, along with the German units, some Italian units paraded, including a battalion of the *Julia Alpini* Division, which had particularly distinguished itself throughout the campaign.

The Occupation of the Ionian Islands

Having completed the occupation of the continental part of Greek territory, the Italian command prepared a number of operations, committing units of the *Regia Aereonautica*, for the conquest of the Ionian islands still in Greek hands: Corfu, Kefalonia, Zakynthos and Ithaca. And so, on 28 April 1941, five Z 506 seaplanes under the orders of *Colonnello* Grande transported an Italian division to Corfu. After negotiations with the Greek forces on the island, their surrender was achieved. The next day, the I Battalion of the 17th Infantry Regiment of the *Acqui* Division, which had landed from two ships, arrived to occupy the island. For the conquest of Cephalonia, it was decided to deploy Italian paratroopers from the 1st Parachute Regiment in combat for the first time. For the action, 75 paratroopers from the 1st Regiment, 2nd Battalion, under the command of *Maggiore* Mario Zanninovich, were committed: 3 S.M.82s were loaded with paratroopers and took off from Galatina Airport, transporting the Italian force to an esplanade not far from the town of Argostoli in the early afternoon. The local garrison, consisting of a few hundred Greek soldiers, surrendered quickly and without any resistance: Zanninovich's paratroopers then disarmed them and the conquest of the island was completed. The next day, 1 May 1941, after requisitioning some boats from the Greek civilians, *Maggiore* Zanninovich's paratroopers went to the islands of Ithaca and Zakynthos, transformed for the occasion into landing infantry, and proceeded to conquer them, without engaging in any armed clashes with the local garrisons.

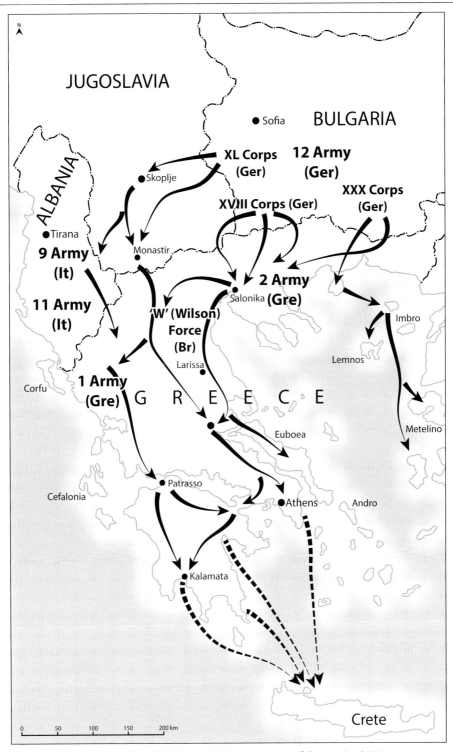

Movement of the Axis Forces in the occupation of Greece, April 1941.

Tanks of the *2.Panzer-Division* in Greek territory, with some New Zealand prisoners, April 1941.

A *s.FH18* heavy howitzer of the *Leibstandarte Adolf Hitler* of the *5.Bttr./SS-Art.Rgt. LSSAH*, April 1941.

Reconnaissance vehicles of the *Leibstandarte Adolf Hitler* and Greek prisoners, April 1941. (NARA)

Leibstandarte Adolf Hitler commander, on the right in the photo, discusses the terms of the surrender of Greek troops with an Italian officer, April 1941. (NARA)

April 1941, Italian infantry units on the march to attack Greek positions. (USSME)

Sergente Maggiore Antonio Mendolicchio of the 47th *Ferrara* Infantry Regiment (www.movm.it).

Tenente Colonnello Achille Lauro, commander of the 1st Battalion of the 139th Infantry Regiment *Bari*. (www.movm.it)

ACHILLE LAURO

Tenente colonnello 130° Reggim. fanteria, da Napoli, alla memoria.

«Ufficiale superiore di elette virtù militari, rimasto ferito il proprio colonnello, assumeva il comando del reggimento durante un aspro combattimento. Due volte ferito, rifiutava di allontanarsi dalle posizioni per dare ancora, in un momento particolarmente delicato, il suo contributo per il conseguimento del successo. Mentre venivano stroncate le ultime resistenze nemiche, veniva nuovamente colpito e cadeva da eroe alla testa dei suoi fanti lanciati verso la vittoria.»

(*Premeti - Zona Ponte Perati, fronte greco, 18-22 aprile 1941-XIX*).

Contemporary postcard commemorating the award of the *Medaglia d'Oro al Valor Militare* to *Tenente Colonnello* Achille Lauro.

Greek soldiers give the Roman salute after surrendering, April 1941. (NARA)

22 April 1941: The Italian Bersaglieri reached the Perati Bridge but were blocked in their advance by the Germans, officially because surrender negotiations with the Greek commanders were in progress. (NARA)

Bersaglieri motorcyclists in pursuit of fleeing Greek units, April 1941. (USSME)

Thessaloniki, 23 April 1941. Generals Tsolakoglou (seated far right), Jodl (seated, second from left) and Ferrero (from behind) sign the Act of Final Surrender of Greece. (NARA)

Italian infantrymen on board trucks during the victory parade through the streets of Athens. (USSME)

Italian troops on the Acropolis in Athens during a ceremony at the end of the Greek campaign, 24 April 1941.

Parachutists of the *Folgore* in Cephalonia, April 1941. (www.congedatifolgore.com)

11

The Conquest of Crete

By the end of April 1941, the Greek campaign could be considered over, but the island of Crete, where the Allied forces had meanwhile taken refuge after fleeing the Hellenic peninsula, still remained to be conquered: more than 40,000 Allied soldiers, 6,000 of whom were unarmed and disorganised, under the orders of General Bernhard Freyberg, commander of the 2nd New Zealand Division, had managed to take refuge on the island. There were 10,000 British regular soldiers, about 14,000 Australian and New Zealand soldiers, over 10,000 Greek soldiers without equipment and heavy weapons, and the Crete gendarmerie forces. The conquest of Crete had been planned by the German command since October 1940, when the Italians started the Greek campaign. The island represented an important strategic position in the defence system in the eastern Mediterranean, especially for the British. The British had landed two infantry battalions on the island as early as 29 October 1940 to prevent any action by the Axis forces. If the Germans or Italians had occupied Crete they would have had air bases close to the North African front. Therefore, the British immediately set about defending Crete at any cost, especially reinforcing its defences in the north-west. Churchill himself had ordered the island, especially the bay of Souda, to be turned into a second Scapa Flow.[1]

Attack on Souda Bay

A first attack against Crete and its naval installations was carried out in March 1941 by the *Regia Marina*, against Souda Bay. On the night of 25/26 March, six raiders of the 10th MAS Flotilla, a special assault unit, aboard as many human torpedo boats, with their explosive warheads, after passing three barrages, sank the British heavy cruiser *York* in Souda Bay on Crete and heavily damaged the Norwegian tanker *Pericles*, which sank later, and a cargo steamer. The Italian raiding party was under the command of *Tenente* Luigi Faggioni. The other boats were piloted by *Sottotenente*

---

1   Scapa Flow is a bay located in the Orkney Islands archipelago, Scotland. The bay is surrounded by the islands of Mainland, Graemsay, Burray, South Ronaldsay and Hoy, and was home to Britain's largest naval base during the First and Second World Wars. Considered impenetrable due to its powerful defences against land, naval and air attacks, in 1939 a German *U-boat*, the U-47, commanded by Günther Prien, managed to penetrate inside the base and sink the battleship *HMS Royal Oak*.

Angelo Cabrini, *Capo Meccanico di Seconda Classe* Alessio De Vito, *Capo Meccanico di Terza Classe* Tullio Tedeschi, *Secondo Capo Meccanico* Lino Beccati, and *Sergente Artigliere* Emilio Barberi, all of whom were decorated with the *Medaglia d'Oro al Valor Militare*. The citation for the medal awarded to Faggioni reads:

> Commanding a unit of Naval Assault Vessels, he penetrated at night, at the head of his units, into the interior of a fortified enemy base and, with exemplary *sang froid*, after having overcome three orders of obstructions and defensive positions, he led them to attack, managing to sink a heavy cruiser and two large steamers. An admirable example of daring, combined with the steadiest and most heroic determination to carry out the mission entrusted to him for the glory of the Homeland and of the Navy. [Souda Bay, 25–26 March 1941]

Operation MERCURY

On 25 April 1941, Hitler issued directive number 28, for the launch of *Unternehmen Merkur* – the conquest of Crete. The date for the start of operations, initially set for 10 May, was finally set for 20 May. For the attack, the Germans mobilised the entire *XI Fliegerkorps* of *General* Kurt Student, which included the *7 Flieger-Division* of *General* Wilhelm Süssmann. The *XI Fliegerkorps* comprised about 22,000 men. Once the main airports on the island had been occupied by dropping paratroopers in several waves, this would be followed by the arrival by air of the *5 Gebirgs-Division*, under the orders of *Generalleutnant* Julius Ringel and, once a landing place was available, the heavy equipment would arrive with the use of a flotilla of small boats, under the protection of the *Regia Marina*, with the reinforcement of another 6,000 men. Thus initially the Italian contribution to the operation was naval support with the dispatch of all Italian torpedo boats to Piraeus and the employment of some submarines from the Leros base. In the afternoon of 20 May, operations began: first with massive *Luftwaffe* bombardment of British positions and then the first airstrikes at the main strategic points.

The Action of Italian Torpedo Boats

Shortly before the attack began, the German commanders had decided to accompany the attacks from the air with a series of secondary landings of mountain troops (*Gebirgsjäger*) and to this end, a series of small convoys were organised by the mass requisitioning of Greek fishing boats and they took on the task of defending them and leading them to the chosen landing sites. Among the various Italian units involved in the operation were the torpedo boats *Lupo* and *Sagittario*.

On 19 May 1941, a convoy of twenty-one caiques[2] left Piraeus: seven were immediately forced to turn back because of breakdowns. At the same time, the torpedo

---

2   The caique is a small fishing boat commonly in use in Greece and the Greek islands (ed.)

boat *Sirius*, which was to act as escort, also complained of starboard propeller failure and was replaced by the torpedo boat *Curtatone*. The latter sank the next day after hitting a mine while on its way to join the convoy. The torpedo boat *Lupo*, under the command of *Capitano di Fregata* Francesco Mimbelli, was then ordered to escort the convoy.

The torpedo boat joined on 21 May 1941 and progress continued smoothly until 22:33, when a lookout signalled the presence of an enemy ship, the destroyer HMS *Janus*, about 1,000 metres to the right. The *Lupo* pulled up and fired two torpedoes, but failed to hit the British ship. It was then ordered to lay a smoke screen to escape enemy observation. Soon afterwards a British cruiser, HMS *Dido*, was sighted 700 metres away and opened fire on the *Lupo*. The Italian torpedo boat responded with all the weapons on board and launched a third torpedo. During this clash, the cruiser HMS *Orion* also appeared on the scene. Mimbelli ordered fire and the *Orion* was hit by a torpedo from the *Lupo*. In turn, the Italian unit took several shells and was subjected to automatic gunfire, which resulted in the death of *Sottocapo Artigliere* Orazio Indelicato, *Artigliere* Nicolò Moccole and 26 others wounded. The fighting in the meantime had become confused because of both the smoke screen and the approach of other British ships. The *Lupo* managed to disengage from the fight and fell back, leaving the enemy units to shoot at each other. Thanks to radar, however, the British eventually managed to locate the now defenceless convoy and attacked it, resulting in the destruction of 10 caiques and the loss of 800 German soldiers. The remnants of the group fell back to the Greek coast. For this action, the *Lupo*'s war flag was decorated with the *Medaglia d'Argento al Valor Militare*, and *Capitano* Mimbelli was awarded the *Medaglia d'Oro al Valor Militare*, with the citation:

> Commander of a torpedo boat escorting a group of motor boats with German troops heading to Crete for the occupation of the island, he clashed at night with an enemy naval formation of three cruisers and some destroyers. When he was hit by violent and concentrated enemy fire at close range, with admirable audacity and exceptional readiness he launched himself into an attack and in a lively melee he hit a cruiser with two torpedoes, sinking it; with a skilful manoeuvre he then managed to disengage his ship from the enemy reaction which, riddled with bullets in the victorious fight, returned to base with its vehicles. [Aegean Sea, night of 22 May 1941]

The Action of the Torpedo Boat *Sagittario*

Another convoy of 38 caiques and small steamers, carrying some 4,000 *Gebirgsjäger*, sailed from the island of Milos at 1 p.m. on 20 May, to meet up with the torpedo boat *Sagittario* of *Tenente* Giuseppe Cigala Fulgosi, which had also sailed from Piraeus. The hospital ship *Brigitte* was also present. At 13:51, the torpedo boat *Curtatone*, which was preceding the *Sagittario*, sank due to hitting a mine and the *Sagittario* rescued 22 survivors, who were then transferred to the minelayer *Rovigno*. At 17:15 the *Sagittario* anchored off Lavrion and waited for the units of the convoy, which had been divided into two groups: the first, coming from the north, arrived almost immediately and at 17:45 the *Sagittario* welcomed *Kriegsmarine Fregattenkapitän* von Lipinski on board.

The second escort, coming from Megara, was sighted at 21:50, so the *Sagittario* sailed to meet it, then set course for Milo with a motor boat with engine problems in tow. Around five o'clock on the morning of 21 May, as the convoy had partially dispersed, the torpedo boat had to return to Lavrion, where several broken-down motor boats had returned, giving them assistance and taking some of them in tow. Eventually, Cigala Fulgosi decided to split the convoy into two groups, the faster ships together with the *Sagittario* and the slower ones in a second group. At 12:40, the torpedo boat *Sirio* and the first group anchored south of Milo, waiting for the other units: the decision was made to depart at 19:00, the time when the second group was expected to arrive, leaving the slower and damaged units at Milo and embarking the troops on board the *Sagittario*. But at 16:00, the North Aegean Naval Group Command (*Marisudest*) ordered the units to remain in Milos for the night, so the torpedo boat and the boats of the first group anchored in Milos harbour, joined in the meantime by the second group. By 18:50, the entire flotilla was assembled in the roadstead.

This halt allowed all the failures of the various boats to be repaired. At 2.30 a.m. on 22 May, the units departed for La Canea, on *Marisudest*'s orders, but at 7.30 a counter-order caused them to reverse course, heading back towards Milos. At 8:35 a.m., after the *Sagittario*'s commander Giuseppe Cigala Fulgosi had sighted a British naval formation, he began to lay a thick smoke screen to protect the small boats and reversed course, retracing the same route to make the screen even thicker and increased his ship's speed. At 09:01, the British sighted the convoy and opened fire. The *Sagittario* responded with her 100mm bow gun and at 9:07, despite being under enemy fire, the *Sagittario* fired her two starboard torpedoes. Standing between the convoy and the British ships, the torpedo boat continued to draw all the fire from the enemy ships. At 09:14 a.m., men spotted two columns rising up on the side of a cruiser and a few minutes later, the British formation was also attacked by *Luftwaffe* planes and turned south and moved away. At 09:22 a.m., a third enemy destroyer, the *Kingston,* was sighted, which attacked the torpedo boat but was hit twice, on the bridge and on the funnel. The *Sagittario*'s action was decisive, since at that point the commander of the British formation, Admiral King, decided not to attack the convoy, continuing its course south. At 09:25 the battle could be considered over. The commander of the *Sagittario*, Giuseppe Cigala Fulgosi, was decorated with the *Medaglia d'Oro al Valor Militare*, with the citation:

> Commander of a torpedo boat escorting a group of motor-sailers with German troops heading to Crete for the occupation of the island, having sighted a significant enemy naval formation of cruisers and destroyers in broad daylight, he manoeuvred with great skill and decision to conceal the convoy from the opposing ships; he then launched himself into the attack with reckless daring, challenging the overwhelming superiority of the enemy and its violent firing, and torpedoing a cruiser that sank, struck full down. With his daring and successful action, he saved the convoy from certain destruction. [Aegean Sea, 22 May 1941]

The Caffaro Landing Party in Crete

While German troops were fighting hard in Crete against the British forces, Mussolini decided to intervene alongside his ally with an expeditionary force, to be landed on the Greek island. Initially, the German command was opposed, but taking into account the failure of the first German attempt to land north of Crete with convoys escorted by the torpedo boats *Lupo* and *Sagittario*, then considering the unforeseen difficulties encountered in the conquest of the island, they accepted the offer. The command of the landing fleet was assigned to *Capitano* Aldo Cocchia, while the command of the troops was entrusted to *Colonnello* Ettore Caffaro. The Italian expeditionary force consisted of around 2,500 men, made up of the following units:

> *Aegean* Platoon/Carabinieri Group
> I Battalion/9th Infantry Regiment *Regina*/50th Infantry Division *Regina*
> II Battalion/10th Infantry Regiment *Regina*/50th Infantry Division *Regina*
> 81st/9th Infantry Regiment *Regina*/50th Infantry Division *Regina* Mortar
>   Company
> 50th 47/32nd/50th Infantry Division *Regina* anti-tank gun company
> 3rd Tank Company CV35/CCCXII Mixed Tank Battalion
> one company/CCI Battalion CC.NN. *Aegean Rhodes* Battalion
> one company/Regiment *San Marco*/*Regia Marina*

The heavy armament available included 46 FIAT 8mm machine guns, 6 x 81mm mortars, 18 x 45mm, 6 x 65/17 and 47/32 cannons, 13 L3 light tanks, nine motorbikes, one truck and 205 mules. The fleet assembled for the landing included four gazolins,[3] two small steamers, the river ship *Porto di Roma*, two refrigerated fishing boats, the lagoon steamer *Giampaolo*, a tanker and two tugs. Some units were equipped with landing gangways, but none of them (except the *Porto di Roma*) was adequate for the purpose in terms of draught, carrying capacity and on-board equipment. Therefore, soldiers were forced to travel on deck with life jackets and without adequate sanitary facilities. The naval escort consisted of the destroyer *Crispi*, the torpedo boats *Lince*, *Libra* and *Lira* plus 6 x MAS.

On 25 May, a landing exercise was carried out in Rhodes, which proved disastrous: nevertheless, it was decided to proceed anyway and on 27 May at 11 a.m., embarkation operations began, which continued until 5 p.m. To save petrol, the smaller and slower ships were taken in tow by the larger ones. At dawn on the 28th, the convoy arrived near the island of Saria (Scarpanto), where it was joined by the larger escort units. Due to the lack of radio equipment in the flotilla, commands were given by a few MAS shuttling between the ships in the convoy. The average speed of the convoy was just over 7 knots but at least the weather conditions were good.

Around 13:00, aerial reconnaissance reported the sighting of a British naval formation that could reach the convoy within four hours. It was therefore decided

---

3   *Gazolin* is a small boat with a gasoline fuelled engine (ed.).

to continue at the maximum possible speed of eight knots, while some units stayed behind and diverted to the island of Kassos and reached Crete the following day. Around 4 p.m. the small fleet arrived in sight of the coast of Cape Sidero: the landing took place in the bay of Sitia without encountering any enemy resistance. The landing operations continued throughout the night. Around 18:00 British naval units were attacked by German aircraft in the Kassos channel. The Italian units started to move at 12 noon on 29 May and during the march there were clashes with armed formations of the Cretan resistance: the enemy forces were overwhelmed without problems.

On 30 May, Italian tanks of the CCCXII Tank Battalion occupied the Ierapetra crossroads, establishing a link with some German motorised units. On 31 May, the Italian troops reached all the established objectives. The conditions under which the Italian soldiers marched were extremely harsh: in two days they covered 60 kilometres, under the scorching sun, with a shortage of water and supplies. Thanks to the iron discipline imposed by *Colonnello* Caffaro, the objectives were achieved without any problems, occupying the eastern part of the island and crushing Hellenic resistance. On 1 June, Italian and German troops advanced on Sfakia, capturing thousands of Allied soldiers as they attempted to board and flee the island.

On 1 June, the Battle of Crete officially ended, with the German troops arriving on the beach of Sfakia, capturing the last 5,000 Allied soldiers who surrendered without a fight. As early as 31 May, in fact, the British command, having managed to embark several thousand soldiers from Sfakia, had decided to stop the evacuation for fear of *Luftwaffe* attacks, especially after the loss of two destroyers. Of the approximately 32,000 Allied soldiers on the island, 1,751 died during the fighting, 18,000 managed to be evacuated by sea and the remainder were taken prisoner by the Germans.

Actions of the *Regia Aeronautica*

The aircraft of the *Regia Aeronautica* took an active part in the operations to conquer Crete, both in attacking British naval formations around the island and in carrying out bombing raids against strategic targets on the island itself. One of the first successes occurred on 21 May, when a formation of Italian high altitude Cant Z. 1007 bis bombers of the 50th Aegean Air Force Group sank the destroyer *Juno* in the Strait of Caso: the formation of five Cant Z. 1007 bis, escorted by four Cr. 42 fighters of 162a Squadron, attacked 80 miles south of the Strait of Caso. The Cant. Z. 1007 bis dropped 10 250-pound bombs and 15 100-pound bombs from an altitude of 5,100 metres against the destroyer *Juno*, which was hit at 12:49 p.m. by two bombs, one of which fell between the engine room and the boiler room, while the other exploded an ammunition depot, dealing the death blow to the ship, which, lurching over on its starboard side, capsized and sank, with it 128 crew members lost their lives. A further 96 survivors were recovered by other British ships.

Several raids against Crete followed in the following days. On the morning of 23 May, nine bombers (four Cant Z. 1007 bis, three S. 84 and two S. 79, from the 50th, 41st and 52nd Groups, respectively) and 12 Cr. 42 fighters from 162a Squadron armed with 100-pound bombs were sent into the attack. All these aircraft, divided into five formations, went to bomb Ieropetra, on the southern coast of Crete, one of the most important strategic targets on the island.

On 24 May, the Aegean Air Force bombarded the targets of Castelli, Mokkos, Ieropetra and Arkalokoui with five S. 79, four S. 84 and three Cant. Z. 1007 bis of the 92nd, 41st and 50th land bombardment groups, while twelve Cr. 42 of the 162nda Fighter Squadron were used to strafe troops. A further seven S. 84 bombers of the 41st B Group and nine Cr 42 fighters of the 162nd Squadron were unable to carry out the actions due to the adverse weather conditions.

On the morning of 25 May, new bombardments were conducted on Ieropetra, with 3 S. 84, 2 S. 79, 3 Cant. Z. 1007 bis of the 41st, 90th and 50th bombardment groups, and 5 Cr. 42 of the 162nda Terrestrial Fighter Squadron, the latter armed with wing bombs.

Crete's strategic position in the eastern Mediterranean.

German mountain troops waiting to board planes for the attack against Crete, May 1941. (NARA)

Nella notte sul 26 marzo 1941-XIX, Mezzi d'Assalto della Marina italiana penetrano nella baia di Suda (Creta) e affondano l'incrociatore
inglese "York", di 10.000 T. e tre grossi piroscafi carichi di materiale bellico

The attack on Suda Bay in a postcard of the time.

Tenente Luigi Faggioni. (www.movm.it)

Capitano di Fregata Francesco Mimbelli.
(www.movm.it)

The torpedo boat *Lupo* at sea, April 1941.

The torpedo boat *Sagittario* at sea, April 1941.

Disembarkation of Italian soldiers from two landing craft in Crete, May 1941. (USSME)

Tenente Giuseppe Cigala Fulgosi. (www.movm.it)

A youthful photo of *Colonnello* Ettore Caffaro.

Italian soldiers during landing operations in Crete, May 1941. (USSME)

Italian troops engaged in combat in Crete, May 1941. (USSME)

Italian bombers flying over Greek territory, 1941. (USSME)

12

Partition of Greece and Balance of Losses

At the end of the hostilities, the Greek territory was militarily occupied by the Axis forces and divided as follows:

> Germany occupied central and eastern Macedonia with the important port of Thessaloniki, the capital Athens, the islands of the North Aegean, the border areas with Turkey and a large part of the island of Crete. Bulgaria obtained Thrace, the north-eastern region of Greece and, later, eastern Macedonia.

> Italy obtained control of most of mainland Greece (the regions of Epirus, Thessaly, Attica and the Peloponnese), as well as the Ionian Islands with Corfu, Zakynthos and Kefalonia, the Cyclades, the Southern Sporades with Samos, Furni and Ikaria and the eastern tip of Crete. In Athens, a Greek military government led by *Genikós* Tsolakoglu was established under the control of Germany and Italy.

The territorial partition of Greece was basically decided by the Germans and communicated to the Italians as a fait accompli, as Mussolini himself acknowledged: '…the Germans communicated a border to us, we could only take note of it.'[1]

Loss Balance Sheet

According to official data from the Ministry of Defence, the Greek campaign cost the Italian forces 13,755 dead, 50,874 wounded, 12,368 suffering from frostbite, 52,108 others sick (hospitalised in nursing homes) and 25,067 missing. As for the fate of the latter, 21,153 were prisoners of war captured by the Greeks and freed in April 1941, the others were mostly unidentified dead: also adding to the number of deaths were those who died in hospitals from wounds or illnesses sustained during the campaign (the number is not accurately recorded); the total number of Italian dead can be estimated at more than 20,000.[2] Among the hardest hit units were the *Julia*

---

1   Giorgio Rochat, *Le Guerre Italiane 1935–1943* (Turin: Giulio Einaudi editore, 2008), p.360.
2   Giorgio Rochat, *Le Guerre Italiane 1935–1943* (Turin: Giulio Einaudi editore, 2008), pp.279–280.

Division with 990 dead, 4,000 wounded and 2,764 missing, the *Ferrara* Division with 522 dead, 2,450 wounded and 2,809 missing and the *Bari* Division with 985 dead, 3,608 wounded and 682 missing.

The *Regia Aeronautica* lost 65 aircraft in action (32 bombers, 29 fighters and 4 reconnaissance aircraft) and 14 destroyed on the ground, plus a further 10 aircraft seriously damaged and 61 slightly damaged; of the airmen, 229 were killed and 65 wounded in action.

Greek losses, according to official data from the Hellenic Ministry of Defence, were 13,408 dead, 42,485 wounded and 218,000 prisoners (partly released by the Germans). Other sources report around 14,000 dead, between 42,500 and 61,000 wounded and 4,250 missing.

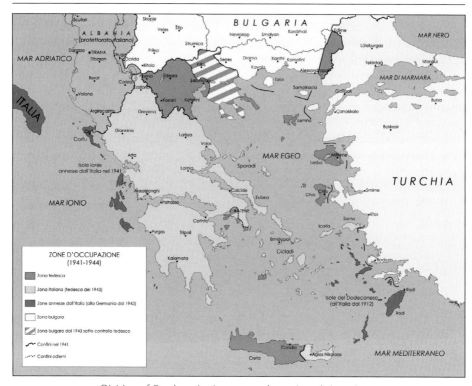

Division of Greek territories among the various Axis nations.

Italian soldiers during a ceremony in memory of the fallen during the Greek campaign, 1941
(USSME).

Appendix I

The Major Italian Units Engaged on the Greek-Albanian Front 1940–1941

Units engaged at the beginning of the attack, October 1940

XXV Army Corps (*Generale* Rossi)
XXVI Army Corps (*Generale* Nasci)
Arezzo Infantry Division (*Generale* Ferone)
Centauro Armoured Division (*Generale* Magli, later *Generale* Pizzolato)
Alpine Division *Julia* (*Generale* Girotti)
Parma Infantry Division (*Generale* Grattarola, then *Generale* Battisti, then *Generale* Adami)
Piedmont Infantry Division (*Generale* Naldi)
Siena Infantry Division (*Generale* Gabutti, then *Generale* Perugi, then *Generale* Carta)
Venice Infantry Division (*Generale* Bonini)

Units added by 31 December 1940

9th Army (*Generale* Vercellino, then *Generale* Pirzio Biroli)
11th Army (*Generale* Geloso)
III Army Corps (*Generale* Arisio)
VIII Army Corps (*Generale* Bancale, later *Generale* Gambara)
Bari Infantry Division (*Generale* Zaccone, then *Generale* D'Havet, then *Generale* Negro)
Modena Infantry Division (*Generale* Gloria, then *Generale* Trionfi, then *Generale* Gloria again)
Pusteria Alpine Division (*Generale* De Cia, then Esposito)
Taro Infantry Division (*Generale* Pedrazzoli)
Alpine Division *Tridentina* (*Generale* Santovito)
Trieste Infantry Division (*Generale* Piazzoni)

Units added between 4 December 1940 and 31 January 1941

IV Army Corps (*Generale* Mercalli)
Special Army Corps (*Generale* Messe)
Acqui Infantry Division (*Generale* Mariotti, later *Generale* Mazzini)
Brenner Infantry Division (*Generale* Berardi)
Generale Infantry Division (Generale Pivano)
Cagliari Infantry Division (*Generale* Gianni, later *Generale* Angioy)
Cuneense Alpine Division (*Generale* Ferrero, then *Generale* Battisti)
Cuneo Infantry Division (*Generale* Melotti)
Legnano Infantry Division (*Generale* Ruggero, then *Generale* De Cia)
Lupi di Toscana Infantry Division (*Generale* Bollea, then *Generale* Reisoli-Mathieu)
Pinerolo Infantry Division (*Generale* De Stefanis)
Sforzesca Infantry Division (*Generale* Ollearo)

Units added between 1 February and 23 April 1941

XIV Army Corps (*Generale* Vecchi)
XVII Army Corps (*Generale* Pafundi)
Casale Infantry Division (*Generale* Navarini)
Firenze Infantry Division (*Generale* Negri)
Forlì Infantry Division (*Generale* Ruggero)
Marche Infantry Division (*Generale* Pentimalli)
Messina Infantry Division (*Generale* Zani)
Puglie Infantry Division (*Generale* D'Aponte)

Bersaglieri motorcyclists on the Greek-Albanian front, spring 1941 (USSME).

Officers of the *Julia* Division in the Primavara 1941 (USSME).

A group of Italian soldiers engaged on the Greek-Albanian front pose for a photo, spring 1941 (USSME).

Appendix II

The *Regia Aereonautica* on the Greek-Albanian front, 1940–1941

In the Italian General Staff's plans, the *Regia Aereonautica* was to play a fundamental role, bombing the Greek airfields from the first days, in order to destroy the enemy air force on the ground, the ports, the main railway junctions, the war factories, the mobilisation and recruitment centres. For this purpose, a deployment of at least 550/600 aircraft was set out. In reality, in the initial phase of the campaign, the force in the field never exceeded 300 aircraft (according to some historians, even less), allowing the Greek Air Force, with its 160/180 aircraft, to face the *Regia Aereonautica*. To this must be added that from 1 November 1940, the Royal Air Force began to transfer its units, such as 30 Squadron equipped with Bristol Blenheim I light bombers, to Greece. On 7 November came 70 Squadron equipped with Vickers Wellington medium bombers, on 8 November 84 and 211 Squadrons equipped with Bristol Blenheims light bombers and on 18 November, 80 Squadron equipped with Gloster Gladiator II fighters. In this way, the initial Italian numerical superiority was immediately lost.

Order of Battle of the *Regia Aereonautica* on 28 October 1940[1]

Headquarters in Tirana, under the orders of *Generale di Squadrone Aereo* Ferruccio Ranza.

38th Land Bombardment Wing on Savoia-Marchetti SM 81 aircraft, based at Valona airfield and made up of the 39th Land Bombardment Group with the 51st and 69th Squadrons and the 40th Land Bombardment Group with the 202nd and 203rd Squadrons

105th Bombardment Group on Savoia-Marchetti SM.79 aircraft in Tirana with the 254th and 255th Squadrons.

---

1   Orazio Ferrara *La Regia Aereonautica alla Guerra di Grecia* (Rome: IBN editore, 2014), pp.21–22.

160th Autonomous Fighter Group at Drenova Airport with the 393rd and 394th Squadrons (Fiat CR.32 aircraft)

72nd Air Observation Group with the 26th Squadron at Koritza, the 42nd at Vlora and the 120th at Gjirokastra on IMAM Ro.37bis aircraft

An overall total of 187 aircraft: 31 Savoia-Marchetti SM.79, 24 Savoia-Marchetti SM.81, 47 G.50, 46 Fiat CR.42 and 25 IMAM Ro.37bis.

Activity report

During the entire Greek campaign, the *Regia Aereonautica* flew

12,000 fighter missions with a total of about 21,000 flying hours
7,777 bomber missions with a total of 17,169 flight hours and a total of 5,456 tons of bombs dropped
1,400 missions by scouts and observers with 99 tons of bombs dropped
77,000 military personnel and approximately 5,000 tons of war material transported.

The loss against both Greek and British opposition was 93 aircraft in total:
36 bombers, 16 shot down by enemy fighters, 10 by anti-aircraft fire and 10 from
        undetermined causes.
29 fighters, 24 in air crashes
5 transport aircraft in accidents
3 Dodecanese Air Force aircraft lost in action against Greek targets
4 reconnaissance aircraft
14 aircraft of various types destroyed on the ground by enemy raids

The losses in the air including both pilots and other personnel was 229 killed and 65 wounded, while on the ground it was 6 killed and 20 wounded.

Italian Aces of the Air War in Greece

Numerous Italian pilots distinguished themselves on the Greek-Albanian front and were decorated with the *Medaglia d'Oro al Valor Militare*.
    Among them was *Tenente* Livio Bassi of the 395th squadron equipped with Fiat G.50s, born in Trapani on 8 October 1918, who achieved a total of six victories, enough to earn him the title of aviation ace. He achieved his first victory on 18 December 1940, shooting down a Bristol Blenheim bomber over the skies of Vlora. On 6 January 1941 he shot down a second Blenheim, and two days later, over Klisura, he took part in combat against a large formation of Gloster Gladiator fighters of the Royal Air Force. On 11 February, his unit carried out an attack against the airport of Janina, destroying 18 enemy aircraft on the ground, while two others were shot down while attempting to take off. On 20 February 1941, he took part in an air

battle between Italian fighters and British bombers and their escorts in the skies over southern Albania.

When *Tenente* Alfredo Fusco of the 361st Squadron, his former course colleague at the Academy, was surrounded by six British Hawker Hurricane fighters, he rushed to his aid. In the ensuing clash, Bassi hit two Hurricanes, but Fusco's plane, hit repeatedly, exploded in flight, killing the pilot instantly. Wounded in turn by the British pilots, Livio Bassi managed to disengage and attempted to make an emergency landing on the field of Berat: his plane overturned catching fire and he suffered severe burns. Livio Bassi died of his severe burns on 2 April 1941 at the Celio Military Hospital in Rome. He was then awarded the *Medaglia d'Oro al Valor Militare alla Memoria*, with the citation:

> A daring fighter pilot of proven valour, he took part in numerous and highly risky military actions carried out by his unit, shooting down four enemy aircraft in individual action. During an aerial bombardment of his own airfield, carried out by a large number of enemy bombers escorted by fighters, he immediately took to the skies, facing the unequal battle with supreme courage and incomparable bravery, contributing to beating off the enemy's attack and shooting down two aircraft. Wounded, and with his aircraft severely damaged, instead of saving himself by parachute, he tried to return to the field, but in his courageous attempt, at the edge of the field, he was enveloped in flames from the perforated fuel tanks. Severely burnt, he was rescued and transported to hospital where, after two months of excruciating suffering, he serenely ended his glorious young life in the vision of the victorious Homeland, which he had so admirably served. [Heaven of Greece, October 1940 – February 1941].

Tenente Alfredo Fusco, too, was also awarded the *Medaglia d'Oro al Valor Militare*, with the citation:

> A Brilliant and daring fighter pilot, in many actions and in bitter fighting, he contributed to the shooting down of ten aircraft, demonstrating the qualities of a superb fighter, contemptuous of danger. On 20 February, in a fight against an overwhelmingly strong enemy fighter formation, although repeatedly hit, he continued to fight until the enemy gave up the fight. In the afternoon of the same day, when an incursion of enemy bombers, escorted by numerous fighters, was reported on the field, he was the first to rise into flight, although he was on rest. Aware of the danger to which he was exposing himself, he immediately took to the skies and single-handedly engaged in combat, drawing the entire enemy formation against him, thus succeeding in diverting them from their intended target. In the unequal struggle, riddled by the volleys of the numerous escorting fighters, he gloriously ended his young existence. [Skies of Greece and Albania, November 1940 – 20 February 1941].

Another decorated airman was *Captitano* Giorgio Graffer, of the 365th Squadron equipped with Fiat CR.42, born in Trento on 14 May 1912. He was credited with three individual kills. He fell in combat on 28 November 1940, in the skies over Albania, during a furious clash with enemy aircraft. He was awarded the *Medaglia d'Oro al Valor Militare alla Memoria*, with the citation:

> Captain pilot, audacious hunter, squadron commander, already distinguished in previous wartime actions, he voluntarily took to the air in the middle of the night, in pursuit of enemy aircraft that were bombing one of our important cities. Having sighted an aircraft, he attacked it decisively, persisting in the fight until, with his own aircraft damaged and his weapons rendered useless by enemy fire, determined to win at all costs, he made his machine and his body the supreme weapon to destroy the enemy with a crash. With a desperate determination, he failed in his first attempt and as his aircraft plummeted to the ground, he found in his parachute the salvation he had so superbly disdained during the fight. Later, in the skies over Albania, in a bitter fight with superior enemies, he plunged into combat at the head of the formation that he led, having already shot down three enemy aircraft. A legendary example of warrior virtue. [Albania sky, 28 November 1940].

Italian and Albanian soldiers by large aircraft bombs at an airfield in Albania in November 1940.
(USSME)

SM 79 bombers of the 253rd squadron of the 104th Land Bombardment Group flying over Greek territory. (USSMA)

CANT Z 1007 aircraft in flight in the skies over Greece winter 1941. (USSMA)

Tenente Livio Bassi.
(www.movm.it)

Livio Bassi on his FIAT G50 *Freccia*.

Tenente Alfredo Fusco.
(www.movm.it)

Capitano Giorgio
Graffer. (www.movm.it)

Appendix III

The Italian Expeditionary Corps in Crete in The War Bulletins of The General Staff of The *Esercito Reale*

The operations of the Italian units during the conquest of Crete were described in the war bulletins published in 1941 by the General Staff of the *Esercito Reale*.

Italian Operations on Crete

Agenzia Stefani informs that yesterday, 28 May, contingents of Italian troops landed on the island of Crete to cooperate with ground forces in the ongoing operations.

Agenzia Stefani informs that, in the afternoon of 28 May, our bombers, in the eastern Mediterranean, attacked an enemy naval formation with bombs, definitely hitting a cruiser. Despite the fierce fire, all the aircraft returned to base unharmed.

In the same afternoon, our torpedo bombers attacked with complete success other British warships sailing in the vicinity of the Caso channel. Three cruisers of over 7,000 tons were certainly hit with torpedoes. All our aircraft returned.

Italian Participation in Operations in the Crete sector

The new methods of combat, already tried elsewhere but which had their consecration in the battle of Crete, confirmed the superiority that in many circumstances that aircraft could acquire over the naval forces, thus subverting every traditional canon of maritime warfare. This new fact will undoubtedly exert an enormous influence on the further development of the conflict and the conquest of Crete has already demonstrated which of the two superiorities, the naval superiority of the British and the air superiority of the Axis, will ultimately prevail. In the meantime, the Crete episode can be considered as completely settled and the island integrates into the Cyclades and Dodecanese system, forming a defensive bastion to Europe and an outpost towards the remaining enemy positions. Our landing units have completed their operational tasks and now complete the occupation of the eastern part, raking every nook and cranny of the coast. In the evening of the 28th, at 6 p.m., our first forces had begun landing in the Bay of Sitia and by 8 p.m. almost all personnel and material were already ashore. During the night, the troops made contact with enemy elements, overwhelming them and beginning the penetration march through rough and difficult terrain. Their task was twofold: to the north, to proceed westwards along the coast, to occupy the many inlets that could aid supply and the enemy's retreat, and to join the German forces operating near Candia; to the south, to quickly target the south coast in order to preclude the British from those landings as well. A first column then headed south-east, driving back the enemy that insistently tried to obstruct the march, and in the afternoon of the 29th reached Exo Mouliani, after overpowering the particularly tenacious resistance organised by the Greeks in that locality, capturing a few hundred prisoners and a plentiful booty of arms and ammunition. A second column moved towards Heraclion (Candia) and during the night of the 31st connected with the German forces just west of Mellion Bay. Meanwhile, the disembarkation of new units, batteries, vehicles, supplies, ovens and anything else an expeditionary force might need continued. All operations were carried out under the constant protection of the air force, which guarded the landing zone and the lines of march, and the light naval units, which ensured the control of that area of the sea. The port of Hierapetra was reached on the 31st, with perfect synchrony, by the Italian and German forces and in this way the ring was tightened around the enemy who, by now disbanded, were still wandering the interior areas of the island.

Bombers in the skies over Greece, spring 1941. (USSMA)

Italian soldiers in Crete, May 1941. (USSME)

Appendix IV

Italian Armour Used in the Greek Campaign

L 3/35 Light Tank

This fast tank was present on the Italian battlefields during World War II and due to its modest technical characteristics earned the nickname 'sardine box'. Its operational history began in 1933, when the Ansaldo company created the Carro Veloce 33 (CV 33), which was so successful due to its extreme manoeuvrability that it was also purchased by several foreign armies. After the CV 33, the basic 35 and 38 versions were produced. The armament, which was initially limited to one machine gun, was increased to two Breda 35 8-calibre machine guns in the L 3/35 model. At the beginning of the Second World War, there were about a thousand examples of this tank available. Its deployment in Ethiopia and Spain highlighted its weakness in armament and armour and it was relegated to becoming a light reconnaissance tank.

Technical data
Weight: 3.1 tonnes
Road speed: 42 Km/h
Autonomy: 120/140 kilometres on the road
Engine: CV3-005 Fiat petrol 4-cylinder in-line engine
Dimensions – length: 3.15 metres, width: 1.40m, height: 1.28m
Armament: 2 Fiat 35 or Breda 38 machine guns
Crew: 2 men
Maximum armour: front 13.5mm, side 8.5mm
Surmountable slope: 46%.

M13/40 Medium Tank

This tank, also produced by Ansaldo, was derived from the 11-ton M11/39, modified by inserting a 47/32 piece in the turret and reinforcing the engine and armour. Around 800 examples were produced and it participated in all Italian military campaigns from 1940 onwards. The M14/41 and the M15/42 models were later developed from the M13/40

Technical data
Weight: 14 tonnes
Road speed: 31.8 km/h
Autonomy: 200 kilometres on the road
Engine: SPA 8 TM 40 diesel with 8 V-cylinders
Dimensions – Length: 4.195m; Width: 2.20m; Height: 2.37m
Armament: 1 semi-automatic 47/32 calibre cannon and 3 Breda 38 calibre machine
    guns
Crew: 4 men
Maximum armour: front 40mm, side 25mm

Centauro L tanks on a Yugoslav road during the march from Shkodra to the north, April 1941.
(USSME)

A medium M13/40 tank engaged in fording a river in the Korcia sector, 1941. (USSME)

Bibliography

Contemporary Studies

Rivista *Cronache della Guerra*, Tumminelli e C Editori, various issues
Silvio Bitocco, *La Guerra Contro la Grecia*, Edizioni Distaptur, 1941

Accounts and Official Publications

Diario Cavallero
Montanari, Mario, *L'Esercito Italiano Nella Campagna di Grecia*, Ufficio Storico Stato Maggiore dell'Esercito

Published Books

AA.VV., *Ottobre 1940: la Campagna di Grecia* (Campobasso: Italia Editrice, 1995)
AA.VV., *La Campagna di Jugoslavia* (Campobasso: Italia Editrice, 2000)
AA.VV., *Il Terzo Reich: la conquista dei Balcani* (Bresso: Hobby & Work, 1993)
Borghese, Junio Valerio, *Decima Flottiglia MAS* (Milan: Garzanti, 1950)
Boschesi, B. P., *Le Armi, i Protagonisti, le Battaglie, gli Eroismi Segreti della Guerra di Mussolini, 1940-1943* (Milan: Gruppo Mondadori, 1984)
Carr, John, *The Defence and Fall of Greece 1940–41* (Barnsley: Pen and Sword, 2013)
Cervi, Mario, *Storia Della Guerra di Grecia* (Milan: Gruppo Mondadori, 1965)
Ciano, Galeazzo, *Diario 1939-1943* (Milan: Rizzoli, 1963)
De Felice, Renzo, *l'Italia in Guerra: 1940-1943* (Turin: Giulio Einaudi editore, 1997)
Ferrara, Orazio, *La Regia Aereonautica alla guerra di Grecia* (Rome: IBN editore, 2014)
Mattesini, F., *La Battaglia di Creta Maggio 1941: il Contributo Italiano*, (Zanica: Soldiershop Publishing, 2020)
Panetta, Rinaldo, *Il ponte di Klisura: i carristi italiani in Albania, 1940-1941* (Milan: Ugo Mursia Editore, 2017)
Raffaelli, Enzo, Gambarotto, Stefano, et al, *Campagna di Grecia, Alpini e Fanti*(Treviso: Editrice Storica, 2010)
Rasero, Aldo, *Alpini della Julia: Storia della Divisione Miracolo* (Milan: Ugo Mursia Editore, 2018)
Rasero, Aldo, *Tridentina Avanti!* (Milan: Ugo Mursia Editore, 2017)

Rocca, Gianni, *I Disperati. La Tragedia dell'Aeronautica Italiana nella Seconda Guerra Mondiale* (Milan: Gruppo Mondadori, 1998)

Rochat, Giorgio, *Le Guerre Italiane 1935-1943* (Turin: Giulio Einaudi editore, 2008)

Romeo di Colloredo Mels, Pierluigi, *Diavoli Bianchi! Il Battaglione alpini sciatori "Monte Cervino" 1941- 1943* (Zanica: Soldiershop Publishing, 2020)

Sadkovich, James, (Mauro Pascolat tr.) *La Marina Italiana nella Seconda Guerra Mondiale* (Milan: Feltrinelli, 2014)

Websites

http://www.regioesercito.it

Gruppo delle Medaglie d'oro al Valor Militare d'Italia (https://www.movm.it/)

About the author

Massimiliano Afiero was born in Afragola (Naples) in 1964. He is an information technology teacher, but above all is a passionate researcher of the Second World War, hawing written many articles in major history journal in Italy and abroad. He is among the few italian historical researchers to have interviewed many veterans of Axis units, in particular of the Waffen SS, publishing their previously unpublished stories. He has written an impressive number of books, in Italian, English and Spanish, and since 2004 he has been director of several periodicals, both in Italian and English, mainly dedicated to Axis formations of the Second World War: *Volontari*, *SGM*, *Ritterkreuz*, *Fronti di Guerra*, *The Axis Forces*.

About the artists

Renato Dalmaso

Renato Dalmaso was born in São Paulo in 1981, where he currently lives with his wife and daughter. Self-taught in drawing and painting, he began his career in illustration at the age of 37, after deciding to change his professional path. Today he illustrates for several publishers in Brazil and around the world. He has been contributing his illustrations and covers to Helion & Company since 2021. In Brazil, he illustrated several graphic novels, such as *Elisio, A Journey To Hell* and *Jambocks!*, about the participation of the Expeditionary Force and the Brazilian Air Force in World War II. He also illustrated comic books about soccer, telling the story of the São Paulo FC and CR Flamengo clubs. In parallel with his work as a book illustrator, he is working on developing his new comic book series, which will tell the story of the Portuguese Great Navigations, in the 16th century.

David Bocquelet

David Bocquelet, webmaster since 1990 and illustrator since 1995, worked at first on ancient ships recreations before starting tank and naval encyclopedia around 2010. Working with many publishers on ground, naval, air and other military hardware since. Early Influences were among others Roy Huxley and Angus McBride.